W9-AUC-502

HOWE · LIBRARY

° HANOVER °
NEW HAMPSHIRE

Yankee Magazine's

NEW ENGLAND
INNKEEPERS'
COOKBOOK

Yankee Magazine's

New England Innkeepers' Cookbook

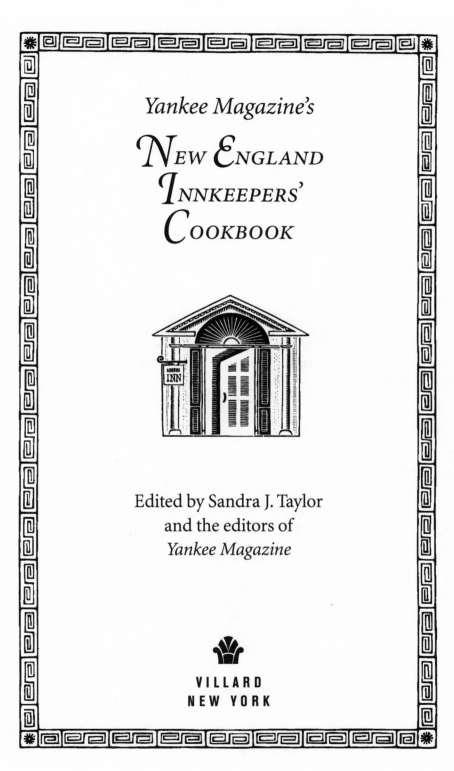

Edited by Sandra J. Taylor
and the editors of
Yankee Magazine

VILLARD
NEW YORK

Yankee Magazine's New England Innkeepers' Cookbook
Edited by Sandra J. Taylor and the editors of *Yankee Magazine*
Design by Jill Shaffer
Illustrations by Beth Krommes
Sidebars by Lori Baird

Copyright © 1996 by Yankee Publishing Inc.
All rights reserved under International and Pan-American Copyright
Conventions. Published in the United States by Villard Books, a division
of Random House, Inc., New York, and simultaneously in Canada by
Random House of Canada Limited, Toronto.

VILLARD BOOKS is a registered trademark of Random House, Inc.

Library of Congress Cataloging-in-Publication Data

Yankee magazine's New England innkeepers' cookbook / compiled and
edited by Sandra J. Taylor.—1st ed.
p.   cm.
ISBN 0-679-43207-8
1. Brunches. 2. Cookery, American—New England style.
I. Taylor, Sandra. II. Yankee (Dublin, N.H.)
TX733.Y36   1995
641.5'3—dc20   95-5248

Manufactured in the United States of America

9 8 7 6 5 4 3 2

First Edition

Contents

*I*NTRODUCTION

I MAGINE THAT you've been spirited away and placed at a dining table in an unknown location somewhere in the country. Only by reading the menu or looking at the dishes in front of you can you tell where you are.

In the age before homogenized fast food and year-round produce from South America, it was pretty simple to figure out your location by paying close attention to the food. Were there grits on the menu or johnnycakes? Did the breadbasket include *sopaipillas* or cranberry muffins? Were there curled green fiddlehead ferns on the plate or simmered collard greens?

Today, in most towns across the United States, the modern taster would have a difficult time determining his or her location: A hamburger is a hamburger is a hamburger.

At any of the New England inns included in this book, though, that task has been made much easier. The reason, I think, has as much to do with what's on the menu as the preservation of the inn itself.

Something comes over a person—whether a native, a transplanted urbanite, or an escapee from another part of the country—once he or she is a New England innkeeper. More often than not the novice innkeeper has just become the owner of the town's primary historic site (and in New England, it's not unusual that the site may even be numbered among the oldest buildings in the country). To acquire such heritage is overwhelming—and inspiring. Longtime residents watch with astonishment as the innkeeper transforms into the most ardent of preservationists.

Scratch the surface of any innkeeper and you'll find an historian lurking. Jack Simko can tell you all about the rare twelve-sided barn that lends its name to his Inn at the Round Barn Farm in northern Vermont. Linda Johnston knows the story behind the haunting murals attributed to the nineteenth-century itinerant painter Rufus Porter in the upstairs bedroom of her New Hampshire John Hancock Inn. Bill Winterer, of Connecticut's Griswold Inn, willingly takes the time to describe how his current taproom was actually built as the town's first schoolhouse.

Fired up with such historic anecdotes, these innkeepers seek to ornament their hostelries with period details and appropriate antiques. I've stayed at inns where I wouldn't have been the least surprised to see Paul Revere wander in through the front door or Louisa May Alcott writing notes on a corner settee.

But decor is only a part of the story. Whether it is a bed and breakfast that serves only a morning meal or a full-service inn that pulls out all the stops for dinner, it's often the food that makes the journey into the past complete. At the best of inns (certainly those included here), the menus play an integral part in reflecting the history.

Just as innkeepers strive for period accuracy in their inns' decor, they try to keep the old-fashioned flavors on their menus. And so at the Old Lyme Inn in Connecticut, you'll find johnnycakes—southern New England's contribution to a great breakfast—that begin with stone-ground cornmeal made from Indian corn. Furthermore, there are four chowder recipes in this book, and not one of them contains a single tomato (anathema to a New England cook).

In the recipes that follow, you'll find lots of the basic tastes that supported the new colony cuisine in America. And in traditional Yankee style, when New Englanders find a good thing they tend to stick with it.

The earliest colonists were introduced to the sweetness of maple syrup by the Indians. Until honeybees were brought over, maple trees provided the only local sweetener. Even after refined sugar was readily available, around the time of the Revolution, many New Englanders stuck with maple syrup: Not only was it cheaper than the heavily taxed import, but its harvest did not rely on "the toil, pain and misery of the wretched," that is, the slaves on the sugar plantations of the West Indies. Maple sugar remained the most popular sweetener in New England until the late 1800s. Today, it is probably the only food in the world that is produced exclusively in New England and Canada. Innkeepers understand the appeal of maple syrup, and it turns up often at the dining table—not only poured over Lemon Soufflé Pancakes and Stillmeadow Stuffed French Toast, but also as a featured ingredient in Tenderloin of Beef with Maple Compote Sauce, Maple Mustard Baked Rabbit, and even tossed with a salad as Mountain Maple Poppy Dressing.

Another important food staple to early New England settlers was apples. Seeds had been brought over from Europe by the earliest English colonists, including the Pilgrims. At one time, there were as many as 150 varieties of apples, and the early settlers could probably have come up with at least as many uses for them. The fruit's best-known fan was Johnny Appleseed, born John Chapman in 1774 in Massachusetts. Although he did not scatter seed willy-nilly as legend has it, his nurseries of apple orchards spread the apple across the country. Today, there are estimated to be seven thousand varieties of apples in the United States, although fewer than a dozen show up at the market. There's a good chance that your New England innkeeper will be using a local variety when mixing apples with granola for breakfast or when combining them with sausage and cheddar cheese to stuff chicken for dinner.

Vermont's green hills lent themselves easily to dairy farming. The English settlers with a dairying background knew that a great cheese requires great milk, and that's just what they had in abundance in Vermont. Perhaps the region's best-known cheese is cheddar, which shows up here in everything from Cheddar Parmesan Muffins to Alehouse Crab, Cheddar, and Cauliflower Soup. Look, too, for goat cheese (chevre), which a handful of enthusiasts produce in New England, from Massachusetts to Maine.

Berries grew in profusion—we have only to think of the names of such places as Strawbery Banke (the original name for Portsmouth, New Hampshire). Blueberries are said to be entirely American in their ancestry, and the small, incredibly sweet wild ones win my vote as a slice of heaven on earth. One innkeeper in Vermont has so many blackberries growing near her inn that she incorporates them into as many recipes as possible and even freezes the bounty for a summertime taste in winter.

Cranberries were eaten by the Indians long before the Europeans arrived. One early colonist reported seeing the Indians eating a cranberry sauce with meat (although this same journalist also went on to report seeing a sea serpent off Cape Ann and a merman in Maine). Whether the Pilgrims actually asked anyone to pass the cranberry sauce at the first Thanksgiving, cranberries assumed an important role in New England commerce: They were the first fruit to be commercially exported from America. Cranberries appear in this cookbook in an Apple and Cranberry Puffed Pancake from the Connecticut Greenwoods Gate Bed and Breakfast Inn, and in Cranberry Orange Glaze for Holiday Duckling at the Norwich Inn in Vermont.

To many northern New Englanders, there is no surer harbinger of spring than the lowly (literally) fiddlehead ferns, whose tightly wound fronds are the first sign of green once the snow has gone. They turn up here in Cream of Fiddlehead Soup from the Combes Family Inn in Vermont.

These menus, using fresh local produce, reflect their New England roots. If you were a blindfolded diner at one of these tables, there would be little doubt that you were in New England.

* * * * *

BUT HISTORY as presented at these dining tables is not confined to regional borders. In many of these recipes, you'll also find threads of family history. There's a simple reason for this: Because most inns are run on a very small scale, it's not unusual to find the innkeeper acting as host, manager, accountant, maintenance worker—and cook. Often without professional training, these people saw innkeeping as a way to turn their love of cooking from a hobby into a vocation. Instead of cordon bleu credentials, they graduated from household kitchens with a family's worth of recipes. Their cooking know-how and expertise were developed in the heat of battle at the stove front.

As a result, most of the following recipes are engagingly uncomplicated. The most obscure ingredient might be the porcini mushrooms called for in the Wild Mushroom Ragout from Vermont's Autumn Crest Inn. In most recipes, the list of ingredients seems to run longer than the instructions—a sure sign of ease in the kitchen. One recipe even calls for a stack of Ritz crackers.

A fair number of the recipes that follow are named in grateful recognition of someone: Nina, Jano, Vince, Mel, Meme, Aunt Rose. Who are these people? Why did they have a recipe named for them? Often it's a family member, or just someone who appreciated that dish more than anyone else. My favorite example of this is the Watch Hill Firehouse Brownies, which were named to honor the fire chief who worked to thaw the inn's pipes with a hair dryer one frigid New Hampshire Christmas Eve.

One thing should remain clear: These are not industrialized meals designed back at some corporate headquarters meant to feed thousands across the country on a single night. These recipes have been concocted through a combination of family lore, trial and error, and a lot of experimentation. That's what makes them so accessible. The ingredients are not fancy and neither are the techniques.

This is home cooking at its best, a little gussied up for company. Not only are these recipes tested and proven crowd pleasers, but they still are flavored by their humble beginnings—in the kitchen, with one cook and one stove. Only at a country inn will you find on the menu a potato salad named Grandma Sally.

* * * * *

IN INVESTIGATING how these innkeepers run their kitchens, we learn their tips on how to make entertaining trouble free.

Innkeepers are, in essence, professional entertainers. What *you* get when you check into an inn is the excuse to indulge in a bit of fantasy: Maybe the inn is an antiques-filled museum, maybe it's the summer estate in the country that you thought you always deserved in life. What the *innkeepers* get when you stay at their inn is the opportunity to put on an exquisite dinner party or open-house breakfast—every day of the season.

By definition, these inns are not equipped with huge staffs of slicing-and-dicing underlings. These double-duty innkeepers do not have the luxury of paying for a cool-eyed maître d'hôtel to breeze through the dining room in starchy tuxedoed perfection. The innkeeper-cook buys the produce, chops the vegetables, beats the eggs, bastes the turkey, whips the cream, makes the coffee, sets the table, arranges the flowers, and plays the perfect host.

Sounds familiar, doesn't it?

Any of us who entertain at home know that Murphy's Law was really formulated to describe the average dinner party: Anything that can go wrong will go wrong. We may not be preparing dinner for paying guests, but who wouldn't appreciate a few tips from an expert before we plunge into our next dinner party?

These innkeepers have not only weathered most conceivable (and some inconceivable) entertaining disasters, they have survived to tell the tale. Here are some thoughts:

* What if the sauce curdles?
* What if you run out of broth halfway through making the soup?
* And what if everything goes right? What do you do with the leftovers? These are frugal Yankee cooks, after all, and they have a few tips about how to use leftover vegetables for soups, leftover roasts in hash (try it with fish next time), and overripe fruit in muffins and pancakes.

Innkeepers are adept at using their time well: Vegetable crudités can be made a day ahead; so can pasta, most vegetables, and potatoes. If like me you'd prefer to be enjoying your guests rather than slaving for them, these are all good suggestions.

And what about everyday questions from the kitchen:

* Why did the cake fall?
* What do I do with a bumper crop of basil?
* Can I substitute phyllo for puff pastry?

Short of having my mother at my elbow every time I step into the kitchen, I wouldn't mind having the advice of these innkeepers there to help me.

❧ ❧ ❧ ❧ ❧

By now, our imaginary diner at the mystery table has probably filled up on Maple-Baked Apples or Apple Cranberry Crumb Pie or Blueberry Buckle or Pumpkin Custard or Firehouse Brownies. One thing is sure: That person's been in New England.

Far from a generic meal in a generic setting, the dishes presented here reflect a very definite taste and a very definite place. And yet they are not limited to being appreciated by New Englanders only.

Anyone looking for their heritage—or the roots of their family's cooking—might begin with these pages.

Anyone looking for something different for dinner, for the family or for friends, can find a dish here that stretches into the past.

Anyone who needs a little bit of help in the kitchen at the last minute—and I don't know anyone who doesn't—should be able to find assistance here; who knows, maybe even from Grandma Sally.

—Janice Brand
Editor, *Yankee Magazine's*
Travel Guide to New England

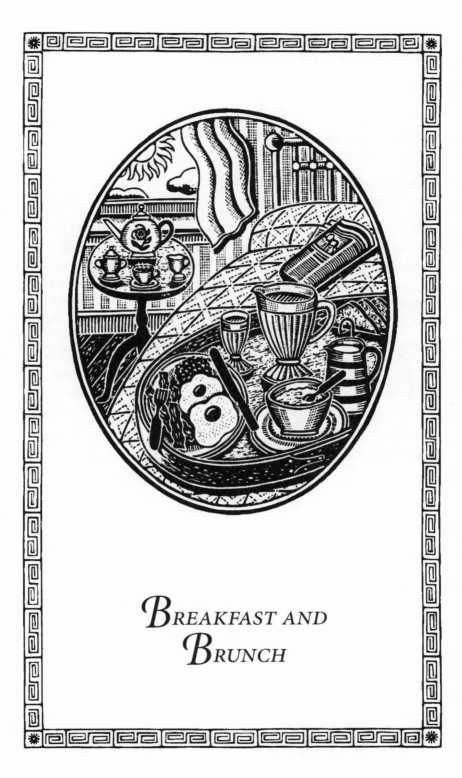

BREAKFAST AND BRUNCH

SUMMER FRUIT COMPOTE WITH STRAWBERRIES AND BLUEBERRIES

A great way to greet the morning, this fresh fruit compote can be varied to whatever is in season and on hand.

1 pint fresh strawberries

2 kiwifruit

1 cup fresh blueberries

1 can (11 ounces) orange segments, drained

¼ cup maple syrup

2 tablespoons light rum or orange juice

Hull the strawberries, cut in half lengthwise, and place in a large serving bowl. Peel the kiwis, cut in half lengthwise, and remove the seeds. Slice thinly crosswise and add to the strawberries along with the blueberries and orange segments. Toss to combine.

In a small bowl, mix the maple syrup and rum or orange juice, blending well, then pour over the fruit and toss to coat thoroughly. Place in the refrigerator and chill before serving.

VARIATION: Try combining 1 cup green grapes, 2 nectarines (peeled and cut into chunks), 1 cup blackberries, and ½ cup raspberries.

SERVES 6.

FERRY POINT HOUSE STUFFED ORANGE CUPS

These orange cups have lots of eye appeal and are ideal for a warm summer morning. Prepare them right before serving and arrange on glass plates, each garnished with a fresh mint leaf.

6 large navel oranges
½ cup chopped dates
½ cup shredded coconut
½ cup chopped pecans or walnuts
Fresh mint leaves for garnish

Cut off the tops of the oranges. Remove the segments with a paring knife and cut up into bite-sized pieces, discarding membranes. Catch any juice in a bowl. In the same bowl, toss the dates, orange pieces, coconut, and nuts.

Spoon the mixture into the hollowed-out orange shells (you may need to cut a thin slice from the bottom of each orange to prevent it from tipping). Garnish with mint and serve immediately.

SERVES 6.

MARLBOROUGH BAKED APPLES

These are appetizing and substantial. For a special touch, top with whipped cream, a fresh sprig of mint, and a light dash of nutmeg.

6 large baking apples (Cortland, Winesap, Red Rome, or Golden Delicious)

¾ cup granola, divided

½ cup chopped dates or raisins

½ cup chopped walnuts

½ teaspoon ground cinnamon

¼ teaspoon ground nutmeg

½ cup honey, divided

4 tablespoons butter

2 to 3 tablespoons lemon juice

1 cup fruit juice (apple, nectarine, etc.)

Core the apples, making the hole large because the filling is so good!

In a small bowl, combine ½ cup of the granola, the dates or raisins, walnuts, cinnamon, and nutmeg with 4 tablespoons of the honey. Spoon the filling into the apples and place them in a shallow baking pan.

Combine the remaining honey with the butter, lemon juice, and fruit juice in a small saucepan and bring to a boil. Pour over the apples, cover the pan with aluminum foil, and bake in a preheated 350°F oven for about 10 minutes.

Remove the cover and baste the apples. Continue baking for about 20 more minutes or until done (they should feel tender when pricked with a fork). Place the apples in individual serving bowls and top each with the remaining ¼ cup granola and juice from the baking pan. Serve warm.

SERVES 6.

ADDISON CHOATE INN GRANOLA

"This is the most asked for recipe at our inn. It freezes well, so make a double batch and freeze half! Enjoy with milk or apple juice poured over the top."

6 cups quick-cooking oats

1 cup firmly packed brown sugar

1 cup oat bran

1 cup Mexican pepita seeds

1 cup sliced almonds

½ cup sesame seeds

½ cup unsweetened coconut

2 teaspoons ground cinnamon

2 teaspoons vanilla extract

¼ cup canola oil

1 cup raisins

Mix all the ingredients except the raisins in a large roasting pan that has been coated with no-stick cooking spray. Bake in a preheated 325°F oven for 20 minutes. Stir and bake another 20 minutes. Stir again, let cool, then mix in the raisins.

MAKES ABOUT 11 CUPS.

THE COMPLETE KITCHEN

*T*HAT THE KITCHEN should be kept sweet and neat, the pots and pans scrupulously clean; that the sieves, strainers, the chopping machine, the cutter, the pastry board or shelf, should be freed from all particles adhering after use; that there should be a place for everything and that everything should be in its place—these are elementary truths.

—Mrs. Henry Reeve, *Cookery and Housekeeping,* 1882

The Victorian Inn Granola

Granola has become a favorite breakfast cereal, but it can be high in fat. This doesn't mean you have to eliminate it entirely, just cut back on certain high-fat ingredients. For example, use only ¼ to ½ cup wheat germ, reduce the quantity of nuts, and add only enough oil to moisten the ingredients and aid in the toasting process.

1½ cups rolled oats

¼ cup sesame seeds

½ cup toasted sunflower seeds

½ cup shredded sweetened coconut

¼ cup bran

½ cup sliced, toasted almonds

½ cup wheat germ

¼ cup honey

¼ cup vegetable oil

½ teaspoon vanilla extract

½ teaspoon almond extract

⅓ cup raisins

Mix the oats, sesame seeds, sunflower seeds, coconut, bran, almonds, and wheat germ together in a large container.

In a small saucepan, heat the honey, oil, vanilla, and almond extract but do not boil. Pour this mixture over the dry ingredients and stir to coat evenly.

Spread in a greased shallow baking dish to a uniform depth. Bake in a pre-heated 300° to 325°F oven, stirring every 5 minutes until golden (approximately 15 minutes). Let cool thoroughly. Add raisins and combine.

Store in an airtight container (glass is best) in the refrigerator until ready to use. Serve with plain yogurt or milk.

Makes about 3½ to 4 cups.

PUMPKIN PIE PANCAKES

Very light, not overly spiced, and so easy.

2 cups all-purpose flour

4 teaspoons baking powder

1 teaspoon ground cinnamon

⅛ teaspoon ground nutmeg

⅛ teaspoon ground allspice

¾ cup sugar

1½ cups mashed, cooked
    pumpkin

3 eggs

1 cup milk

¾ cup vegetable oil

1 teaspoon vanilla extract

In a medium-sized bowl, sift together the flour, baking powder, cinnamon, nutmeg, allspice, and sugar. In a large bowl, beat together the pumpkin, eggs, milk, oil, and vanilla. Add the dry ingredients and blend thoroughly.

Pour ¼ cup batter on a hot greased griddle. Cook until the bottom is lightly browned and bubbles form. Turn and finish cooking on other side. Serve with hot syrup.

SERVES 8.

LEMON SOUFFLÉ PANCAKES

These airy pancakes are fantastic. Maple syrup complements the tangy tartness of the lemon.

3 eggs, separated

2 tablespoons vegetable oil

¼ teaspoon salt

2 teaspoons baking powder

1 cup cottage cheese

1 tablespoon maple syrup

2 tablespoons lemon juice

2 tablespoons lemon zest

½ cup all-purpose flour

Beat the egg whites until stiff, then set aside.

Combine in a food processor or blender the egg yolks, oil, salt, baking powder, cottage cheese, maple syrup, lemon juice, lemon zest, and flour, blending until smooth. Pour the batter into a bowl and fold in the egg whites.

Cook on a hot greased griddle and serve with warm maple syrup.

SERVES 6.

LEMON COTTAGE PANCAKES WITH RASPBERRY MAPLE SYRUP

"Our guests' favorite and most requested breakfast by repeat customers."

1 cup cottage cheese

4 eggs

½ cup all-purpose flour

6 tablespoons butter, melted and cooled

2 tablespoons lemon juice

A pinch of lemon zest

Raspberry Maple Syrup (recipe follows)

With a mixer, blend the cottage cheese in a large bowl. With the mixer running, add the eggs and flour, then slowly pour in the butter. Stir in the lemon juice and zest by hand. The mixture should be thick.

Cook on a hot greased griddle until golden, but be careful not to overcook. The pancakes should be moist and should spring back to the touch. Serve with Raspberry Maple Syrup.

RASPBERRY MAPLE SYRUP

1 cup Vermont maple syrup (grade B dark amber has the best flavor for cooking)

⅔ cup raspberries, fresh or frozen

2 tablespoons raspberry jam

Combine the maple syrup, raspberries, and jam in a medium-sized no-stick saucepan and bring to a boil, stirring constantly. Remove from the heat and let sit for a few minutes until the mixture has thickened.

SERVES 4.

CARROT CAKE PANCAKES WITH CREAM CHEESE BUTTER

If bulgur and soy milk (found in any health food store) are not usually in your kitchen cupboard, they will become staple ingredients once you make these pancakes—ideal for a weekend when there's time for a leisurely breakfast or brunch.

½ cup bulgur (cracked wheat)

1½ cups all-purpose flour

1 cup whole wheat flour

⅓ cup firmly packed brown sugar

4 teaspoons baking powder

½ teaspoon ground allspice

1 teaspoon ground cinnamon

½ teaspoon salt

4 egg whites

2 cups soy milk

2 tablespoons vegetable oil

½ teaspoon vanilla extract

1½ cups shredded carrot

½ cup chopped walnuts or pecans

Cream Cheese Butter (recipe follows)

Soak the bulgur in 1 cup water for 45 to 60 minutes, then drain. (The larger the grains, the longer it will take; this can be done the night before, but refrigerate after draining.)

Combine the all-purpose flour, whole wheat flour, brown sugar, baking powder, allspice, cinnamon, and salt in a large bowl. In a small bowl, beat together the egg whites, soy milk, oil, and vanilla. Fold the wet ingredients into the flour mixture, then fold in the carrot, nuts, and bulgur.

Cook on a lightly greased griddle and serve with Cream Cheese Butter.

CREAM CHEESE BUTTER

½ cup butter or margarine, softened

1 small package (3 ounces) cream cheese, softened

¼ cup maple syrup

In a small bowl, beat the butter or margarine, cream cheese, and maple syrup until smooth. For a special effect, we like to put this in a pastry bag and pipe it onto the pancakes. *SERVES 4.*

CINNAMON APPLE PANCAKES

Apples and spice and everything nice—that's what these pancakes are made of.

2 cups all-purpose flour

1 teaspoon baking soda

2 teaspoons baking powder

1 tablespoon brown sugar

1 teaspoon salt

1 teaspoon ground cinnamon

2 eggs, beaten

1½ cups buttermilk

½ cup sour cream

¼ cup butter or margarine, melted

1 large apple, peeled, cored, and grated

In a large bowl, mix together the flour, baking soda, baking powder, brown sugar, salt, and cinnamon. Mix the eggs, buttermilk, sour cream, and butter in a separate bowl and add to the flour mixture, stirring just until moistened. Fold in the apple.

Using ¼ cup batter per pancake, pour onto a hot, lightly greased griddle. Cook, turning once, until golden brown.

SERVES 4.

ORANGE, WHOLE WHEAT, AND BLUEBERRY PANCAKES

"Here at Churchill House, we use wild, local blueberries. They are small and tender, giving this flavorful pancake an extra twist."

1½ cups whole wheat flour

½ cup all-purpose flour

½ teaspoon baking powder

½ teaspoon salt

2 eggs

2 cups orange juice, divided

¼ cup vegetable oil

1 tablespoon vanilla extract

1 teaspoon almond extract

1 pint fresh blueberries

Sift together the whole wheat flour, all-purpose flour, baking powder, and salt.

Beat the eggs in a mixing bowl, add 1¾ cups of the orange juice, the oil, and vanilla and almond extracts and mix well. Stir in the flour mixture and remaining orange juice, blending just until smooth. Fold in the blueberries.

Using about ¼ cup batter for each pancake, cook on a lightly greased griddle until brown on both sides. Serve with hot syrup.

MAKES 15 TO 20 PANCAKES.

SOUR CREAM BLUEBERRY PANCAKES

"These are light and fluffy pancakes. Our guests love them smothered in local Barre pure maple syrup."

½ cup all-purpose or whole wheat flour

½ teaspoon salt

½ teaspoon baking soda

2 eggs, beaten

1 cup sour cream

1 cup blueberries, fresh or frozen

Combine the flour, salt, and baking soda in a bowl. Add the eggs and sour cream, blending well. Fold in the blueberries.

Cook on a lightly greased griddle until lightly browned, about 3 minutes per side. Serve with bacon or sausage and plenty of maple syrup.

SERVES 2 TO 4.

COOKS' Q & A

Is it true that egg whites beat better in a copper bowl? And what exactly does "stiff but not dry" mean?

FIRST, IT IS TRUE that egg whites beat more quickly in a copper bowl. According to Chef Matt Delos at Edson Hill Manor in Stowe, Vermont, copper has an acid quality that egg whites react to in the same way they react to cream of tartar.

"Stiff but not dry" means that the egg whites look moist. Soft peaks form when the beaters are lifted out of the whites and the whites don't slide when the bowl is tipped.

Before you beat egg whites, make sure that the eggs are at room temperature and that the bowl and beaters are clean and dry. Even a little oil will prevent the whites from beating up well. If the recipe calls for the addition of cream of tartar or sugar, don't add it until after you've beaten the whites for a few seconds.

APPLE AND CRANBERRY PUFFED PANCAKE

Attractive and easy, this will be well received by kids as well as adults.

3 eggs, room temperature

½ cup all-purpose flour

½ cup milk

2 to 4 tablespoons butter

2 medium-sized Granny Smith apples, sliced (or 1 Red Rome and 1 Granny Smith)

½ cup chopped fresh cranberries

1¼ teaspoons ground cinnamon

1 tablespoon granulated sugar

Lemon juice (optional)

Confectioners' sugar

In a medium-sized bowl, thoroughly whisk the eggs. Slowly add the flour, whisking all the while to prevent lumps. Gradually add the milk and whisk to form a smooth batter. Set aside.

In a medium-sized skillet, melt 2 tablespoons butter, then add the apples, cranberries, cinnamon, and granulated sugar. Cook over medium heat until the apples are fork tender, about 15 minutes.

In a 9-inch pie plate, melt the remaining 2 tablespoons butter, being careful not to burn it (or spray with a no-stick cooking spray). Fill the plate with the apple mixture and top with the batter. Bake in a preheated 450°F oven for 15 to 20 minutes or until puffed and golden.

Top the pancake with a sprinkling of lemon juice, if desired, and finish off with a liberal dusting of confectioners' sugar. Slice into portions and serve immediately.

SERVES 2 TO 4.

APPLE WAFFLES WITH APPLE CIDER SYRUP

For an extra-special treat on the weekend, make these for your family. The waffles have a subtle apple flavor; the syrup is sweet, spicy, and intense.

3 eggs, separated

1 cup milk

½ cup butter, melted and cooled

½ cup grated apple

1 cup all-purpose flour

½ cup whole wheat flour

1 tablespoon baking powder

1 tablespoon sugar

1 teaspoon salt

1 teaspoon ground nutmeg

½ teaspoon ground cinnamon

Craignair Inn Apple Cider Syrup (recipe follows)

Beat the egg whites into stiff peaks and set aside.

In a small bowl, stir the egg yolks, milk, butter, and apple until well mixed. In a large bowl, combine the all-purpose flour, whole wheat flour, baking powder, sugar, salt, nutmeg, and cinnamon. Carefully combine the dry ingredients and apple mixture until just moistened. Gently fold in the egg whites.

Cook the waffles according to the manufacturer's instructions on the iron. Serve garnished with apple slices and accompanied by Craignair Inn Apple Cider Syrup.

CRAIGNAIR INN APPLE CIDER SYRUP

2 cups apple cider

1 teaspoon ground nutmeg

½ teaspoon ground cinnamon

½ cup maple syrup

In a small saucepan, combine the cider, nutmeg, and cinnamon. Bring to a boil, lower the heat, and simmer until reduced approximately by half. Stir in the maple syrup and simmer until slightly thickened.

SERVES 4.

Stuffed French Toast with Sautéed Apples and Apple Cider Syrup

Rich and delicious, this hearty breakfast will sustain you on a cold fall morning when your list of chores includes raking the leaves and stacking firewood.

1 package (8 ounces) cream cheese, softened

2 teaspoons vanilla extract, divided

½ cup finely chopped walnuts

1 loaf (1 pound) Italian bread, unsliced

4 eggs

1 cup heavy cream

½ teaspoon ground nutmeg

Sautéed Apples (recipe follows)

Admiral Farragut Inn Apple Cider Syrup (recipe follows)

In a medium-sized bowl, beat the cream cheese and 1 teaspoon of the vanilla until fluffy. Stir in the nuts and set aside.

Cut the bread into eight 2-inch slices and cut a pocket in each (sideways through upper crust). Fill each pocket with 2 tablespoons of the cream cheese mixture, then set aside while preparing the batter.

In a second medium-sized bowl, beat the eggs, cream, nutmeg, and remaining 1 teaspoon vanilla until well blended. Dip both sides of the bread in the egg mixture, being careful not to squeeze out the filling.

Cook on a lightly greased griddle until golden brown on both sides. Place on an ungreased cookie sheet and bake in a preheated 300°F oven for 20 minutes. Place 2 slices each on 4 plates and top each with 2 tablespoons Sautéed Apples. Serve warm with Admiral Farragut Inn Apple Cider Syrup.

SAUTÉED APPLES

4 medium-sized apples, peeled, cored, and cut into thin slices

1 ounce rum

2 tablespoons orange juice

1 tablespoon butter

¼ cup firmly packed brown sugar

Combine the apples, rum, orange juice, butter, and brown sugar in a large skillet and sauté gently over medium heat until the apples are tender, stirring frequently.

ADMIRAL FARRAGUT INN APPLE CIDER SYRUP

¼ cup firmly packed brown sugar

2 tablespoons cornstarch

¼ teaspoon ground allspice

⅛ teaspoon ground nutmeg

2 cups apple cider or apple juice

In a small saucepan, combine the brown sugar, cornstarch, allspice, and nutmeg. Slowly add the cider or juice. Cook over medium heat until slightly thickened, stirring constantly.

SERVES 4.

BANANA-STUFFED FRENCH TOAST WITH BLUEBERRY COMPOTE

For a pleasant alternative to white bread, try honey whole wheat or raisin bran bread.

4 ounces cream cheese, softened

3 large ripe bananas, mashed

¼ teaspoon ground nutmeg

24 slices white bread, crust removed

6 eggs

3 cups half-and-half

2 teaspoons vanilla extract

Confectioners' sugar

Blueberry Compote (recipe follows)

In a medium-sized bowl, beat together the cream cheese, banana, and nutmeg. Spread 12 slices of bread with the cream cheese mixture and sandwich with the remaining 12 slices.

In a blender, combine the eggs, half-and-half, and vanilla. Pour into a shallow dish. Dip the sandwiched bread into the egg batter and cook on a lightly greased griddle until brown on both sides. Serve immediately on warmed plates and sprinkle with confectioners' sugar. Accompany with Blueberry Compote.

BLUEBERRY COMPOTE

2 cups blueberries, fresh or frozen

¼ cup sugar

1½ teaspoons lemon juice

1 tablespoon cornstarch

Blend the blueberries, sugar, lemon juice, and cornstarch together in a medium-sized saucepan. Cook over low heat until thickened and serve warm.

SERVES 6.

OVEN-BAKED CARAMEL FRENCH TOAST

Absolutely delicious just the way it is, but for a variation place a layer of Granny Smith apple slices between the sandwiched bread.

1 cup firmly packed brown sugar

½ cup butter

2 tablespoons light corn syrup

1 cup finely chopped pecans

12 to 18 slices Italian or French bread

6 eggs

1½ cups milk

1 teaspoon vanilla extract

¼ teaspoon ground nutmeg

1½ teaspoons ground cinnamon

¼ teaspoon salt

Graycote Inn Caramel Sauce (recipe follows)

Combine the brown sugar, butter, and corn syrup in a small saucepan and cook over medium heat until thickened, stirring constantly. Pour into a 13- by 9-inch baking dish and sprinkle half the pecans over the syrup. Place 6 to 9 slices of bread on top of the syrup mixture and sprinkle the remaining pecans on top of the bread. Top with the remaining 6 to 9 slices of bread.

Combine the eggs, milk, vanilla, nutmeg, cinnamon, and salt in a blender. Pour evenly over the bread slices, cover the baking dish, and chill 8 hours.

Bake uncovered in a preheated 350°F oven for 40 to 45 minutes or until lightly browned. Drizzle the sauce over the toast right before serving.

GRAYCOTE INN CARAMEL SAUCE

½ cup firmly packed brown sugar

¼ cup butter

1 tablespoon light corn syrup

In a small saucepan, combine the brown sugar, butter, and corn syrup and cook until thickened, stirring constantly.

SERVES 6 TO 9.

STILLMEADOW STUFFED FRENCH TOAST

"This is an overnight recipe that allows us more time to spend with guests! It is excellent with fruit compote or with extra warmed syrup on the side."

12 to 16 slices raisin or cinnamon bread, depending on size

½ cup cream cheese, softened

Cinnamon-sugar mixture

8 eggs

½ cup milk or heavy cream

½ cup maple syrup

Confectioners' sugar

Grease or spray a 13- by 9-inch casserole dish (glass works best). Arrange a layer of bread slices on the bottom of the dish, covering completely. Spread each slice with a generous layer of cream cheese, then sprinkle liberally with cinnamon-sugar mixture. Top with the same arrangement of remaining bread slices.

In a large bowl, mix the eggs, milk or cream, and syrup, then pour over the bread. If it floats, push the bread down to immerse it in liquid. Cover with plastic wrap and refrigerate overnight.

Bake uncovered in a preheated 350°F oven for 45 minutes or until golden and puffy. To serve, cut through bread slices diagonally, creating triangles. Sprinkle with confectioners' sugar and serve while puffed.

SERVES 4 TO 6.

MARLBOROUGH ZUCCHINI FRITTATA

"This is one of those wonderful recipes that isn't adversely affected if substitutions are made with low-fat ingredients. Use egg substitute and egg whites instead of whole eggs, margarine instead of butter, and low-fat/low-sodium cheese instead of regular cheese. Make a dramatic statement by bringing this brown and puffy egg dish to the table in the skillet right from the broiler."

2 cups chopped zucchini

3 tablespoons butter

12 eggs, beaten

⅓ cup chopped green onion or
  ¼ cup chopped fresh chives

1 cup grated Monterey Jack
  cheese

1 tablespoon chopped fresh dill

Sauté the zucchini in 1 tablespoon of the butter for about 3 minutes. Do not overcook. Remove from the pan and set aside to cool.

Mix the cooled zucchini into the beaten eggs. Melt the remaining 2 tablespoons butter in a heavy 10- or 12-inch skillet until very hot but not burning. Slowly pour in the egg and zucchini mixture and reduce the heat to medium. As the eggs begin to set around the perimeter of the skillet, use a spatula to lift the edges, letting the eggs flow underneath. Repeat until the eggs are set, but not dry. Turn off the heat.

Sprinkle the eggs with the onion, cheese, and dill. Place under a preheated broiler until puffy, brown, and bubbly. Cut into 4 wedges and serve on warmed plates.

SERVES 4.

Left Over but Not Forgotten

*L*EFTOVERS—you can barely live with 'em, but you can't bear to toss 'em out either. Here are some innkeepers' tips for transforming last night's dinner into today's repast:

* Rare roast beef makes a wonderful base for salads. Slice the meat thinly, grill or reheat it, and place it on a bed of greens. Serve with a light dressing.

* Toss your leftover cooked vegetables in with chicken, beef, or fish stock to make a quick soup. Don't heat the soup too long or the vegetables will overcook.

* Almost any leftover meat, cheese, or fresh vegetable makes a good filling for omelets.

* Combine leftover meats with pasta, mix in some Mozzarella or provolone cheese, perhaps some tomatoes or tomato sauce, and heat in a casserole dish.

* Substitute leftover poached salmon for beef in breakfast hash.

* Chop up fresh fruit that's become slightly overripe and add it to pancake or muffin batter.

* Spread a thin layer of Dijon-style mustard on leftover crepes. Roll them up and cut them into 1-inch slices to make a snack or hors d'oeuvres.

* Save leftover French toast batter—milk, eggs, cinnamon, and sometimes other spices—and use as the basis for bread pudding.

* Coarsely chop leftover chicken or meat, blend with either cooked long-grain white or brown rice, and you've got a tasty filling for burritos. Just add lettuce, salsa, and cheese.

* Mix coarsely chopped leftover chicken or meat and vegetables, add your favorite spices, top with a layer of mashed potato—or puff pastry or biscuit dough—and heat in the oven.

FESTIVE HOLIDAY EGGS

"This is a very old family recipe that is traditionally served on Christmas morning."

8 slices maple-smoked bacon
12 eggs
Garlic salt
Seasoned pepper
Crushed red pepper flakes
Dried parsley

Cut the bacon crosswise into 1-inch squares and place five squares evenly around the edge of each cup in a greased 12-cup muffin tin, keeping half the bacon inside and half outside each cup. Break 1 egg into each cup, add a dash of seasonings to taste, and bake in a preheated 325°F oven for 25 minutes.

Carefully loosen the egg-bacon mixture with a sharp knife, then lift from the cups with a tablespoon onto paper towel to blot. Serve hot with fresh-baked bread or hot English muffins, strawberries, butter, and jams.

MAKES 12.

EGGS DIJON

Breakfast, brunch, lunch, or supper, this dish fits any meal. It's easy to make, attractive, and delicious.

½ cup mayonnaise or salad dressing

1 teaspoon maple syrup

1 teaspoon Dijon-style mustard

6 hard-boiled eggs

4 English muffins, split

8 thin slices ham

½ cup grated cheddar cheese

Freshly ground pepper

Combine the mayonnaise, maple syrup, and mustard in a saucepan and blend well. Chop the eggs into rough chunks and stir into the mayonnaise mixture. Cook over medium heat until hot but do not boil.

Toast the muffins very lightly. Top each muffin half with a slice of the ham, then ¼ cup of the egg mixture. Sprinkle the cheese over the top.

Bake in a preheated 350°F oven for 8 to 10 minutes or until thoroughly heated and the cheese is melted. Sprinkle with pepper and serve.

SERVES 4.

TAMWORTH BAKED EGGS

"This is a very reliable and extremely popular breakfast dish with our guests. It makes approximately 10 to 12 servings and can be doubled or cut in half. We usually make one with ham and one vegetarian, using mushrooms, spinach, or other vegetables."

1 loaf French bread
½ cup chopped onion
1 cup chopped ham
1 cup grated cheddar cheese
15 eggs
2 to 3 cups milk
½ teaspoon mustard
Salt and pepper to taste
A dash of Tabasco sauce
Crushed red pepper flakes
Sour cream
Parmesan cheese

Tear the bread into small pieces and layer in the bottom of a greased 13- by 9-inch baking pan. Sprinkle onion, ham, and cheese over the bread. Beat the eggs with the milk, mustard, salt, pepper, Tabasco, and red pepper flakes until frothy. Pour over the mixture in the pan, cover tightly with aluminum foil, and refrigerate overnight.

In the morning, remove from the refrigerator and let stand at room temperature for 30 minutes. Bake in a preheated 350°F oven for approximately 45 minutes or until the eggs are almost set. Uncover and spread a layer of sour cream over the eggs, then sprinkle with Parmesan cheese and return to the oven for approximately 15 minutes.

SERVES 10 TO 12.

ON CRANBERRY POND EGG CASSEROLE

In addition to breakfast, this makes a great supper as well.

1 pound ground pork sausage
(the chef uses Sardinha
sausage because it's low-fat)

1 small onion, chopped

½ teaspoon garlic powder

2¼ cups milk

10 eggs

1½ teaspoons dry mustard

½ teaspoon salt

1½ cups grated cheddar cheese

2 cups flavored croutons

Cook the sausage, onion, and garlic powder in a large skillet over medium heat until the sausage browns. Drain well.

In a large bowl, combine the milk, eggs, mustard, and salt and beat for 1 minute. Stir in the cheese, croutons, and sausage. Pour into an ungreased 13- by 9-inch pan and bake uncovered in a preheated 350°F oven for 30 to 40 minutes or until a knife inserted in the center comes out clean.

NOTE: This recipe can be prepared the night before, refrigerated, and then baked in the morning, but extend the cooking time by about 10 minutes.

SERVES 6 TO 8.

BAKED EGGS

Onions, chives, and cheese enliven this elegant dish, which appeals to all ages. Serve it with homemade applesauce and sausage.

6 eggs

½ cup sour cream

¼ teaspoon white pepper

1 teaspoon chopped onion

1 ounce diced ham

1 teaspoon chopped dried chives

1¼ cups grated Havarti cheese, divided

Beat the eggs, then add the sour cream, pepper, onion, ham, chives, and 1 cup of the cheese, stirring to blend (the mixture will be lumpy).

Pour into a greased 8-inch baking dish and bake in a preheated 375°F oven for 35 minutes. When set, remove from the oven, sprinkle with the remaining ¼ cup cheese, and return to the oven for 3 minutes or long enough to melt the cheese topping. Serve hot.

SERVES 4.

The Inn on Sea Street

HYANNIS, MASSACHUSETTS

CRAB SCRAMBLE

"Decidedly rich, but a favorite with all our guests. Not only a breakfast dish but wonderful for brunch with salad and French bread."

4 tablespoons butter

9 eggs

½ cup milk

½ teaspoon salt

¼ teaspoon pepper

1 can (6 ounces) crabmeat, drained

1 package (8 ounces) cream cheese, cut into ½-inch cubes

1 tablespoon dill, fresh or dried

Melt the butter in a 12- by 8-inch glass baking dish. In a bowl, beat the eggs, milk, salt, and pepper. Stir in the crabmeat and cream cheese. Pour over the melted butter and sprinkle dill over the top.

Bake in a preheated 350°F oven for 20 minutes, then lower the heat to 300°F and bake for 10 minutes or until firm in the center.

SERVES 6.

THE CAPTAIN'S EGGS

"This recipe is great for breakfast right out of the oven and works beautifully for brunch, since it keeps well on a warming tray. For a light supper, use a mix of red and green peppers and shredded cheddar cheese in place of the Monterey Jack. Top with garden-fresh tomatoes."

5 eggs

¼ cup all-purpose flour

½ teaspoon baking powder

¾ cup cottage cheese

8 ounces grated Monterey Jack cheese

½ cup sliced fresh mushrooms

½ cup broccoli florets, cut into small pieces (or other seasonal vegetables such as zucchini or green or red bell pepper)

Beat the eggs with a whisk, then add the flour and baking powder, mixing well. Stir in the cottage cheese, Jack cheese, mushrooms, and broccoli and pour into a greased or sprayed 8-inch square baking dish.

Bake in a preheated 375°F oven for 25 to 30 minutes or until set. Garnish with bacon or sausage links (cut in half).

SERVES 4 TO 6.

RIVER BEND FARM MASTER EGG CASSEROLE

"One of the hardest things for an innkeeper or hostess is finding an egg recipe that will hold well. This one will keep on the table for about an hour!"

3 cups 2 percent milk

6 large eggs

1 teaspoon dry mustard (Coleman's is recommended)

Unsalted butter

Stuffing mix (Pepperidge Farm herbed stuffing is recommended, but even stale bread will work, cut into ½-inch cubes, but the cook will need to improvise with herbs and spices)

12 ounces mild sausage meat (Jimmy Dean is recommended)

10 ounces whole leaf spinach, fresh or frozen

Pepper

8 ounces grated Vermont sharp cheddar cheese

Whisk the milk, eggs, and mustard in a bowl and set aside.

Butter an 8-cup-capacity oval gratin dish or other suitable refrigerator-to-oven-to-table container. Cover the bottom with half the stuffing mix or bread pieces.

In a medium-sized saucepan, boil the sausage briefly in water. Drain in a colander, breaking up the meat, and let cool. Distribute the meat in an even layer over the top of the stuffing or bread, spread the spinach over that, and gently pour the egg-milk mixture over all. Grind pepper over the top and sprinkle with the cheese. Cover with plastic wrap and refrigerate 8 hours or more.

Bake in a preheated 350°F oven for 60 to 75 minutes or until the top is brown and puffy. Serve immediately.

VARIATION: Substitute ham for sausage, shredded zucchini for spinach, change the cheese, add a little nutmeg; it's versatile, easy, and fun. The important things are to use what's seasonally available, use the 2 eggs to 1 cup milk custard ratio, and allow the casserole to sit for at least 8 hours to soak the bread and blend the flavors.

SERVES 12.

Eggemoggin Reach Bed and Breakfast

DOWNEAST SAUSAGE AND EGGS

This scrumptious and simple one-dish breakfast cuts neatly into generous-sized portions that are easy to serve.

6 to 8 ounces loose sausage, cooked and drained

1½ cups grated sharp cheddar cheese

2 eggs, beaten

1 cup milk

1¼ tablespoons all-purpose flour

Salt and pepper to taste

Spread the sausage evenly over the bottom of a 13- by 9-inch buttered casserole. Sprinkle cheese over the sausage. Beat the eggs, milk, flour, salt, and pepper together and pour over the sausage-cheese mixture.

Bake in a preheated 350°F oven for 35 to 40 minutes.

NOTE: The night before you plan to serve this recipe, prepare it up to where the cheese is added, then place in the refrigerator. The next morning, simply proceed with the rest of the directions, put it in the oven, and let bake while you make toast and coffee, pour the juice, and set the table.

SERVES 6 TO 8.

WATCH HILL SAVORY HOLIDAY STRATA

Fresh herbs add flavor as well as color to this splendid dish.

⅓ cup butter

1 pound sausage (preferably homemade)

3 to 4 cups dried white bread, crust removed and cut into 1-inch cubes

1 tablespoon shredded fresh basil or 2 teaspoons dried

1 tablespoon chopped fresh dill or 1 teaspoon dried

1 tablespoon chopped fresh chives

1 cup grated sharp cheddar cheese

1 cup corn kernels, fresh or frozen

¼ cup chopped red bell pepper

6 eggs

2 cups milk

Salt and pepper to taste

Melt the butter in a 13- by 9-inch baking dish, tilting it so the butter coats the bottom. Brown the sausage in a skillet, drain thoroughly, and set aside.

Layer half of the bread cubes in the buttered baking dish and sprinkle with half of the basil, dill, chives, cheese, corn, and bell pepper. Then layer with the remaining bread cubes, basil, dill, chives, cheese, corn, and bell pepper. Sprinkle the sausage over all.

Beat the eggs, then add the milk, blending well. Season with salt and pepper and pour over the casserole.

At this point, you may bake it immediately or cover with plastic wrap and refrigerate overnight. If it has been refrigerated, let stand at room temperature ½ to 1 hour before you bake it.

Bake in a preheated 350°F oven for 1 hour, then let set for 10 minutes before serving.

SERVES 6.

CHEDDAR AND PESTO STRATA

Morning or evening, this will be a big hit. Accompany with sausage for breakfast and at suppertime include a salad to complete the meal.

½ loaf Italian bread, cut into
   1-inch cubes

¾ cup chopped onion

¾ cup diced red bell pepper

¾ cup diced green bell pepper

⅓ cup grated Romano cheese

2 cups grated cheddar cheese

1 cup sliced fresh mushrooms

7 eggs

1 teaspoon salt

3 cups milk

1 teaspoon chopped garlic

1 tablespoon chopped fresh
   basil or 1½ teaspoons dried

Place the bread on the bottom of a greased 13- by 9-inch pan. Top with a layer of onion, red and green bell pepper, cheeses, and mushrooms. Beat the eggs, salt, milk, garlic, and basil together and pour over all. Let set in the refrigerator overnight.

Bake in a preheated 325°F oven for 1 hour.

SERVES 6.

BRIE STRATA WITH FRUIT SALSA

"This strata is a favorite at Watch Hill. I served it at the occasion of the restoration of our landmark Kona Fountain, which graces the center of Center Harbor."

Butter, softened

8 to 10 slices white bread, crust removed

1 pound Brie, rind removed and well chilled

4 eggs

1½ cups milk

1 teaspoon salt

Paprika

Fruit Salsa (recipe follows)

Butter one side of the bread slices and place half of them, buttered side up, in a greased 9-inch square baking pan.

Cut the Brie into ½-inch cubes and sprinkle half over the bread. Repeat with the remaining bread and Brie.

Beat the eggs, milk, and salt together and pour over the bread and cheese. Sprinkle with paprika and let stand 30 minutes before baking.

Bake in a preheated 350°F oven for 35 to 40 minutes. To serve, cut the strata into squares and top with Fruit Salsa.

FRUIT SALSA

1 pint fresh strawberries, hulled and diced

1 medium-sized Anjou pear, cored and diced

1 medium-sized red apple, cored and diced

1 tablespoon honey

1 tablespoon freshly squeezed lime juice

Combine the strawberries, pear, apple, honey, and lime juice in a medium-sized bowl, stirring to blend. Serve at room temperature.

NOTE: This recipe can be prepared the night before serving, but be sure to remove from the refrigerator 30 minutes before baking.

SERVES 6.

CAPTAIN BILLY'S BREAKFAST

"This sausage-egg strata was first served to us by a Navy friend (presently a captain and still on active duty) at a Sunday brunch during an Army–Navy football weekend (Navy won). We have modified the recipe somewhat, substituting potatoes for bread and using low-fat sausage, and have been serving it at the Graycote since we took over in 1992."

5 to 6 medium-sized potatoes, peeled, boiled, and chopped

1 cup flavored croutons

¼ cup dried chopped onion

2 cups grated hard cheese (or combination of cheddar, Monterey Jack, and provolone)

1 pound low-fat turkey sausage, fully cooked, either sliced or crumbled (any kind of sausage will do)

10 eggs, beaten

2 cups half-and-half or milk

Salt

¼ teaspoon cayenne pepper

1 cup crushed cornflakes cereal

Layer the potato, croutons, onion, half of the cheese, sausage, and remaining cheese in a 13- by 9-inch baking dish coated with no-stick cooking spray.

Beat the eggs, half-and-half or milk, salt, and cayenne together and pour over the layered ingredients. Cover and refrigerate overnight.

Remove the dish from the refrigerator 15 minutes before baking. Sprinkle cornflakes over the top and bake in a preheated 350°F oven for 45 minutes or until set (may have to cover with aluminum foil last 15 to 20 minutes). Let stand 5 minutes before slicing.

SERVES 6 TO 8.

The Richards Bed and Breakfast

NARRAGANSETT, RHODE ISLAND

Breakfast Strudel

When you're hankering for something different for breakfast, make this easy and unusual dish. It can be partially prepared in advance, then assembled right before baking.

3 tablespoons butter, divided

2 tablespoons all-purpose flour

1 cup milk

½ cup grated cheddar or Swiss cheese

A pinch of pepper

A pinch of ground nutmeg

¼ pound sausage

6 eggs

½ teaspoon dried thyme

¾ cup butter, melted

8 phyllo dough sheets

½ cup dried bread crumbs

1 tablespoon chopped fresh parsley for garnish

Melt 2 tablespoons of the butter over low heat, add the flour, and cook, stirring constantly, for 3 minutes. Gradually whisk in the milk, increase the heat, and cook until the mixture comes to a boil. Remove from the heat, stir in the cheese, pepper, and nutmeg, and pour into a bowl.

Crumble the sausage into a skillet and cook over medium heat until it is no longer pink, but do not brown. Drain and add to the cheese sauce.

Beat the eggs and thyme together and cook in the remaining 1 tablespoon butter until just set. Add to the sausage-cheese sauce and cool completely. (This may be done the night before, refrigerated, and brought to room temperature when ready to bake.)

Brush 1 sheet of phyllo dough with some of the melted butter. Sprinkle with 1 tablespoon bread crumbs and fold in half lengthwise. Brush with butter and spoon about ⅓ cup of the sausage-cheese filling along one short end, leaving a ¾-inch border along the edges empty. Fold the edges over, starting at the end with the filling, and roll to make a neat package. Place on a greased cookie sheet and brush with butter. Repeat with the remaining ingredients.

Bake in a preheated 375°F oven for 15 minutes. Garnish with the parsley.

SERVES 8.

STRAWBERRY SWIRL COFFEE CAKE

Quick and simple to prepare yet elegant in taste and appearance. Freeze the extra loaf for later use or wrap it in aluminum foil, attach a colorful bow, and present it as a hostess gift.

¾ cup butter or margarine, softened

1½ cups sugar

3 eggs

1½ teaspoons vanilla extract

3 cups all-purpose flour

1½ teaspoons baking powder

1½ teaspoons baking soda

¼ teaspoon salt

1½ cups sour cream

Strawberry preserves

Sugar

Cream the butter or margarine and sugar in a large bowl. Add the eggs and vanilla and beat for 2 minutes. Combine the flour, baking powder, baking soda, and salt, and add to the creamed mixture alternately with the sour cream. Spoon most of the batter into two greased 9- by 5-inch loaf pans, reserving just enough to layer the tops.

Distribute a thin layer of strawberry preserves over the batter in each pan and then swirl slightly with a fork, but do not blend the preserves into the batter. Cover the preserves with the reserved batter and dust tops lightly with sugar.

Bake in a preheated 350°F oven for about 1 hour or until a toothpick inserted in the center comes out clean. Cool slightly in pans before removing.

MAKES 2 LOAVES.

Eggemoggin Reach Bed and Breakfast

BROOKSVILLE, MAINE

delicious

JANO'S BLUEBERRY COFFEE CAKE

Simple and sweet, this should be served soon after it is made; it does not keep particularly well, but it tastes so good that there's seldom any left over.

2 cups all-purpose flour

2 cups sugar, divided (1½ + ½)

2 teaspoons baking powder

1 teaspoon salt

⅓ cup butter

2 eggs

1 cup milk

2 cups fresh blueberries

1 teaspoon ground cinnamon

Mix the flour, 1½ cups of the sugar, baking powder, and salt together. Cut in the butter until crumbly in consistency. Add the eggs and milk, beating until smooth. Pour into a greased 13- by 9-inch pan. Distribute the blueberries over the top of the batter.

Combine the remaining ½ cup sugar with the cinnamon and sprinkle over the top of the berries and batter. Bake in a preheated 350°F oven for 35 to 40 minutes.

SERVES 8 TO 10.

Sour Cream Coffee Cake

"Many years ago, I received a chain letter requesting a recipe. I dutifully followed the directions and sent my recipe out. This was the only recipe I received in return, but it has certainly paid off. I make it often at the inn."

1 cup sugar, divided

1 teaspoon ground cinnamon

½ cup chopped walnuts

1 cup sour cream

1 teaspoon baking soda

¼ pound butter, softened

2 eggs

½ teaspoon vanilla extract

2 cups all-purpose flour

1½ teaspoons baking powder

Mix ½ cup of the sugar, cinnamon, and walnuts in a small bowl and set aside. Combine the sour cream and baking soda in a small bowl and set aside.

Cream the butter and remaining ½ cup sugar in a large bowl. Beat in the eggs and vanilla. Sift the flour and baking powder together and add alternately with the sour cream mixture to the butter-egg mixture.

Spread half the batter in a greased and floured 9- by 5-inch loaf pan. Sprinkle half the sugar, cinnamon, and nut mixture over the top and gently incorporate some of it into the batter, using a fork. Add the remaining batter, and then the remaining sugar, cinnamon, and nut mixture, blending as before.

Bake in a preheated 350°F oven for 45 to 60 minutes or until golden brown.

Serves 8.

The Village House

ALMOND COFFEE CAKE

Rich and sweet, this is a multipurpose cake. For a more pronounced almond flavor, use almond extract instead of vanilla or half of each.

½ cup butter, softened

1 cup sugar

2 eggs

1 cup milk

2 cups all-purpose flour

2 teaspoons baking powder

1 teaspoon vanilla extract

Almond Topping (recipe follows)

Cream the butter and sugar in a large bowl. Add the eggs, milk, flour, baking powder, and vanilla, blending thoroughly. Pour into a greased 11- by 7-inch pan.

Spread the topping evenly over the batter and bake in a preheated 350°F oven for 30 minutes or until golden brown. Let cool before cutting.

ALMOND TOPPING

1 cup sugar

½ cup butter

1 teaspoon vanilla extract

1 teaspoon ground cinnamon

1 cup slivered almonds

Combine the sugar, butter, vanilla, and cinnamon in a medium-sized saucepan. Cook until melted and just beginning to bubble. Remove from heat and stir in almonds.

SERVES 10.

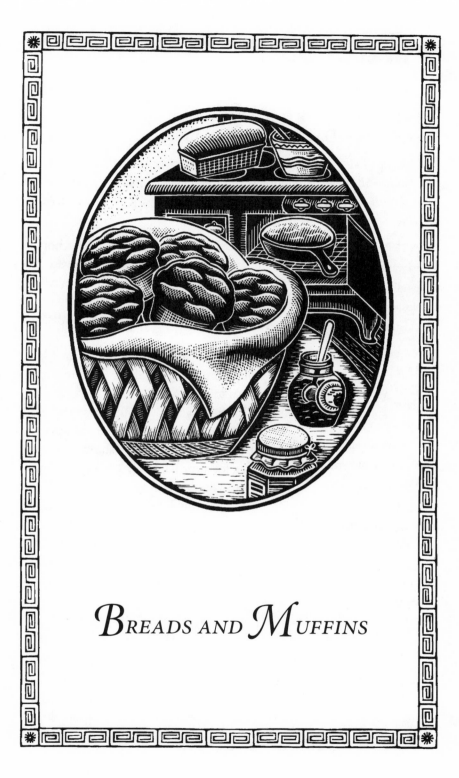

BREADS AND MUFFINS

VINCE'S FIVE-DAY SOURDOUGH BREAD

"It looks just like bread looks in books," said one six-year-old who sampled this bread. Although it requires five days' advance planning, this recipe rewards you with big, beautiful loaves, the flavor of which is enhanced by toasting.

STARTER

3 cups warm water

4 cups all-purpose flour

2 tablespoons honey

1 package (1 tablespoon) dry yeast

BREAD

1 package (1 tablespoon) dry yeast

½ cup warm water

3 tablespoons nonfat dry milk

4 tablespoons butter, melted

4 tablespoons sugar

3 teaspoons salt

5 to 7 cups all-purpose flour

Vegetable oil

In a large bowl, mix the water, flour, honey, and yeast together and leave uncovered in a warm place for 1 day, stirring down several times. The next day, cover with a towel and let sit for another 2 to 4 days, stirring twice a day.

Combine the yeast with the water, dry milk, butter, sugar, salt, and 3 cups flour. Let sit for 5 minutes.

In the large bowl with the starter, add the yeast mixture and beat until smooth. Cover with a cloth and let stand in a warm place for approximately 1 hour until bubbly and double in size.

Stir in enough flour to make a workable dough, turn out onto a lightly floured surface, and knead for 10 minutes or until smooth, adding additional flour if needed.

Divide in two pieces and let rest while you grease two 9- by 5-inch bread pans. Form into two loaves, place in pans, and brush the tops with oil. Cover with a cloth and let rise approximately 1½ hours until double.

Bake in a 375°F oven for 45 to 55 minutes or until golden brown. Remove from pans and place on wire racks to cool.

VARIATION: For a better sour flavor, add 3 tablespoons of any or all of the following: buttermilk, plain yogurt, or sour cream. You may also substitute 2 cups rye and/or whole wheat flour for 2 cups all-purpose flour.

MAKES 2 LOAVES.

ITALIAN BREAD

"We serve this bread warm with dinner. Wrapped in foil, it may be reheated at 375 degrees for 10 minutes. We also use the dough for our homemade pizza."

4½ to 5½ cups all-purpose flour

1 tablespoon salt

1 tablespoon sugar

2 packages (2 tablespoons) dry yeast

1 tablespoon butter or margarine

1¾ cups hot water

Cornmeal

Corn or other vegetable oil

1 egg white lightly beaten with 1 tablespoon cold water

Place 3 cups flour, the salt, sugar, yeast, and butter or margarine in the bowl of a food processor fitted with a metal blade. Pulse the machine on and off rapidly two or three times or until the butter is thoroughly cut into the dry ingredients. Add half the water and pulse four times. Add 1½ cups more flour and the remaining water and pulse four times. Let the processor run until a ball of dough forms on the blades. If the dough is too sticky, add some of the remaining flour, a few tablespoons at a time, then let the processor run 40 to 60 seconds to knead the dough.

Turn the dough out onto a lightly floured surface and knead several times to form a smooth ball. Cover with plastic wrap and a towel. Let rest for 20 minutes. Divide the dough in half and roll each half into a rectangle about 15 by 10 inches. Beginning on the long side, roll up the dough tightly. Pinch the seams to seal and taper the ends by rolling gently back and forth.

Place the dough on greased baking sheets sprinkled with cornmeal, brush with oil, and cover loosely with plastic wrap. Refrigerate 2 to 24 hours. When ready to bake, remove from the refrigerator, uncover carefully, and let stand at room temperature for 10 minutes. Make 3 or 4 cuts across the top of each loaf with a sharp knife.

Bake at 425°F for 20 minutes. Remove from the oven and brush with the egg white–water mixture. Return to the oven and bake 5 to 10 minutes longer or until golden brown. Let cool on a wire rack.

MAKES 2 LOAVES.

SAUSAGE BREAD

This flavorful, hearty bread makes a fine accompaniment to soups and salads. It's great for picnics and tailgate parties, too.

6 cups all-purpose flour (approximate)

1 package (1 tablespoon) dry yeast

2 cups hot water

⅓ cup butter or margarine, melted

1 tablespoon sugar

1½ teaspoons salt

1 link sweet Italian sausage

1 link hot Italian sausage

1 medium-sized onion, chopped

2 cloves garlic, minced

Dried oregano, basil, tarragon, salt, and pepper to taste (optional)

½ cup chopped green bell pepper

½ cup chopped red bell pepper

1½ cups grated Mozzarella cheese

3 tablespoons all-purpose flour

1 egg white lightly beaten with 1 tablespoon water

In a large bowl, or in a food processor, combine 3 cups of the flour and the yeast. In a separate bowl, combine the water, butter or margarine, sugar, and salt and add to the dry ingredients, mixing well. Add 1 cup of the flour and blend well. Stir in the remaining flour ½ cup at a time until the dough leaves the sides of the bowl. (At this point, you will have used about 5 cups flour.) Remove the dough from the bowl and knead by hand on a lightly floured surface, adding flour as needed, until the dough is smooth and elastic. (If you mixed the dough by hand, the kneading will take about 5 to 8 minutes. If you mixed the dough in a food processor, only a brief kneading is necessary.)

Altogether you will use about 6 cups flour, but each loaf is different so don't rely too heavily on the measurements. Add just enough flour to take out the stickiness. Let the dough rest under a clean towel while you prepare the filling or for at least 15 minutes.

Remove the casings from the sausages and brown the meat in a skillet with the onion and garlic. Season to taste with oregano, basil, tarragon, salt, and pepper, if desired (since the sausage is already seasoned, you may not want to add more). Drain the sausage well on several layers of paper towel or a clean cloth.

Combine the green and red bell pepper and cheese in a medium-sized bowl and toss with the 3 tablespoons flour. Add the drained sausage mixture and toss again.

Knead the dough briefly in a little more flour and divide it into two pieces. Roll each piece into a rectangle approximately 15 by 12 inches. Sprinkle each rectangle with half of the sausage mixture, leaving a 1-inch border on all sides. Starting with a long side near you, roll each rectangle tightly into a jelly roll. Pinch the seams and both ends to seal. Place the loaves in an ungreased French bread pan or on a cookie sheet. Cover with a clean towel and let rise for about 1 hour.

Brush the loaves with the egg white–water mixture and bake in a preheated 425°F oven until they are light and shiny brown, approximately 30 minutes. Remove from oven and place on wire racks to cool.

MAKES 2 LOAVES.

MANNA FROM THE FREEZER

*M*ARION HEBERT of Edgewater Farm Bed and Breakfast in Sebasco Estates, Maine, always freezes her homemade bread after she bakes it. She says that freezing improves the flavor and makes the bread easier to slice when it thaws. If you double-wrap the bread in heavy-duty aluminum foil, it will keep for months.

APPLE RAISIN BREAD

"Over the years, our afternoon tea at the Jefferson Inn has grown in popularity. We offer numerous baked goods, but there are certain recipes that have been the crowd favorites, like the one included here."

3 cups peeled, cored, and chopped apple

3 cups all-purpose flour

1½ teaspoons baking soda

½ teaspoon baking powder

⅔ cup raisins

½ cup chopped walnuts

1½ teaspoons salt

2 cups sugar

1¼ cups vegetable oil

4 eggs

1 tablespoon plus 1 teaspoon vanilla extract

2 teaspoons ground cinnamon

Combine the apple, flour, baking soda, baking powder, raisins, nuts, salt, sugar, oil, eggs, vanilla, and cinnamon in a large bowl and beat on low speed for 1 minute. Increase the speed to medium and beat for 1 more minute, scraping the bowl constantly.

Pour into two greased 9- by 5-inch bread pans and bake in a preheated 325°F oven for 1 hour. Cool for 10 minutes, remove from pans, and cool completely before slicing.

MAKES 2 LOAVES.

CRANBERRY BREAD

A moist, dense loaf that can be served with breakfast, lunch, or dinner or as a snack any time of day.

1 cup sugar

2 tablespoons butter, softened

1 egg

2 cups all-purpose flour

½ teaspoon baking soda

1 teaspoon baking powder

½ teaspoon salt

1 cup chopped fresh
   cranberries

¾ cup orange juice

½ cup chopped walnuts

Cream the sugar and butter until smooth. Beat in the egg. Add the flour, baking soda, baking powder, salt, cranberries, orange juice, and nuts and blend well.

Pour into a greased 9- by 5-inch loaf pan and bake in a preheated 350°F oven for 50 minutes or until a toothpick inserted in the center comes out clean.

MAKES 1 LOAF.

AUNT ROSE'S FAMOUS DATE AND NUT BREAD

"My Aunt Rose was a sensational cook and baker. She loved to visit unexpectedly, but she was always welcome—and always brought a freshly baked loaf of this bread. Although raisins were usually substituted for dates, in our family it was always called date and nut bread. Cream cheese is delicious on this bread. At the inn, we serve it at breakfast made up into miniature sandwiches."

1 teaspoon baking soda

1 cup boiling water

1 cup chopped dates or raisins

1 tablespoon shortening

¾ cup sugar

1 egg

1 teaspoon vanilla extract

½ teaspoon unsweetened cocoa powder

1¾ cups all-purpose flour

½ cup chopped walnuts

Dissolve the baking soda in the boiling water, add the dates or raisins, and let soak for half an hour.

Cream the shortening and sugar. Add the egg, vanilla, cocoa, and date or raisin mixture. Blend in the flour, then add the nuts.

Pour the batter into a greased and floured 9- by 5-inch loaf pan. Bake in a preheated 350°F oven for 45 to 55 minutes.

MAKES 1 LOAF.

THE FOREST'S LEMON TEA BREAD

Golden brown and nicely shaped, this tasty bread is ideal not only for teatime but also for breakfast or brunch.

1¼ cups sugar, divided

½ cup shortening

½ cup milk

2 eggs

1½ cups all-purpose flour

1 teaspoon baking powder

½ teaspoon salt

Grated rind and juice of
    1 medium-sized lemon

In a large bowl, cream together 1 cup of the sugar and the shortening. Beat in the milk and eggs. Stir in the flour, baking powder, salt, and lemon rind.

Pour into a greased 8½- by 4½-inch loaf pan. Bake in a preheated 350°F oven for 30 to 40 minutes. Mix the remaining ¼ cup sugar with the lemon juice and spoon over the bread while it is still warm.

MAKES 1 LOAF.

POPPY SEED BREAD

Flavorful and aromatic, this attractive bread resembles pound cake. It's an excellent accompaniment to any meal.

3 cups all-purpose flour

2½ cups sugar

1 teaspoon salt

1½ teaspoons baking powder

3 eggs, beaten

1½ cups milk

1½ cups vegetable oil

1½ tablespoons poppy seeds

1½ teaspoons vanilla extract

1½ teaspoons almond extract

In a large bowl, sift the flour, sugar, salt, and baking powder together. In a separate bowl, combine the eggs, milk, oil, poppy seeds, and vanilla and almond extracts and add to the flour mixture, beating well.

Pour into two greased 9- by 5-inch loaf pans and bake in a preheated 350°F oven for 1 hour.

MAKES 2 LOAVES.

Lemon Poppy Seed Bread

Baked in a Bundt pan, this has a fancy presentation and could be served for dessert.

3 cups all-purpose flour

1½ teaspoons baking powder

1¼ cups sugar

1 teaspoon salt

1 cup milk

1 cup butter, softened

3 eggs

2 tablespoons poppy seeds

2 tablespoons lemon juice

Lemon Glaze (recipe follows)

In a large bowl, combine the flour, baking powder, sugar, salt, milk, butter, eggs, poppy seeds, and lemon juice. Beat at medium speed until well mixed, about 2 to 3 minutes.

Pour the batter into a greased 12-cup Bundt pan and bake 40 minutes in a pre-heated 350°F oven. Cool in the pan 10 minutes, then remove the bread to a serving plate, pour the glaze over the warm bread, and let cool completely.

Lemon Glaze

⅓ cup sugar

3 tablespoons butter, melted

1½ tablespoons lemon juice

In a small bowl, stir together glaze ingredients.

Serves 16 to 20.

Sugar Hill Inn

FRANCONIA, NEW HAMPSHIRE

IRISH TEA BREAD

Golden in color, chewy in texture, and chockful of raisins, this is great toasted for breakfast or served as a treat with afternoon tea. It also makes an excellent alternative to traditional fruitcake.

2 cups golden raisins

2 cups dark raisins

2 cups firmly packed light brown sugar

1 cup cold breakfast tea

½ cup Irish whiskey

4 cups all-purpose flour

3 eggs, beaten

3 teaspoons baking powder

Grated rind of 1 medium-sized lemon

1 teaspoon ground nutmeg

1 teaspoon ground allspice

1 tablespoon honey dissolved in a little warm water, for glazing

Combine the golden and dark raisins, sugar, tea, and whiskey in a large bowl. Cover and let soak overnight or about 12 hours.

Add the flour, eggs, baking powder, lemon rind, nutmeg, and allspice to the raisin mixture, blending well.

Pour into a greased 9- or 10-inch round cake pan and bake in a preheated 350°F oven for 80 to 90 minutes or until nicely browned or a toothpick inserted in the center comes out clean.

Remove the bread from the pan and let cool on a wire rack. Brush the cooled loaf with the warm honey mixture for a shiny glaze.

SERVES 15 TO 20.

APPLE CINNAMON MUFFINS

These muffins are moist, tasty, and aromatic and don't need butter or cream cheese. Children enjoy them as much as adults do.

1 cup all-purpose flour

¾ teaspoon baking soda

¾ teaspoon baking powder

½ teaspoon ground cinnamon

¾ cup firmly packed brown sugar

1 cup rolled oats

½ cup chopped walnuts

1 egg

¾ cup milk

⅓ cup vegetable oil

¾ cup peeled, cored, and finely chopped apple

Brown sugar for sprinkling tops

Sift the flour, baking soda, baking powder, and cinnamon into a large bowl. Combine the brown sugar and oats and add to the flour mixture. Beat the egg, milk, and oil together and add to the flour-oats mixture, blending well. Fold in the apple.

Spoon into paper-lined muffin tins or tins that have been greased or coated with no-stick cooking spray and sprinkle tops with additional sugar. Bake in a preheated 350°F oven for 15 to 20 minutes.

MAKES 12.

BANANA NUT MUFFINS

These have a nice firm texture that allows them to be served warm and spread with butter without falling apart.

2½ cups all-purpose flour

¾ cup sugar

1 tablespoon baking powder

¾ teaspoon salt

¼ cup plus 2 tablespoons
  shortening

1 cup chopped walnuts

3 ripe medium-sized bananas,
  mashed

2 eggs

⅓ cup milk

½ teaspoon vanilla extract

In a large bowl, mix the flour, sugar, baking powder, and salt. With a pastry blender, work in the shortening until mixture is crumbly. Stir in the nuts.

In a separate bowl, combine the banana, eggs, milk, and vanilla. Stir the banana mixture into the dry ingredients until well blended.

Spoon into paper-lined muffin tins or tins that have been greased or coated with no-stick cooking spray and bake in a preheated 400°F oven for 25 to 30 minutes.

MAKES 14 TO 16.

MUFFIN MAGIC

*W*HEN SHE'S MAKING muffins or quick breads that call for the addition of plain yogurt, Marnie Duff of the 1811 House in Manchester, Vermont, substitutes flavored yogurt instead. Blueberry muffins get an extra flavor boost from blueberry yogurt, and lemon yogurt gives lemon tea cake or poppy seed bread a zing. Use your imagination, but be sure to maintain the ratio of dry to wet ingredients called for in the recipe.

APRICOT CRANBERRY MUFFINS

Serve these well-formed, light-brown, moist, and fruity muffins with any meal.

⅓ cup butter or margarine, softened

½ cup plus 1 tablespoon sugar, divided

1 teaspoon vanilla extract

2 eggs

1⅓ cups all-purpose flour

1 teaspoon baking powder

¾ teaspoon baking soda

⅔ cup lemon yogurt

¼ cup finely diced dried cranberries

¼ cup finely diced dried apricots

1 tablespoon grated lemon rind

Cream together the butter or margarine, ½ cup of the sugar, and vanilla until fluffy. Add the eggs one at a time, beating well after each addition. Combine the flour, baking powder, and baking soda and gradually add to the egg mixture alternately with the yogurt.

Toss the cranberries and apricots with a little flour and fold into batter. In a small bowl, mix the remaining 1 tablespoon sugar and the lemon rind.

Fill greased or paper-lined muffin tin two-thirds full, sprinkle tops with the sugar mixture, and bake in a preheated 350°F oven for 20 to 25 minutes.

MAKES 12.

THE MOST IMPORTANT MEAL

*M*OST MORTALS lack the manual dexterity required to prepare hot muffins at 7:00 A.M. But up in the White Mountains of New Hampshire, guests at the Village House Inn in Jackson feast on poppy seed bread, pumpkin and blueberry muffins, and almond coffee cake. Yet Robin Crocker doesn't bake all night, and she doesn't get up at the crack of dawn. She mixes the batter ahead of time and freezes it. Here's how it works: Prepare the batter as usual, then line the cake pan with heavy-duty aluminum foil or muffin tins with paper cups. Pour the batter into the pan or cups, then put in the freezer uncovered until the batter is set. Remove the frozen cake or muffins from the pan or tins, wrap well in plastic wrap, and return to the freezer for up to a month. When you're ready to bake, unwrap, place in the pan or tins, and bake as usual. You will have to add around 10 minutes to the baking time.

RIVER BEND FARM ORANGE CRANBERRY MUFFINS

"This is a favorite of our guests."

6 ounces fresh cranberries

8 ounces bran flakes cereal

2½ cups all-purpose flour

1½ cups sugar

2½ teaspoons baking soda

1 teaspoon salt

2 large eggs

1 pint buttermilk

½ cup vegetable oil

¼ teaspoon orange oil or grated rind of ½ medium-sized orange (see Note)

In a colander, wash and pick through the cranberries. Combine the cereal, flour, sugar, baking soda, and salt in a large bowl. In a separate bowl, whisk the eggs with the buttermilk, oil, and orange oil or rind.

Add the cranberry-egg mixture to the cereal-flour mixture and stir to moisten. Fill greased or paper-lined muffin tins two-thirds full and bake in a preheated 450°F oven for 20 minutes or until a toothpick inserted in the center comes out clean. (The batter will keep in the refrigerator for two or three days.)

NOTE: Boyajian's Pure Orange Oil, available at Williams Sonoma, is recommended by the inn, but the grated rind of ½ orange may be substituted. Use only the orange part, however, not the bitter pith. Use canola oil spray to grease the muffin tins, whose cups should have a 5-ounce capacity, and scoop up the mixture with a 3-ounce ice cream scoop so the muffins will be uniform in size. Bake them for 25 minutes

MAKES 24 REGULAR OR 12 LARGE MUFFINS.

MORNING GLORY MUFFINS  *excellent*

High-energy food, one of these muffins will get you off to a good start in the morning or give you an extra boost midafternoon.

2 cups all-purpose flour

1¼ cups sugar

2 teaspoons baking soda

2 teaspoons ground cinnamon

½ teaspoon salt

2 cups grated carrot

½ cup raisins

½ cup shredded coconut

1 medium-sized apple, peeled, cored, and grated

3 large eggs

1 cup vegetable oil

2 teaspoons vanilla extract

In a large bowl, sift together the flour, sugar, baking soda, cinnamon, and salt. Stir in the carrot, raisins, coconut, and apple. In another bowl, beat the eggs, oil, and vanilla. Stir into the flour mixture until the batter is just moistened.

Spoon the batter into greased or paper-lined muffin tins and bake in a preheated 350°F oven for 35 minutes or until springy to the touch.

MAKES 12 TO 18.

ONE-BOWL LEMON POPPY SEED MUFFINS

"Our guests can never get enough of these! Allowing two muffins per person, we are lucky if there are any left over for our own breakfast!"

2 eggs

1 cup milk

1 tablespoon lemon juice

2 tablespoons grated lemon rind

¼ cup canola oil

2 cups all-purpose flour

¼ cup sugar

2½ teaspoons baking powder

¼ teaspoon ground nutmeg

2 tablespoons poppy seeds

½ cup chopped walnuts

In a large bowl, beat the eggs, milk, lemon juice, lemon rind, and oil together until well blended. Add separately the flour, sugar, baking powder, nutmeg, and poppy seeds, stirring well after each addition. Fold in the walnuts.

Spoon the batter into greased or paper-lined muffin tins, filling about three-fourths full. Bake in a preheated 400°F oven for about 20 minutes or until a toothpick inserted in the center comes out clean.

MAKES 12.

not lemony enough.

RASPBERRY LEMON MUFFINS

Light, slightly tart muffins complemented by a sweet, crunchy topping.

1½ cups all-purpose flour

½ cup sugar

2 teaspoons baking powder

¼ teaspoon salt

1 egg, slightly beaten

¼ cup plus 2 tablespoons butter, melted and cooled

½ cup milk

2 teaspoons lemon juice

1½ cups raspberries, fresh or frozen

1 teaspoon grated lemon rind

Streusel Topping (recipe follows)

In a large bowl, sift together the flour, sugar, baking powder, and salt and stir to combine. In a small bowl, beat together the egg, the butter, milk, and lemon juice. Make a well in the center of the flour mixture, pour in the egg mixture, and stir with a fork until just combined. Lightly fold in the raspberries and lemon rind.

Spoon into greased or paper-lined muffin tins, filling three-fourths full, and sprinkle with Streusel Topping. Bake in a preheated 350°F oven for 20 minutes.

STREUSEL TOPPING

½ cup chopped pecans

½ cup firmly packed light brown sugar

½ cup all-purpose flour

2 tablespoons butter, melted

1 teaspoon grated lemon rind

Combine the pecans, brown sugar, flour, butter, and lemon rind and proceed as directed above.

NOTE: The topping makes a lot, so you may want to reduce the amounts called for by half.

MAKES 12.

STRAWBERRY MUFFINS WITH STRAWBERRY CREAM CHEESE SPREAD

High, light, and lovely, these have just a hint of orange flavor, which blends beautifully with the strawberries.

1 cup chopped fresh strawberries

1 tablespoon plus ¾ cup sugar, divided

2 cups all-purpose flour

2 teaspoons baking powder

1 teaspoon salt

3 eggs

¼ cup vegetable oil

½ cup milk

1 teaspoon grated orange rind

12 whole fresh strawberries, cut fan-shaped (for garnish)

Strawberry Cream Cheese Spread (recipe follows)

In a small bowl, sprinkle the chopped strawberries with 1 tablespoon of the sugar and set aside.

In a large bowl, sift together the flour, remaining ¾ cup sugar, baking powder, and salt. In another bowl, beat the eggs, oil, milk, and orange rind together and add to the flour mixture, stirring until just moistened. Drain the chopped berries and fold into the batter.

Fill greased or paper-lined muffin tins two-thirds full and bake in a preheated 400°F oven for 20 minutes or until a toothpick inserted in the center comes out clean. Garnish each muffin with a fan-shaped strawberry and serve warm or cool with Strawberry Cream Cheese Spread.

STRAWBERRY CREAM CHEESE SPREAD

1 package (8 ounces) cream cheese, softened

¼ cup crushed or chopped fresh strawberries

Combine the cream cheese and strawberries in a bowl, beating until fluffy. Proceed as directed above.

MAKES 12.

TRADE WINDS MUFFINS

"These muffins are always a big hit with our guests. They are moist and freeze well."

1 small package (3 ounces) cream cheese, softened

1 cup sugar

2 teaspoons vanilla extract

1 large egg, beaten

2 cups sifted all-purpose flour

1 teaspoon baking soda

1 teaspoon salt

½ cup sour cream

1 large can (20 ounces) crushed pineapple, drained

½ cup sliced almonds or chopped walnuts

In a bowl, beat the cream cheese, sugar, and vanilla together until smooth. Blend in the egg. Sift the flour, baking soda, and salt together in a separate bowl and add to the sugar-egg mixture alternately with the sour cream. Fold in the drained pineapple.

Sprinkle the nuts in the bottoms of greased or paper-lined muffin tins and fill three-fourths full with batter. Bake in a preheated 350°F oven for 25 to 30 minutes.

MAKES 12 TO 14.

extra

OATMEAL BUTTERSCOTCH MUFFINS

Kids love these sweet treats, which are ideal for packing into school lunches and carrying on picnics.

1 box (18 ounces) rolled oats

1 quart buttermilk

1 box (16 ounces) brown sugar

1½ cups margarine

3 cups all-purpose flour

4 teaspoons baking powder

1½ teaspoons baking soda

1 teaspoon salt

6 large eggs

2 cups butterscotch chips

In a large bowl, mix the oats and buttermilk. Crumble the brown sugar over the mixture and set aside 1 hour.

Melt the margarine and set aside to cool.

In a separate bowl, sift together the flour, baking powder, baking soda, and salt.

Beat the cooled margarine and eggs together and stir into the oats mixture, blending well. Add the flour mixture and stir to combine. Fold in the butterscotch chips.

Spoon the batter into greased or paper-lined muffin tins, filling two-thirds full, and bake in a preheated 400°F oven for 15 to 20 minutes or until a toothpick inserted in the center comes out clean.

NOTE: The batter for these muffins can be made a day in advance and refrigerated until used. Measure out the batter with an ice cream scoop. The baked muffins freeze beautifully, so you can always have extras on hand.

MAKES 3 DOZEN.

CHEDDAR PARMESAN MUFFINS

Tasty and easy to make, these go well with chili, soups, and stews.

2 cups all-purpose flour

1 tablespoon sugar

1 tablespoon baking powder

¼ teaspoon white pepper

½ teaspoon salt

1¼ cups milk

¼ cup vegetable oil

1 egg

1¼ cups grated cheddar cheese, divided

½ cup grated Parmesan cheese

In a large bowl, combine the flour, sugar, baking powder, pepper, and salt. In a small bowl, beat together the milk, oil, and egg. Add the egg mixture to the flour mixture and stir just until blended. Do not overmix. Fold in 1 cup of the cheddar cheese and all the Parmesan cheese.

Spoon the mixture into greased or paper-lined muffin tins and sprinkle with the remaining cheddar cheese. Bake in a preheated 400°F oven for 15 to 20 minutes.

MAKES 12.

GOLDEN HARVEST MUFFINS

The combination of winter squash, molasses, and raisins creates a hearty treat with a terrific taste. Moist and cakelike, these muffins fit any occasion.

½ cup butter or margarine, softened

¾ cup sugar

1 egg

¼ cup light molasses

1 cup mashed, cooked winter squash

1¾ cups all-purpose flour

1 teaspoon baking soda

1 teaspoon baking powder

¼ teaspoon salt

½ cup raisins

In a large bowl, cream together the butter or margarine and sugar. Add the egg, molasses, and squash and beat until well blended. In another bowl, sift together the flour, baking soda, baking powder, and salt. Stir into the squash mixture. Add the raisins and mix gently.

Spoon the batter into greased or paper-lined muffin tins and bake in a preheated 375°F oven for 30 minutes.

MAKES 16 TO 18.

PUMPKIN GINGER MUFFINS

One of the great things about this recipe is you can take out a few muffins to bake at a time. The frozen batter will keep in the freezer for up to six weeks.

1½ cups sifted all-purpose flour

1¾ teaspoons baking powder

½ teaspoon baking soda

½ teaspoon salt

¾ teaspoon ground ginger

½ teaspoon ground cinnamon

⅛ teaspoon ground cloves

¾ stick margarine, softened

⅓ cup granulated sugar

⅓ cup firmly packed light brown sugar

1 egg

½ cup canned pumpkin

½ cup milk

½ cup currants (optional)

In a large bowl, sift together the flour, baking powder, baking soda, salt, ginger, cinnamon, and cloves. Beat the margarine, granulated sugar, and brown sugar in a medium-sized bowl until light and fluffy. Beat in the egg and pumpkin. Add the flour mixture alternately with the milk, blending well. Fold in the currants, if desired.

With an ice cream scoop, fill paper-lined muffin tins three-fourths full. Place in the freezer until solid. Remove the frozen batter in their paper cups from the muffin tins and seal in Ziploc bags or covered plastic containers.

When ready to bake, remove the paper cups from the freezer and place in a muffin tin. Bake in a preheated 350°F oven for 30 to 40 minutes or until the muffins spring back to the touch.

MAKES 12.

PUMPKIN CHOCOLATE CHIP MUFFINS

Chocolate chips add a new twist to an old favorite.

3⅓ cups all-purpose flour

1½ cups sugar

2 tablespoons pumpkin pie spice

2 teaspoons baking soda

1 teaspoon baking powder

½ teaspoon salt

4 large eggs, beaten lightly

2 cups canned pumpkin

1 cup butter, melted and cooled

1½ cups chocolate chips

In a large bowl, thoroughly mix the flour, sugar, pie spice, baking soda, baking powder, and salt. In a medium-sized bowl, combine the eggs, pumpkin, and butter and blend well. Stir in the chocolate chips. Pour the pumpkin mixture into the dry ingredients and fold in with a spatula until the dry ingredients are just moistened.

Spoon into greased or paper-lined muffin tins and bake in a preheated 350°F oven for about 25 minutes.

MAKES 16 TO 18.

Old Lyme Inn
OLD LYME, CONNECTICUT

JOHNNYCAKES

An alternative to baking the batter is to spoon silver dollar–sized cakes onto a hot greased griddle or skillet. Cook on both sides until golden brown.

1 cup all-purpose flour

2 cups cornmeal

½ teaspoon salt

2 teaspoons sugar

1 teaspoon baking powder

3 tablespoons butter

3 tablespoons shortening

1 egg, separated

1½ cups milk or sour milk

1 teaspoon baking soda

2 tablespoons hot water

In a large bowl, combine the flour, cornmeal, salt, sugar, and baking powder. Cut in the butter and shortening until crumbly. In a small bowl, beat together the egg yolk and milk and stir into the cornmeal mixture along with the baking soda dissolved in hot water. Whip the egg white until stiff but not dry and fold into the batter.

Pour into a greased 8-inch square pan and bake in a preheated 325°F oven for 30 to 40 minutes.

SERVES 9 TO 12.

BISCUITS

*"These are one of our most often requested recipes. The biscuits aren't diffi-
cult to make, but they do require careful handling and the use of cake flour
is essential. To keep from rerolling and overworking the dough, I incorporate
the scraps that are left between biscuits by sweeping them into the dough
where I'm cutting the next biscuit."*

4 cups cake flour (preferably
    Soft as Silk)

1½ teaspoons salt

¼ cup sugar

¼ teaspoon ground nutmeg

2½ tablespoons baking powder

1 cup shortening

3 eggs

1 cup buttermilk

7 tablespoons water

2 tablespoons milk

Sift the flour, salt, sugar, nutmeg, and baking powder together in a large bowl. Cut in
the shortening, using a pastry cutter or
working lightly with your fingers, until the
mixture is crumbly. In a small bowl, whisk
2 of the eggs with the buttermilk and
water. Make a well in the dry ingredients
and add the liquid mixture all at once.
Working lightly with your fingers, use a
fluffing motion to combine the ingredients until they are just moistened. Don't
overwork.

Turn out onto a floured surface and
using the fingers of both hands spread (or rake) the dough gently to a 1½-
inch thickness. (When combining dry and wet ingredients, and when
spreading the dough, remember that it's the air in the dough that makes
the biscuits light. Never knead, overwork, or compress the dough, as this
removes the air.) Let the dough sit for a couple of minutes.

Dip a 2-inch biscuit cutter into water, then flour, and starting from
the edge of the dough and working toward the center cut and shake out
the biscuits, placing them in a baking pan. Beat together the remaining
egg and the milk and brush lightly over the biscuit tops.

Bake in a preheated 400°F oven for about 15 minutes or until nicely
browned.

MAKES 18 TO 24.

ORANGE ROLL-UPS

"We make double and triple batches of these, alternating the filling with cinnamon-sugar mixture, and freeze the unbaked roll-ups. The frozen roll-ups go into the same oven and take only a minute or two longer, so this is a great last-minute menu enhancer!"

Zest of 1 large orange

¾ cup plus 2 tablespoons sugar, divided

2 cups all-purpose flour

1 tablespoon baking powder

½ teaspoon salt

⅓ cup butter, softened

1 egg

¾ cup milk

In a small bowl, mix the orange zest and ¾ cup of the sugar and set aside.

In a large bowl, sift together the flour, remaining 2 tablespoons sugar, baking powder, and salt, blending well. Cut in the butter until crumbly. Beat together the egg and milk and add to the flour mixture. Stir gently to form a soft dough. (Add a little more milk, if needed.)

Turn out onto a floured surface and knead gently three or four times, using enough flour to prevent sticking. Pat the dough into a 14- by 8-inch rectangle. Sprinkle the orange zest–sugar mixture over the dough. Starting on a long side, roll up the dough jelly-roll fashion, making it as even as you can. With the seam side down, cut the roll into sixteen equal slices and place them on a greased cookie sheet.

Bake in a preheated 375°F oven for 15 minutes or until golden brown. Remove from the sheet and serve.

MAKES 16.

CURRANT BUTTERMILK SCONES

"These golden brown scones, studded with currants, are tender and just crumbly enough. Any leftovers (rare) can be used to make fabulous French toast."

3 cups all-purpose flour

½ cup sugar

2½ teaspoons baking powder

½ teaspoon baking soda

6 ounces unsalted butter, chilled and cut into small chunks

¾ cup currants

1 cup buttermilk

Zest of 1 small orange

2 tablespoons heavy cream or half-and-half

In the bowl of a food processor, mix the flour, sugar, baking powder, and baking soda. Add the butter and combine, pulsing on and off, until the mixture resembles coarse meal. Transfer to a large bowl, add the currants, buttermilk, and orange zest, and mix with a fork until just combined.

Turn out the dough onto a floured surface and knead 8 to 10 times. Shape it into a 10-inch circle about ¾ inch thick. Cut into 10 to 12 wedges and place on a greased baking sheet. Brush the tops with heavy cream or half-and-half and bake in a preheated 425°F oven for 15 to 20 minutes.

MAKES 10 TO 12.

APRICOT SCONES

Moist and rich but only subtly sweet, these scones are pretty as a picture.

4 ounces dried apricots

¼ cup water

1 tablespoon lemon juice

2 tablespoons honey

2 sticks margarine, softened

¼ cup sugar

3 large eggs

1 teaspoon vanilla extract

3 cups all-purpose flour

1 tablespoon baking powder

¼ teaspoon salt

⅔ cup plain yogurt

Put the apricots, water, lemon juice, and honey in a food processor and mix until the consistency of a thick puree. Set aside.

In a large bowl, beat the margarine until creamy. Add the sugar, eggs, and vanilla and beat until fluffy. In another bowl, combine the flour, baking powder, and salt and stir into the creamed mixture until well blended. Add the yogurt and mix well. Then fold the apricot puree into the batter until just swirled through.

Using an ice cream scoop, put the batter on ungreased cookie sheets, placing the mounds about 2 inches apart. Loosely cover with plastic wrap and freeze overnight.

Bake in a preheated 350°F oven for 15 minutes. Reduce the heat to 325°F and bake 10 minutes longer or until light golden brown. Cool on a wire rack.

NOTE: After freezing the batter, the individual unbaked scones can be transferred to a plastic bag or airtight container and stored in the freezer for up to six weeks. This allows you to bake only as many scones as you need at a time.

MAKES 12 TO 14.

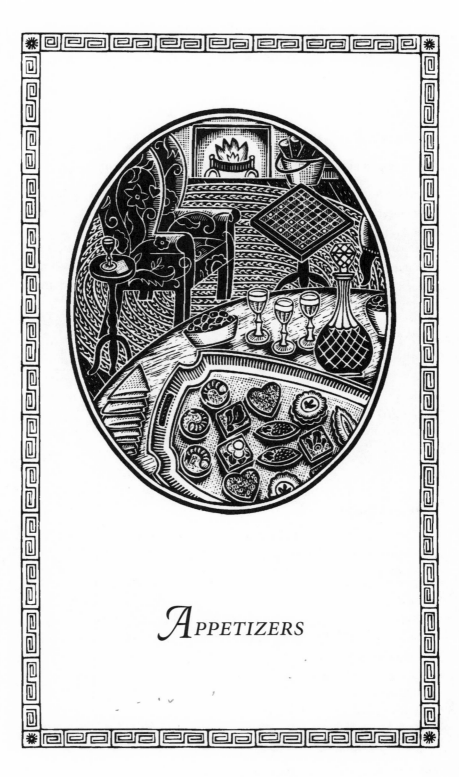

*A*PPETIZERS

CANDIED PECANS

Serve these to nibble on at a party or use them as a dessert topping.

1 egg, beaten

¾ cup sugar

2 heaping teaspoons ground
cinnamon

1 scant teaspoon salt

1 pound pecan halves

In a medium-sized bowl, mix together the egg, sugar, cinnamon, and salt. Add the nuts and toss to coat.

Bake on an ungreased cookie sheet in a preheated 275°F oven for 30 to 45 minutes, stirring frequently. Cool. Store in an airtight container.

MAKES ABOUT 2 CUPS.

 *Old Lyme Inn*

OLD LYME, CONNECTICUT

CORN RELISH

The bright and festive combination of colors and the sweet-tart taste make this an attractive and delectable addition to any table.

2 cups whole kernel corn

½ cup chopped green bell
pepper

½ cup chopped red bell pepper

¼ cup chopped green onion

1 cup raspberry or apple cider
vinegar

2 teaspoons coarse mustard

2 tablespoons sugar

Combine the corn, green and red bell pepper, onion, vinegar, mustard, and sugar in a shallow dish, blending thoroughly. Cover well and refrigerate 24 hours before serving.

MAKES ABOUT 4 CUPS.

Party Marinade

"This is the most carefree recipe I know. Serve in a footed truffle dish, sit back, and relax! Leftovers will keep refrigerated for a week."

1 jar (4½ ounces) marinated mushrooms, drained

1 can (16 ounces) pineapple chunks, drained

½ pound boiled ham, cut into 1-inch cubes

½ pound sharp cheddar cheese, cut into 1-inch cubes

1 pound seedless green grapes

1 pound seedless purple grapes

1 jar (2½ ounces) ripe pitted olives, drained

1 jar (2½ ounces) stuffed green olives, drained

Mix together the mushrooms, pineapple, ham, cheese, grapes, and olives and chill for 2 hours. Serve in a shallow bowl with toothpicks.

SERVES 8 TO 10.

Stonecrest Farm Bed and Breakfast

FIVE ONION MARMALADE

For a unique addition to beef, pork, or game, serve these sweet, spiced onions.

2 to 3 tablespoons vegetable oil

1 medium-sized Spanish onion, sliced

1 medium-sized purple onion, sliced

2 leeks, cleaned and sliced

3 shallots, sliced

½ cup firmly packed brown sugar

½ cup apple cider vinegar

½ cup chicken broth or water

2 whole cloves

1 cinnamon stick

Salt and freshly cracked pepper to taste

2 to 3 tablespoons chopped fresh chives

Heat the oil in a large saucepan. Add the onions, leeks, and shallots and sauté/sweat until limp.

Stir in the brown sugar, vinegar, broth or water, cloves, and cinnamon and bring to a boil. Reduce the heat to low and let cook until the liquid evaporates and the onions glisten, stirring occasionally. Add the salt, pepper, and chives and serve warm or at room temperature.

MAKES 2½ TO 3 CUPS.

MACADAMIA GOAT CHEESE WITH CHERRY CHUTNEY

Elegant and unusual, this may be served as a first course for a romantic dinner for two. It's easy to prepare but may require a trip to a specialty foods store to find all the ingredients.

8 ounces aged chevre (goat cheese), round or wedge-shaped

1 egg, beaten

4 ounces chopped macadamia nuts

Cherry Chutney (recipe follows)

Dip the cheese in the egg, coat with the nuts, and bake in a preheated 425°F oven for 15 minutes. Serve with croustades or crackers and Cherry Chutney.

CHERRY CHUTNEY

½ pound dried cherries

¼ cup chopped celery

2 tablespoons minced candied ginger

½ teaspoon minced garlic

½ teaspoon ground allspice

½ cup sugar

½ cup raspberry vinegar

½ cup raisins

¼ cup chopped walnuts

2 tablespoons lemon juice

½ cup Kirsch (cherry liqueur) or cherry brandy

Combine the cherries, celery, ginger, garlic, allspice, sugar, vinegar, raisins, walnuts, lemon juice, and Kirsch or brandy in a large saucepan and cook to a syrupy consistency. Serve at room temperature.

SERVES 2.

Mad River Inn Dip

This gets better the longer it sits, so you may want to make it the day before you serve it.

1 package (10 ounces) frozen spinach, thawed and thoroughly drained

2 cups plain yogurt

¼ pound finely crumbled feta cheese

¼ teaspoon freshly ground pepper

1 clove garlic, finely chopped

1 small onion, finely chopped

1 teaspoon salt

1 teaspoon sugar

½ teaspoon dry mustard

¼ teaspoon dried tarragon

Combine the spinach, yogurt, and cheese in a bowl. Add the pepper, garlic, onion, salt, sugar, mustard, and tarragon, blending well.

Makes about 3 cups.

LEMON CAPER DIP

Creamy and smooth, this dip can be made four to five days in advance.

1 cup mayonnaise

⅓ cup chopped shallots

1 tablespoon Dijon-style mustard

2 tablespoons lemon juice

2 tablespoons olive oil

2 tablespoons capers, rinsed and drained

¼ cup shredded fresh basil leaves

¼ cup chopped fresh parsley

2 cloves garlic, chopped

Salt and pepper to taste

Combine the mayonnaise, shallots, mustard, lemon juice, oil, capers, basil, parsley, garlic, and salt and pepper, mixing well. Refrigerate until thoroughly chilled and serve with pita chips and fresh vegetables such as sliced cucumbers, endive spears, red bell peppers, and fennel or anise strips.

MAKES 1½ CUPS.

High Meadows Bed & Breakfast
ELIOT, MAINE

RIPE OLIVE CANAPÉ

Engligh muffin halves are spread with a smooth topping enlivened with curry, then broiled briefly in the oven. These can be cooked, frozen, and reheated for later use.

1½ cups grated cheddar cheese

½ cup mayonnaise

2 teaspoons grated onion

1 teaspoon curry powder

1 cup chopped ripe olives

6 English muffins, split

Mix the cheese, mayonnaise, onion, curry powder, and olives together and spread on the muffins. Place under the broiler and cook until brown, watching closely. Cut into pie-shaped wedges and serve hot.

MAKES 48.

Combes Family Inn
LUDLOW, VERMONT

APPETIZER PIZZA

Fresh basil, ripe tomatoes, and a good-quality olive oil are essential for this high-summer appetizer.

2 medium-sized (6 inch diameter) pita breads

4 cloves garlic, minced

1 bunch fresh basil

12 tomato slices

½ cup shredded Mozzarella cheese

8 teaspoons extra-virgin olive oil, divided

Split each pita in half. Spread one-fourth of the minced garlic on each round, arrange 4 to 6 basil leaves over the garlic, and top with 3 tomato slices. Sprinkle with one-fourth of the shredded cheese and drizzle with 2 teaspoons oil.

Bake on a cookie sheet in a preheated 400°F oven for about 15 minutes or until the cheese melts and is bubbly. Serve immediately. *MAKES 4.*

GOVERNOR'S CROUTONS

"This is named after the late Vermont governor James Hartness, for his unique and eccentric ways."

6 slices (½ inch thick) French bread

6 slices (1 ounce) Vermont chevre (goat cheese)

¼ cup olive oil

2 teaspoons chopped garlic

½ cup sun-dried tomatoes (lightly poached to soften)

2 small fresh sprigs of rosemary

Place the bread slices in a small pie plate or on a baking sheet and toast lightly in a preheated 350°F oven. Put a slice of cheese on each crouton and bake for 5 to 10 minutes.

Meanwhile, combine the oil, garlic, tomatoes, and rosemary in a small sauté pan and cook over medium heat until the garlic just begins to turn light golden. Do not let it brown. Remove from the heat.

Place the croutons on a serving plate and top with the tomato mixture. Serve immediately.

MAKES 6.

BROWN SUGAR BACON

"You can never make enough of this!"

½ cup firmly packed light brown sugar

8 to 12 slices thickly sliced bacon (2 to 3 slices per person)

Orange or lemon slices for garnish (optional)

Fresh parsley for garnish (optional)

Spread the brown sugar on a platter and dip the bacon slices into it, coating both sides and gently patting on the sugar so it adheres to the bacon. (Go easy on the sugar as any excess melts off and drips onto the pan bottom.) Place the slices on a cookie sheet or cake rack in a shallow, aluminum foil–lined pan.

Bake in a preheated 375°F oven for 20 to 25 minutes, checking frequently. Serve on another platter, garnished with orange or lemon slices and sprinkled with the parsley, if desired.

SERVES 4 TO 6.

MARLBOROUGH QUICK AND EASY ROLL-UPS

"A lot of recipes I use at the inn are tried-and-true dishes that I've served to my family and guests for years—long before I became an innkeeper. This one has always been a great favorite with my children."

8 spears fresh asparagus

2 tablespoons butter

1 large onion, sliced into rings

2 tablespoons all-purpose flour

1 cup milk

A dash of dried basil

Salt and pepper to taste

4 slices (⅛ inch thick) deli ham
   or turkey

4 slices (⅛ inch thick) deli
   Swiss cheese

If asparagus spears are longer than 6 inches, trim to that length. Drop the spears into boiling water and cook only until slightly done (about 3 to 4 minutes). Drain.

In the meantime, melt the butter in a large skillet and sauté the onion slices until they begin to soften. Sprinkle in the flour and cook, stirring, until the mixture is hot and bubbly. Pour in the milk and stir over medium heat until thickened. Mix in the basil and salt and pepper, remove from the heat, and set aside.

To assemble the roll-ups, top each slice of meat with 1 slice of cheese and 2 asparagus spears. Roll up, secure with a toothpick, and place seam side down in a shallow baking pan. Top with the onion mixture, cover the baking pan with aluminum foil, and bake in a preheated 350°F oven for 30 minutes.

NOTE: This is an ideal dish for making ahead and preparing for large groups. Leftovers can be frozen.

SERVES 4.

Roast Beef and Horseradish Pinstripes

"This recipe may be adjusted to serve as many or as few as you wish. You can make it several days ahead, but store it tightly wrapped in plastic wrap and slice just before serving."

1 package (8 ounces) cream cheese, softened

1 tablespoon prepared horseradish

2 teaspoons Dijon-style mustard

½ teaspoon salt

¼ teaspoon freshly ground white pepper

16 paper-thin slices cooked roast beef (see Note)

Fresh parsley for garnish

Combine the cream cheese, horseradish, mustard, salt, and pepper, blending well. On a cutting board, overlap 2 slices of beef to form a rectangle about 8 by 4 inches. Using a long, thin spatula, spread 2 tablespoons of the cream cheese mixture over the beef, then beginning with the long side tightly roll it up and wrap in plastic wrap. Repeat with the remaining slices of beef. Refrigerate until ready to serve.

Using a sharp knife, cut each roll crosswise on the diagonal into ½-inch-thick slices. Garnish with parsley.

NOTE: Ask your butcher to slice the beef as thinly as possible without it breaking and to place a piece of deli paper between the slices.

SERVES 10.

Kitchen Tool Hall of Fame

*W*HAT *ONE* kitchen tool would New England innkeepers and chefs take with them to a desert island? Their answers are the key to a well-equipped kitchen.

* *Knives.* The first item on most lists is a set of good, sharp knives. This is no place for the serious cook to scrimp. Hold the knife before you purchase it. As one innkeeper put it, "Shake hands with the knife. You're going to buy it."

* *Food processor.* The versatility of this tool makes it popular among chefs and innkeepers. It does everything the old blender used to do and more, including making pastry dough.

* *Wooden spoons.* Some things never go out of style. In addition to being inexpensive, these handy utensils won't scratch expensive no-stick finishes.

* *KitchenAid mixer.* Long the choice of serious cooks. This heavyweight, heavy-duty mixer beats batter, kneads dough, and best of all its design keeps your hands free.

* *Mandoline.* No, not the stringed instrument, the French slicer. Another extremely versatile tool. It slices, it juliennes, it cuts shoestrings.

* *Convection oven.* This oven cooks with forced hot air. Food prepared in a convection oven cooks more quickly and evenly at a lower temperature.

* *Microwave oven.* For defrosting, *not* for cooking.

* *Around-the-neck timer.* This kitchen timer comes equipped with a cord so that you can wear it around your neck. Handy for when you can't wait around in the kitchen.

SWEDISH MEATBALLS

Don't let the long list of ingredients discourage you from trying this simple dish. It's great as an appetizer, but equally satisfying for dinner—just make the meatballs larger and extend the cooking time.

MEATBALLS

3 tablespoons chopped onion

5 tablespoons butter, divided

¾ cup light cream

¾ cup water

¾ cup bread crumbs

1½ pounds ground round

½ pound ground pork

2 eggs, slightly beaten

2 teaspoons salt

½ teaspoon pepper

¼ teaspoon ground allspice

A dash of ground cloves

SAUCE

2 tablespoons all-purpose flour

½ cup light cream

1½ cups water

1 teaspoon salt

A dash of pepper

1½ cups tomato sauce

2 tablespoons minced fresh parsley

To make the meatballs, sauté the onion in 1 tablespoon of the butter until golden. In a large bowl, combine the cream, water, and bread crumbs. Add the onion, ground round, ground pork, eggs, salt, pepper, allspice, and cloves and mix well.

Shape into very small balls (¾ inch diameter) and brown in a skillet in the remaining butter. Remove with a slotted spoon and set aside on paper towel. Save the drippings for the sauce.

To make the sauce, pour off all but 2 tablespoons of the drippings, stir in the flour, and cook for 1 to 2 minutes. Stir in the cream and water and bring to a boil, stirring constantly. Add the salt, pepper, tomato sauce, and parsley and stir until smooth.

Transfer the meatballs to the sauce and heat until cooked through, about 20 minutes. Serve with long toothpicks.

MAKES ABOUT 75 SMALL OR 36 LARGE MEATBALLS.

New London County Mushrooms with Sausage and Apple Stuffing

Moist, rich, and hearty, this finger-licking fare is perfect for a party.

1 pound mushrooms (about 24)

½ pound sausage

2 tablespoons butter or margarine

½ medium-sized onion, finely chopped

1 stalk celery, finely chopped

½ medium-sized tart apple, peeled, cored, and finely chopped

2 tablespoons finely chopped fresh parsley

2 cloves garlic, minced

½ cup crushed Ritz crackers (about 10)

¾ teaspoon salt

½ teaspoon pepper

⅓ cup grated sharp cheddar cheese

Clean the mushrooms, remove the stems, finely chop the stems, and set aside.

Brown the sausage in a large skillet over medium heat, then drain thoroughly and set aside in a bowl.

Melt the butter or margarine in the same skillet, add the onion and celery, and cook until translucent. Add the mushroom stems, apple, parsley, garlic, and browned sausage and cook for 5 minutes. Stir in the crushed crackers, blending thoroughly, and transfer the mixture to a large mixing bowl.

Add the salt, pepper, and cheese and blend well. Firmly fill each mushroom cap with about 1 tablespoon of the stuffing. Place in a large, lightly greased baking pan and bake in a preheated 325°F oven for 15 minutes. Serve hot.

Serves 4 to 6.

GRILLED WILD MUSHROOMS WITH POLENTA

Sure to earn you rave reviews, these have a dramatic presentation, sensational combination of textures, and delectable flavor. What more could you ask for? Second helpings, perhaps.

1½ cups water

1½ cups milk

Salt and pepper to taste

1 cup yellow cornmeal

1 tablespoon unsalted butter

½ cup grated Parmesan cheese

Bread crumbs

2 pounds assorted fresh
   mushrooms (oyster, shiitake,
   cremini, chanterelle)

1 tablespoon minced shallots

1 tablespoon minced garlic

¼ cup extra-virgin olive oil

Chopped fresh herbs for
   garnish

Bring the water and milk to a boil. Season with salt and pepper to taste and slowly add the cornmeal in a steady stream, whisking vigorously. Stir with a wooden spoon until the polenta starts to dry and pull away from the sides of the pot. Stir in the butter and cheese and adjust the seasonings, if necessary.

Pour the polenta into a large shallow baking pan and smooth over into a uniform thickness. Let cool, then cut into desired shapes and dredge with bread crumbs.

Trim the mushrooms and lightly brush off any dirt. Cut large mushrooms into smaller pieces. Toss in a bowl with the shallots, garlic, and oil. Season with salt and pepper.

Place the mushrooms in a hinged grill basket and grill until tender and golden brown, about 10 to 15 minutes.

Sauté the polenta in oil over low heat until golden brown on both sides. Place it in the center of a serving platter and arrange the mushrooms around it. Sprinkle with chopped herbs and serve.

SERVES 8 TO 10.

BAKED SHRIMP WITH DIJON-SMOKED GOUDA

Serve this heavenly dish with a crusty bread so you can soak up every last bit of the luscious sauce.

1 tablespoon finely chopped shallots

3 ounces white wine

1 pound fresh large shrimp (about 16 to 20), peeled and deveined

1 pint heavy cream

2 heaping tablespoons Dijon-style mustard

Salt and white pepper to taste

1 cup grated smoked Gouda cheese

½ cup finely chopped scallions

In a large saucepan, sauté the shallots in the wine and cook until the liquid is reduced by half. Add the shrimp, cream, and mustard and stir to blend. Poach the shrimp in the simmering sauce uncovered for 3 to 4 minutes until only partially cooked.

Remove the shrimp from the saucepan and arrange 4 to 5 each in small individual casserole dishes. Reduce the sauce further until it is slightly thickened. Season with salt and pepper, stirring with a whisk. Pour the sauce over the shrimp and top with the cheese.

Bake in a preheated 450°F oven for about 4 to 5 minutes or place under the broiler until bubbling and golden. Do not overcook.

Serve on a napkin-lined plate and garnish with the scallions.

SERVES 4.

Mountain Top Inn

CHITTENDEN, VERMONT

Bay Scallops with Dijon and Apple Chutney

You will find that you have more than enough chutney for this recipe, but it keeps well in the refrigerator and is great to have on hand.

1 pound fresh bay scallops

All-purpose flour for dredging

1 teaspoon butter

2 ounces white wine (preferably sauterne)

1 tablespoon Dijon-style mustard

2 ounces Apple Chutney (recipe follows)

Dredge the scallops with flour and shake off excess. Melt the butter in a large sauté pan and cook the scallops only until partially done. Add the wine, mustard, and chutney and simmer until the scallops are cooked through.

Apple Chutney

½ cup chopped red or green seeded tomatoes

1 cup mild apple cider vinegar

½ cup firmly packed brown sugar

3 medium-sized apples, peeled, cored, and diced

½ cup diced onion

½ cup raisins

Salt, pepper, and fresh ginger to taste

Place the tomato, vinegar, brown sugar, apple, onion, raisins, salt, pepper, and ginger in a medium-sized saucepan and cook until the apple and onion are soft.

Serves 4.

SCALLOPS, SPINACH, AND GOAT CHEESE IN PUFF PASTRY

"It is fun to use different shapes of pastry for different occasions. We prepare this dish as an appetizer for Valentine's Day in the shape of a heart, with separate top and bottom pastries."

1 package (16 ounces) frozen puff pastry sheets, thawed

1 package (10 ounces) frozen spinach, thawed and drained

1½ pounds fresh sea scallops (about 30)

8 ounces chevre (goat cheese)

1 egg, beaten

Dijon Beurre Blanc Sauce (recipe follows)

Roll out the puff pastry to a ⅛-inch thickness. Cut out eight 6-inch circles. Place a mound of spinach on half of each circle, top with 3 to 4 scallops, then 1 ounce of the cheese. Brush some of the beaten egg around the rim of each pastry and fold over the top half. Crimp the edges and brush additional egg over the top.

Bake on a greased cookie sheet in a preheated 425°F oven for 15 minutes or until golden brown. Serve with warm Dijon Beurre Blanc Sauce.

DIJON BEURRE BLANC SAUCE

5 ounces cold butter, divided

½ teaspoon minced shallots

1 teaspoon Dijon-style mustard

½ cup white wine

1 cup heavy cream

Salt and pepper to taste

In a medium-sized sauté pan, heat 1 ounce of the butter and sauté the shallots until they just start to brown. Add the mustard and wine and simmer until reduced by half. Add the cream and reduce by one-third. Divide the remaining cold butter into six pieces and slowly mix into the cream over low heat until the sauce is smooth. Season with salt and pepper. Serve immediately.

SERVES 8.

Pilgrim's Inn
DEER ISLE, MAINE

SESAME GINGER MUSSELS

After assembling this dish, either serve it immediately or refrigerate until ready to serve.

2 dozen mussels, debearded and cleaned

1 cup white wine

2 tablespoons chopped fresh ginger, divided

¼ cup tamari (soy sauce)

1 teaspoon sesame oil

1 teaspoon red wine vinegar

1 teaspoon sugar

1 tablespoon chopped fresh cilantro

1 small red onion, chopped

1 tablespoon dry mustard

Combine the mussels, wine, and 1 tablespoon of the ginger in a large pot and cook covered over medium heat until the mussels open, about 5 minutes. Remove from the heat and cool.

Remove the mussels from their shells, place them in a large bowl, and reserve the shells.

In a food processor, combine the tamari, oil, vinegar, sugar, remaining 1 tablespoon ginger, cilantro, onion, and mustard and process for 10 seconds. Pour this marinade over the mussels and allow to sit at room temperature for 1 hour.

Spoon the mussels with some of the marinade into the mussel shells and serve.

SERVES 6.

SALADS AND DRESSINGS

WARM SHRIMP AND LOBSTER SALAD WITH "CUCUMBER SPAGHETTI"

For sheer presentation, this is a visual knockout. And it tastes great, too.

1 bunch fresh dill, thicker stems removed

1 bag (3½ ounces) fresh enoki mushrooms

5 tablespoons unsalted butter, divided

4 cucumbers, peeled, seeded, and cut into ⅛-inch-wide strips

¼ cup heavy cream

Salt and white pepper to taste

1 pound fresh medium-sized shrimp, peeled and deveined

1¼-pound fresh lobster, cooked, meat removed, and sliced

2 medium-sized tomatoes, peeled, seeded, and diced

2 medium-sized red bell peppers, peeled and diced, or use bottled roasted sweet red peppers (see Note)

1 bunch fresh chives, chopped

Beurre Blanc Sauce (recipe follows)

Arrange the dill and mushrooms around the edge of four salad plates and set aside.

Melt 2 tablespoons of the butter in a medium-sized sauté pan over medium-high heat. Add the cucumbers and cream. When the cream has reduced and the cucumbers are lightly cooked, remove from the heat, season with salt and pepper, then place equal portions on the plates, making a "bed" for the shrimp and lobster.

In a large skillet, melt 2 more tablespoons of the butter over high heat. Add the shrimp, stir-tossing frequently so it will cook evenly (the shrimp cook *very* quickly and are done when they begin to turn a milky white and pink color). Just before the shrimp are cooked through, add the lobster. Stir-toss until the lobster is warm, then place equal portions of the shrimp and lobster on top of the bed of cucumbers.

In the same skillet, melt the remaining 1 tablespoon butter over medium-high heat. Sauté the tomato and bell pepper until just tender, season with salt and pepper, and add half of the chives. Stir in the Beurre Blanc Sauce, then spoon the mixture in equal portions over the shrimp and lobster. Garnish with the remaining chives.

BEURRE BLANC SAUCE

¾ cup white wine

2 shallots, finely diced

¾ cup heavy cream

¾ pound unsalted butter, softened

Salt and white pepper to taste

Combine the wine and shallots in a small saucepan. Cook over medium-high heat until the mixture is reduced by half. Add the heavy cream and continue cooking until the mixture is reduced by one-third.

Take the pan off the heat and add the butter bit by bit (about a tablespoon at a time), making sure each bit has melted before adding the next. Swirling the butter in the pan (rather than stirring or whisking it) will produce a smooth sauce.

Strain the sauce to remove the shallots and season with salt and pepper.

NOTE: To prepare peeled bell peppers, place them under the broiler until their skins "blister." Remove from the oven, and when they are cool enough to handle pull off and discard the skins, membrane, and seeds and dice the pulp.

SERVES 4.

The Boulders Inn

NEW PRESTON, CONNECTICUT

FENNEL AND SEARED SHRIMP SALAD WITH BLOOD ORANGE VINAIGRETTE

This imaginative and colorful dish is perfect for a festive dinner party.

2 fennel bulbs, trimmed and thinly sliced

2 tablespoons minced fresh chives

Salt and freshly ground pepper to taste

3 medium-sized blood or red navel oranges

6 tablespoons extra-virgin olive oil, divided

16 fresh medium-sized to large shrimp, peeled and deveined

1 tablespoon finely minced shallots

Fennel leaves for garnish

Steam the fennel until crisp-tender. Cool, then add the chives and season with salt and pepper.

Peel 2 oranges with a knife, holding the fruit over a bowl to catch the juice. Remove the segments from each orange and set them aside. Measure the juice in the bowl and add just enough from the third orange to equal 6 tablespoons.

Heat 2 tablespoons oil in a large skillet. Add the shrimp, season with salt and pepper, and cook through, turning once. Add the shallots and deglaze the pan with the orange juice.

Remove the skillet from the heat and use a slotted spoon to remove the shrimp. Arrange the shrimp on a plate with the fennel.

Add the remaining 4 tablespoons oil to the skillet, stirring to blend. Taste for seasonings and pour over the salad. Garnish with fennel leaves.

SERVES 4.

My Garden Overfloweth

*H*AVE YOU a bumper crop of basil growing in your garden? Is your cilantro as high as an elephant's eye? Chef Roger Keroack of the Griswold Inn in Essex, Connecticut, has some ingenious methods for storing extra herbs that you've grown (or purchased at the store).

 Wash the herbs and let them dry thoroughly, then pull the leaves from the stems. Chop the leaves and store in the refrigerator in an airtight crock filled with olive oil. The herbs will keep for a year, and flavored oil—especially basil-flavored—is terrific for sautéing chicken breasts.

 Wash the herbs and let them dry. Layer the leaves between sheets of waxed paper and roll the sheets up into a cigar-shaped tube. Wrap the tube in plastic wrap and store in the freezer. Just pull the herbs from the freezer as you need them, there's no need to thaw.

 Wash and dry the herbs. Put the leaves in the food processor with a few drops of water and puree. Pour the puree into ice cube trays and place in the freezer until just set. Remove the herb cubes from the trays, transfer to Ziploc bags, and store in the freezer.

TAMWORTH INN CHICKEN SALAD VERONIQUE

"This is a very popular brunch salad. We accompany it with our homemade rolls."

3 cups cooked cut-up chicken

½ cup low-fat mayonnaise

½ cup plain low-fat yogurt

¾ cup diced celery

1 teaspoon dried thyme

¼ cup finely chopped onion (optional)

¼ cup chopped walnuts

A dash of curry powder

Salt and pepper to taste

1 cup sliced seedless green grapes

Fresh lettuce leaves

Whole grapes for garnish (optional)

Combine the chicken, mayonnaise, yogurt, celery, thyme, onion (if desired), nuts, curry powder, salt and pepper, and sliced grapes in a large bowl, mixing well. Line a serving bowl with lettuce or arrange leaves on individual salad plates. Top with the chicken mixture and garnish with grapes, if desired.

NOTE: The flavor of this salad improves if kept in the refrigerator 2 to 3 hours before serving.

SERVES 6.

GRANDMA SALLY'S POTATO SALAD

"Grandma Sally passed this and many other fine recipes down through the family. This one dates from about 1936!"

8 large potatoes

2 hard-boiled eggs, chopped

2 dill pickle spears, chopped

2 tablespoons dill pickle juice

1 cup mayonnaise

2 tablespoons light cream

2 tablespoons chili sauce

1½ teaspoons paprika

1½ teaspoons dried dill

½ teaspoon pepper

¼ cup chopped onion

2 tablespoons finely chopped celery

2 tablespoons finely chopped green bell pepper

1 tablespoon sugar

Peel the potatoes, cut them in half, and boil in salted water until tender. Let cool, then dice into bite-sized pieces.

In a large bowl, combine the eggs, pickles, pickle juice, mayonnaise, cream, chili sauce, paprika, dill, pepper, onion, celery, bell pepper, and sugar, blending thoroughly. Fold in the diced potato.

NOTE: This salad is best if refrigerated overnight and then served near room temperature.

SERVES 10.

TURNER SALAD

Chunky and chewy, with a sweet-tart dressing, this salad is substantial. Serve it with a cup of soup and bread or rolls for a complete and satisfying lunch or supper.

DRESSING

1 large egg

1 large egg yolk

½ cup sugar

½ teaspoon dry mustard

1½ teaspoons cornstarch

¼ cup distilled white vinegar

¼ cup water

¼ teaspoon salt

2 tablespoons unsalted butter, softened

½ cup mayonnaise

SALAD

4 to 5 cups broccoli florets, blanched if desired

1 cup raisins

1 to 2 cups sliced fresh mushrooms

½ cup chopped red onion

6 slices bacon, cooked crisp and crumbled

Salt and pepper to taste

For the dressing, whisk together the whole egg, egg yolk, sugar, mustard, and cornstarch in a small bowl. In a saucepan, combine the vinegar, water, and salt and bring to a boil over moderate heat. Slowly add the egg mixture, whisking constantly, and cook 1 minute or until thickened. Remove the saucepan from the heat and whisk in the butter and mayonnaise. Cover and chill.

To make the salad, combine the broccoli, raisins, mushrooms, onion, and bacon in a large bowl. Pour the dressing over the salad and toss well. Add salt and pepper and serve.

SERVES 4 TO 6.

INDIAN SPINACH SALAD

An attractive combination of colors and appealing mix of textures, this salad can be enjoyed any time of the year.

½ cup white vinegar

¼ cup vegetable oil

2 tablespoons chutney

2 teaspoons sugar

½ teaspoon salt

1½ teaspoons curry powder

1 teaspoon mustard

1 bag (10 ounces) fresh spinach, rinsed and stems removed

1½ cups peeled, cored, and chopped apple

½ cup raisins

½ cup peanuts

Combine the vinegar, oil, chutney, sugar, salt, curry powder, and mustard in a jar with a tight lid and shake well to blend. Chill.

In a large salad bowl, combine the spinach, apple, raisins, and peanuts and toss well. Pour on some of the dressing and toss to coat the ingredients, reserving any leftover dressing for later use.

SERVES 8 TO 10.

Salad Days

*I*N AN EFFORT to get preparations for a dinner party done ahead of time, you may be tempted to toss a green salad and stow it in the refrigerator until the next evening. But Chef Jacques Thiebeult of the Homestead Inn in Greenwich, Connecticut, advises against making a salad until just before you're ready to serve it. If you're strapped for time and need to prepare the salad early, follow his advice: Wash and cut the greens and vegetables and allow them to dry completely—a salad spinner for lettuce is the tool of choice. Store them separately in airtight containers or in Ziploc bags. Assemble the salad just before you serve it, and never put dressing on a green salad until the last minute.

Does it matter whether you cut the lettuce or tear it? Since it doesn't affect the taste, it's more a matter of personal preference than anything else. Some cooks feel that cut lettuce makes the salad look as if it's come off an assembly line.

MEDITERRANEAN SALAD

For lunch, dinner, or a potluck supper, this is an adaptable salad. Serve it as is, or turn it into a main dish by adding strips of grilled chicken breast.

1 bunch fresh frisée or chicory, rinsed and dried

1 bunch fresh watercress, rinsed, stemmed, and dried

1 small bunch fresh red leaf lettuce, rinsed and dried

1 bulb fennel, trimmed and thinly sliced

2 medium-sized navel oranges, peeled and cut into sections

1 small purple onion, thinly sliced

½ cup pitted black olives

¼ cup balsamic vinegar

¼ cup olive oil

½ cup salad oil

Salt and cracked pepper to taste

In a large salad bowl, combine the frisée or chicory, watercress, and lettuce. Toss the greens with the fennel, orange pieces, onion, and olives.

In a small bowl, beat the vinegar, olive oil, and salad oil together and add enough of the dressing to the salad ingredients to coat lightly but thoroughly. Season with salt and pepper and serve.

SERVES 6 TO 8.

MARLBOROUGH CRANBERRY AND FETA SALAD

This is a beautiful salad—with green lettuce, bright red cranberries, snowy white feta cheese, and translucent onion slices. Combining cranberries with feta creates a great taste, too. Any type of lettuce will work here, but curly leaf or Boston lettuce is recommended.

1 cup fresh lettuce, rinsed and dried

1 cup fresh spinach, rinsed and stems removed

4 tablespoons dried cranberries

4 tablespoons crumbled feta cheese

4 to 8 thin slices Bermuda onion

Sweet and Sour Dressing (recipe follows)

Arrange the greens on two salad plates. Sprinkle with the cranberries and cheese and top with the onion slices. Drizzle with dressing.

SWEET AND SOUR DRESSING

1 cup canola oil

¼ cup apple cider vinegar

¼ cup lemon juice

1 teaspoon salt

½ teaspoon dry mustard

½ teaspoon paprika

1 tablespoon maraschino cherry juice (optional)

2 tablespoons honey

Mix the oil, vinegar, lemon juice, salt, mustard, paprika, cherry juice (if desired), and honey in a jar with a tight lid. Shake well and refrigerate until ready to use.

SERVES 2.

CRUNCHY CUCUMBER SALAD WITH BLUE CHEESE

A fine addition to lunch or dinner, this salad needs to be made a few hours in advance so it has time to chill thoroughly in the refrigerator.

¼ cup mayonnaise

¼ cup plain yogurt

¼ cup cottage cheese

¼ cup crumbled blue cheese

1 teaspoon tarragon vinegar

Freshly ground pepper to taste

1 large European cucumber, partially peeled, halved lengthwise, and sliced

1 bunch fresh red or green leaf lettuce, rinsed and dried

Red bell pepper slices (optional)

Combine the mayonnaise, yogurt, cottage cheese, blue cheese, vinegar, and pepper in a large bowl, whisking thoroughly. Add the cucumbers and stir to coat all slices. Chill several hours.

Place the lettuce leaves on individual salad plates, top with the cucumbers and dressing, and garnish with bell pepper slices, if desired.

SERVES 5 TO 6.

 *Bernerhof Inn*

GLEN, NEW HAMPSHIRE

BERNERHOF HOUSE DRESSING

Creamy and piquant, this dressing gets a subtle boost from the liqueur.

½ cup heavy cream

½ cup milk

½ cup apple cider vinegar

1 tablespoon Dijon-style
  mustard

1 tablespoon Crème de Cassis

½ tablespoon Maggi Seasoning
  (a natural, vegetable-derived
  protein flavoring)

Salt and pepper to taste

Combine the cream, milk, vinegar, mustard, Crème de Cassis, Maggi Seasoning, and salt and pepper in a blender and mix well. Refrigerate until thoroughly chilled. Serve over Boston lettuce.

MAKES ABOUT 1½ CUPS.

 Hartness House Inn

SPRINGFIELD, VERMONT

MOUNTAIN MAPLE POPPY DRESSING

"This excellent salad dressing uses Vermont maple syrup and poppy seeds, creating a slightly sweet and different taste for any salad you choose."

2 cups mayonnaise

¼ cup plus 2 tablespoons maple
  syrup

¼ cup red wine (Burgundy)

2 tablespoons red wine vinegar

2 tablespoons sugar

1 tablespoon poppy seeds

In a large bowl, combine the mayonnaise, maple syrup, wine, vinegar, sugar, and poppy seeds and mix thoroughly.

MAKES ABOUT 2½ CUPS.

FINES HERBES HORSERADISH VINAIGRETTE

Versatile and tasty, this is terrific not only on salad greens but also for sautéing various foods like pork cutlets and assorted fresh vegetables.

3-inch piece fresh horseradish

1 cup plus 3 tablespoons olive oil, divided

½ medium-sized onion or 5 shallots, sliced

7 fresh sprigs of sage, finely chopped

7 fresh sprigs of rosemary, finely chopped

7 fresh sprigs of tarragon, finely chopped

¼ cup balsamic vinegar

¼ cup tarragon vinegar

Roughly chop the horseradish and simmer in 1 cup of the oil for about 20 minutes. Strain and set aside.

Sauté the onion or shallots in the remaining 3 tablespoons oil over medium heat for 4 minutes. Add the sage, rosemary, and tarragon and heat for 2 minutes. Let cool, then add the balsamic vinegar, tarragon vinegar, and horseradish oil, stirring well.

Refrigerate until thoroughly chilled, but serve at room temperature.

MAKES 1½ CUPS.

PARSLEY CHIVE DRESSING

"I make this dressing with fresh herbs from my garden and often use low-fat ingredients."

2 cloves garlic, chopped

½ cup chopped fresh parsley

¼ teaspoon dried tarragon

¼ cup chopped chives

1 cup mayonnaise or low-fat
mayonnaise

2 tablespoons red wine vinegar

2 teaspoons sugar

¼ teaspoon salt

¼ teaspoon dry mustard

A pinch of pepper

½ cup plain yogurt or low-fat
yogurt or sour cream

Place the garlic, parsley, tarragon, and chives in a food processor and process until minced. Blend in the mayonnaise, vinegar, sugar, salt, mustard, pepper, and yogurt or sour cream. Pour into a bowl, cover, and chill.

MAKES ABOUT 1½ CUPS.

SOUPS AND CHOWDERS

The Tamworth Inn

TAMWORTH, NEW HAMPSHIRE

TAMWORTH INN CURRIED APPLE AND CELERY SOUP

Granny Smith, McIntosh, or Cortland apples work best.

1 medium-sized onion, chopped

1 cup chopped celery

4 tablespoons butter or margarine

¼ cup white wine

3 medium-sized apples, peeled, cored, and sliced

1 tablespoon curry powder (or to taste)

2 cups chicken broth

Salt and pepper to taste

1 cup half-and-half

Sauté the onion and celery in the butter or margarine and wine over low heat, stirring, until the vegetables are softened. Add the apples and cook until they begin to soften. Stir in the curry and cook for 3 minutes. Add the broth, bring to a boil, and simmer until the apples are tender, approximately 30 minutes. Cool the mixture slightly, then process in a food processor or blender until smooth. Season with salt and pepper, if desired.

At this point, the soup can be frozen for later use. If serving immediately, add the half-and-half and heat until hot, stirring frequently. If frozen, thaw the soup, add the half-and-half, heat thoroughly, and serve.

VARIATION: For a low-fat version of the recipe, eliminate the butter or margarine and substitute white wine and a small amount of chicken broth. Also low-fat plain yogurt can be substituted for the half-and-half.

SERVES 6.

MARLBOROUGH BROCCOLI BISQUE

"I have been making and serving this recipe for years—even long before I became an innkeeper. It has a positively wonderful flavor and is economical and very heart-healthy. What's more, it takes less than twenty minutes to prepare from start to finish, it can be served hot or cold, and it freezes well. What more could anyone ask for?"

1¼ to 1½ pounds fresh broccoli or 2 packages (10 ounces each) frozen

2 cans (13¾ ounces each) chicken broth

1 medium-sized onion, quartered

2 tablespoons butter

Salt to taste

A dash of pepper

1 teaspoon curry powder

2 tablespoons lime juice

Lemon slices and sour cream for garnish

In a large saucepan, cook the broccoli, broth, onion, butter, salt, pepper, and curry powder at a simmer for about 8 to 12 minutes or until the broccoli is just tender. Cool slightly, then puree in a blender. Heat or chill, depending on your preference, stir in the lime juice, and garnish with lemon slices and sour cream to serve.

SERVES 4 TO 6.

Combes Family Inn
LUDLOW, VERMONT

CREAM OF FIDDLEHEAD SOUP

"Spring in Vermont and fiddleheads are synonymous. I pick the ferns myself, wash and clean them to remove the paper-thin membrane that clings to the coiled fern, and make gigantic portions of the soup base to use during the year, but I don't add the cream until later."

2 quarts chicken stock

1 quart (1 pound) coarsely chopped fiddlehead ferns (see Note)

1 medium-sized onion, chopped

1 bay leaf

4 tablespoons butter or margarine

4 tablespoons flour

2 cups milk

1 cup half-and-half

Salt and pepper to taste

Heat the stock in a large soup pot. Add the fiddleheads, onion, and bay leaf and simmer for 1 hour.

In another large pot, melt the butter or margarine and stir in the flour to make a roux. Cook over low heat for 5 minutes but do not brown. Add the stock mixture to the roux gradually, stirring constantly, and simmer until slightly thickened and smooth, about 30 minutes.

Remove the bay leaf and pass through a food mill or process in a blender or food processor. (At this point, the soup can be frozen for use later.) If serving immediately, add the milk, half-and-half, and salt and pepper and serve.

NOTE: If you're unable to obtain fiddleheads, you may use broccoli, zucchini, cauliflower, spinach, or Swiss chard instead.

SERVES 6 TO 8.

GAZPACHO

"Our first summer at the inn, our niece was overcome with kitchen creativity. The following spectacular summer soup was the result of her enthusiasm and culinary efforts."

1 medium-sized cucumber

1 medium-sized green bell pepper

1 pound tomatoes

2 scallions, coarsely chopped

1 medium-sized lemon

2 cups tomato juice

¼ cup olive oil

2 tablespoons chopped fresh dill

Salt and pepper to taste

4 fresh medium-sized shrimp, cooked, split, and chilled

Fresh sprig of dill

Peel and seed the cucumber and cut it into chunks. Remove the stem, seeds, and membrane from the bell pepper, then cut into chunks. Quarter and seed the tomatoes. Whirl the vegetables and scallions in a food processor until finely chopped, then transfer to a large bowl.

Squeeze 1 tablespoon lemon juice and stir into the vegetable mixture. Add the tomato juice, oil, dill, salt, and pepper. Stir to blend and refrigerate for at least 3 hours.

Pour into individual soup bowls, top each with a split shrimp and sprig of dill, and serve.

SERVES 4.

CREAM OF ROASTED SWEET RED PEPPER SOUP

Rich and satisfying, this attractive soup can be ready to serve in less than half an hour.

1 can (16 ounces) roasted sweet red peppers

¼ cup butter

½ cup all-purpose flour

4 cups light cream

1 tablespoon paprika

2 tablespoons favorite dried herb (tarragon is good)

6 cups chicken broth

1 teaspoon chopped garlic in oil

½ cup white wine of your choice (Marsala is good)

Sea salt and pepper to taste

Diced red bell pepper or flavored croutons for garnish

Puree the sweet red peppers in a food processor fitted with a metal blade. Set aside.

Melt the butter in a large saucepan, add the flour to make a roux, and stir constantly over moderate heat for about 1 minute. Do not let the mixture brown.

Add the cream, paprika, and herb of your choice and whisk over moderate heat until the mixture thickens. This will take 3 to 5 minutes. (Use a spatula to scrape the bottom corners and sides of the pan to prevent browning.)

Whisk in the chicken broth, pureed peppers, garlic, and wine. Cook for 10 minutes, stirring frequently. Season with salt and pepper. Garnish with diced pepper or croutons.

VARIATION: Substitute beef broth for chicken, red wine for white, and add 2 cups of chopped, sautéed steak for a robust steak soup.

SERVES 8 TO 10.

CURRIED EGGPLANT SOUP

"Our guests rave about this soup and frequently ask for the recipe."

3 tablespoons canola oil

1½ cups chopped onion

2 cloves garlic, minced

1½ teaspoons curry powder

6 cups chicken stock

1 cup peeled and grated carrot

1½ pounds eggplant (1 large), peeled and finely chopped

1 pound potatoes (2 large), peeled and chopped

2 cups milk

2 tablespoons minced fresh cilantro

Salt and pepper to taste

Fresh cilantro leaves for garnish

In a large soup pot, heat the oil and sauté the onion until translucent, about 15 minutes. Add the garlic and curry powder and sauté 1 minute more. Whisk in the chicken stock, add the carrot, eggplant, and potato, and mix well. Bring to a boil, reduce the heat, and simmer partially covered for about 30 minutes or until the vegetables are soft. Remove from heat and let cool slightly.

Puree the mixture in batches in a food processor or blender, then return to the pot. Add the milk and reheat but do not boil. Whisk in the cilantro and salt and pepper. Pour the soup into bowls, garnish each with a cilantro leaf, and serve.

SERVES 8 TO 10.

ZUCCHINI SOUP

What to do with all of that zucchini getting bigger by the day? This soup manages to use up a few, and it is also delicious.

1 large onion, chopped

2 tablespoons butter or margarine

2 cups chicken broth

¼ cup white wine

4 cups unpeeled, diced zucchini

½ teaspoon salt

⅛ teaspoon celery salt

½ teaspoon pepper

⅛ teaspoon garlic powder

¼ cup fresh parsley, washed but not chopped

2 tablespoons sour cream

In a large saucepan, sauté the onion in the butter until tender. Add the broth, wine, zucchini, salt, celery salt, pepper, and garlic and cook over low heat for 15 minutes or until the zucchini is tender. Cool slightly, then pour half the mixture into a blender and process. Pour in the remainder and add the parsley while blending. If the soup is too thick, add more chicken broth.

Heat the soup through and serve with a dollop of sour cream.

SERVES 6.

CREAM OF TOMATO AND ZUCCHINI SOUP

The recipe requires the vegetables to be ground up, which can be a tedious job, but it pays off in the end.

1 medium-sized carrot

1 small onion

1 stalk celery

3 medium-sized zucchini (or 4 small)

½ stick butter

¼ teaspoon garlic powder

1 tablespoon dried basil

½ cup all-purpose flour

2 quarts chicken stock

14 ounces canned whole plum tomatoes, drained and diced

Salt and pepper to taste

1 cup light cream

Finely grind the carrot, onion, and celery; coarsely grind the zucchini.

In a large soup pot over medium heat, sweat the vegetables in the butter for about 20 minutes or until soft. Add the garlic and basil, stir in the flour to make a thick roux, and cook for about 5 minutes. Add the chicken stock and the tomatoes and simmer for 1 hour.

Check the seasonings and add salt and pepper. At this point, the soup can be frozen and held for later use. If serving immediately, add the cream and continue to simmer for an additional 10 minutes or until the soup is hot.

SERVES 10 TO 12.

Too Thin and Not Rich Enough

*T*HERE ARE lots of ways to thicken homemade soups without thickening your waistline, too. The next time your potage needs a pick-me-up, try one of these tips:

  ❧ Scott Laviana of the Mountain Top Inn in Chittenden, Vermont, likes to use a slurry—a mixture of cornstarch and water—to thicken clear soups and consommés because it doesn't cloud the liquid. To prepare the mixture, add a little cornstarch to a little cold water until it reaches the consistency of heavy cream. Pour the slurry slowly into the hot soup, but be patient because the soup won't start to thicken until it comes to a boil.

  ❧ A simple way to enrich and fortify soups such as cream of broccoli, cream of leek, or cream of tomato is to puree extra quantities of the cooked vegetables—broccoli, leeks, tomatoes—and add them in.

  ❧ At the Governor's Inn in Ludlow, Vermont, guests might be surprised to find that their pumpkin soup has been thickened with mashed potatoes. Chef and innkeeper Deedy Marble uses plain potatoes (without cream or butter). The spuds add lots of texture but no fat. Cooked rice and lentils add richness in the same way. Add them at the end of cooking.

  ❧ Don't throw your bread heels out! Use the crumbs—dried or fresh, plain or flavored—in soups. Flavored crumbs add a kick: Try oregano- or basil-flavored crumbs in tomato soup.

BAKED ONION SOUP

An all-time favorite.

3 tablespoons butter

1 tablespoon vegetable oil

2 pounds onions, thinly sliced

¼ teaspoon sugar (optional, for browning)

3 tablespoons all-purpose flour (optional, for thicker soup)

½ cup sherry or sweet vermouth

2 quarts boiling rich brown stock (made from beef, chicken, and veal bones)

6 to 8 slices French bread

Grated Parmesan and Swiss cheeses

Heat the butter and oil in a large soup pot, add the onion, and cook slowly covered for 15 minutes. Uncover and cook for another 30 minutes or until brown (add the sugar at this point, if desired). Sprinkle in the flour, if desired, and stir until well blended. Deglaze the pan with the sherry or vermouth. Stir in the stock and cook for 45 minutes, skimming as necessary.

Pour into ovenproof bowls, top with a slice of bread, and sprinkle with the cheeses. Bake or broil until the cheese is brown and bubbly.

SERVES 6 TO 8.

Mushroom Dill Soup

A wonderful, flavorful, comforting soup that will make you feel warm and cozy when it's cold or rainy outside.

4 tablespoons butter, divided

2 cups chopped onion

Salt and freshly ground pepper

¾ pound fresh domestic mushrooms, sliced

1 tablespoon finely minced fresh dill or ½ teaspoon dried

2 cups chicken broth, divided

1 tablespoon tamari (soy sauce)

1 teaspoon sweet Hungarian paprika

3 tablespoons all-purpose flour

1 cup milk

2 teaspoons lemon juice

½ cup sour cream

½ cup chopped fresh parsley for garnish

In a medium-sized saucepan, melt 2 tablespoons of the butter and sauté the onion until soft but not brown, stirring occasionally. Sprinkle lightly with salt and pepper. Add the mushrooms, dill, ½ cup broth, tamari, and paprika. Cover the pot and simmer for 15 minutes.

Heat the remaining 2 tablespoons butter in a large saucepan. Whisk in the flour, stirring until the mixture foams and bubbles. Remove from the heat. Add the milk all at once and whisk vigorously to blend well. Return to moderate heat and continue to whisk until the sauce is thick and smooth.

Stir in the mushroom mixture and remaining 1½ cups broth. Cover the pot and simmer for 10 to 15 minutes. Just before serving, add salt and pepper, lemon juice, sour cream, and extra dill, if desired. Blend well and heat through but do not boil. Serve garnished with parsley.

Serves 6.

WILD MUSHROOM BARLEY SOUP

Three kinds of mushrooms, fresh herbs, and a splash of sherry give this soup character as well as flavor. Serve it with a crusty French bread and fresh green salad, and you have a complete meal.

½ cup diced onion

¼ cup diced celery

¼ cup diced carrot

3 tablespoons butter

2 tablespoons diced shallots

2 tablespoons minced garlic

1 cup sliced fresh domestic
 mushrooms

½ cup sliced fresh shiitake
 mushrooms

½ cup sliced fresh chanterelle
 mushrooms

¼ cup barley

1½ quarts chicken stock

2 tablespoons sherry

2 tablespoons rice wine vinegar

¼ cup cream

1 tablespoon chopped fresh
 sage

1 tablespoon chopped fresh
 chives

Salt and pepper to taste

In a large saucepan, sauté the onion, celery, and carrot in the butter over medium heat, stirring occasionally. Add the shallots and garlic and cook for about 4 minutes. Add the domestic, shiitake, and chanterelle mushrooms and cook until tender. Stir in the barley, sauté for 2 minutes, then add the stock and bring to a boil. Reduce the heat and simmer for 30 minutes. Add the sherry, vinegar, cream, sage, and chives, season with salt and pepper, and serve hot.

SERVES 6 TO 8.

PUMPKIN BISQUE

"A lavish, festive, cold-weather soup, especially nice for the holidays. Best of all, it's fast. Once the ingredients are prepared, it only takes about 20 minutes to assemble the soup, and it can be done two days ahead of time."

3 slices bacon, diced

1 cup diced onion

4 cups chicken stock

2 cloves garlic, minced

1 tablespoon minced fresh ginger

30 ounces pumpkin puree

¼ cup plus 2 tablespoons maple syrup

¼ cup Marsala wine

2 tablespoons brandy (optional)

A dash of cayenne pepper

1 cup heavy cream

Salt to taste

In a large saucepan, brown the bacon until crisp. Remove with a slotted spoon and set aside to drain on paper towel.

In the bacon fat, sauté the onion until translucent, about 5 minutes, adding 2 to 3 tablespoons of the stock, if needed. Add the garlic and ginger and sauté 1 minute.

Add the pumpkin, stock, maple syrup, wine, brandy (if using), cayenne, and bacon. Whisk until smooth, bring to a boil, reduce the heat, and simmer for 5 minutes to blend the flavors. Add the cream, reheat but do not boil, and add salt.

Serve soup garnished with a dollop of sour cream or yogurt, sprinkled with a little cinnamon, or topped with a little chopped green onion, chives, or parsley or toasted pumpkin seeds.

SERVES 8.

Brass Lantern Inn ❧

STOWE, VERMONT

BRASS LANTERN BUTTERNUT SQUASH SOUP

"The wafting aroma of this soup will draw a crowd. It's a tradition at the inn at Thanksgiving."

2 pounds butternut squash, peeled, seeded, and cut into chunks

1 quart water

½ teaspoon salt

½ cup diced celery

½ cup diced onion

½ cup diced green bell pepper

½ cup butter, melted and divided

⅓ cup white wine

1 teaspoon chopped fresh tarragon

½ teaspoon ground nutmeg

4 cups chicken stock

¼ cup all-purpose flour

⅓ cup sherry

½ cup maple syrup

Combine the squash, water, and salt in a large saucepan and cook covered until soft. Drain, reserving 2 cups of the cooking liquid.

In a separate saucepan, sauté the celery, onion, and pepper in ¼ cup of the butter until softened. Add the wine, tarragon, nutmeg, and stock and simmer for about 10 minutes. Stir in the squash and reserved cooking liquid.

In a small pan, combine the flour and remaining ¼ cup butter and cook, stirring constantly, for about 1 minute. Add the sherry, maple syrup, and some liquid from the squash mixture, stirring to blend. Pour into the squash mixture, blend well, then remove from the heat and cool slightly. Puree in a blender, return to the saucepan, and simmer for 20 minutes uncovered.

SERVES 12.

❧ *Sugar Hill Inn*
FRANCONIA, NEW HAMPSHIRE

BUTTERNUT BISQUE

Butternut and other winter squashes provide a springboard for all manner of soups. This one is sweetened with apples and apple juice and enlivened with curry powder.

4 tablespoons unsalted butter

2 cups finely chopped yellow onion

4 to 5 teaspoons curry powder

2 medium-sized butternut squash (about 3 pounds)

3 cups chicken stock

2 medium-sized apples, peeled, cored, and chopped

1 cup apple juice

Salt and freshly ground pepper to taste

1 medium-sized Granny Smith apple, unpeeled and shredded, for garnish

Melt the butter in a large soup pot. Add the onion and curry and cook covered over low heat until the onion is tender, about 25 minutes.

Meanwhile, peel the squash (an ordinary vegetable peeler works best), scrape out the seeds, and chop the flesh.

When the onion is tender, pour in the stock, add the squash and chopped apple, and bring to a boil. Reduce the heat and simmer partially covered until the squash and apple are very tender, about 25 minutes.

Pour the soup through a strainer, reserving the cooking liquid, and transfer the solids to the bowl of a food processor fitted with a metal blade or use a food mill fitted with a medium disk. Add 1 cup of the cooking liquid and process until smooth.

Return the pureed soup to the pot and add the apple juice and additional cooking liquid, about 2 cups, until the soup is of the desired consistency. Season with salt and pepper.

Simmer briefly to heat the soup through and serve immediately, garnished with the shredded apple.

SERVES 4 TO 6.

AUTUMN POTAGE

"A favorite at Churchill House. This squash, apple, and carrot soup is spiced with cinnamon and ginger."

2 pounds butternut squash, peeled, seeded, and diced

2 medium-sized apples, peeled, cored, and quartered

1 medium-sized onion, chopped

2 large carrots, peeled and chopped

2 medium-sized parsnips, peeled and chopped

4 cups chicken stock

1 whole cinnamon stick

1 teaspoon minced fresh ginger

1 teaspoon ground nutmeg

¼ cup maple syrup (or to taste)

1 cup heavy cream

Salt and pepper to taste

2 tablespoons sliced almonds, toasted

¼ teaspoon ground cinnamon

Place the squash, apple, onion, carrot, and parsnip in a large soup pot, add the stock, and bring to a boil. Reduce to a simmer and add the cinnamon stick, ginger, nutmeg, and maple syrup. Simmer covered until the vegetables are tender.

Remove the cinnamon stick and puree the mixture in a food processor. Pour the puree into the soup pot, add the cream and salt and pepper, and heat through. Garnish with almonds tossed in cinnamon.

SERVES 6.

GARLIC BREAD SOUP

Your guests will give this a unanimous "thumbs up." Serve it for lunch with a sandwich or in small portions with dinner.

½ loaf white bread (about 10 inches long)

1½ tablespoons butter

1 medium-sized onion, diced

2 cloves garlic, peeled and crushed

3 quarts chicken stock

A pinch of dried thyme

Salt and white pepper to taste

1½ cups half-and-half

Slice the bread and heat in a slow oven until crusty but not browned. Cut into 1-inch cubes.

Melt the butter in a large soup pot, add the onion and garlic, and sauté until softened. Add the bread cubes and sauté briefly. Stir in the stock and thyme and simmer 1 hour.

Pass the mixture through a food mill, season with salt and pepper, and add the half-and-half. Heat through but do not boil.

SERVES 10 TO 12.

BLACK BEAN SOUP

"This is my favorite soup. I puree it in a food processor, but some people like the texture of the whole beans. What makes it extra special, as far as I'm concerned, is the dollop of sour cream."

1 pound dried black beans

6 slices bacon, chopped

2 large onions, chopped

3 cloves garlic, crushed

1 large carrot, peeled and diced

1 medium-sized green bell pepper, seeded and diced

1 tablespoon chili powder

1 to 2 teaspoons dried oregano

1 teaspoon ground cumin

1 bay leaf

Salt and freshly ground pepper to taste

9 to 10 cups hot chicken broth or water

½ cup dry sherry

Juice of 1 medium-sized lemon

Sour cream and minced onion for garnish

Rinse and pick over the beans. Pour into a large bowl, cover with water, and soak overnight; or place in a 3-quart microwave-proof casserole with 6 cups hot water and microwave for 18 minutes on high. Let stand covered for 1 hour.

In a large soup pot, sauté the bacon until crisp. Add the onion, garlic, carrot, and bell pepper and cook until the vegetables are softened.

Drain the beans and add to the vegetable mixture. Stir in the chili powder, oregano, cumin, bay leaf, salt, and pepper. Add the broth or water and simmer for 2 hours, or until the beans are tender.

Cool slightly and puree in batches in a food processor or blender. Return to the pot, stir in the sherry and lemon juice, and heat but do not boil.

Ladle into bowls, spoon on a dollop of sour cream, sprinkle with onion, and serve immediately.

SERVES 8.

JARLSBERG VEGETABLE BISQUE

"We can never make enough of this soup—either for family or for guests. It's very special. Our Michael always knows when this is on the stove. It's his favorite."

3 tablespoons butter

3 tablespoons all-purpose flour

4 cups hot chicken broth

2 cups coarsely chopped broccoli

¾ cup chopped carrot

½ cup chopped celery

1 small onion, chopped

1 clove garlic, minced

¼ teaspoon dried thyme

½ teaspoon salt

⅛ teaspoon freshly ground pepper

1 cup heavy cream

1 egg yolk

1½ cups grated Jarlsberg cheese

In a large soup pot, melt the butter. Add the flour and whisk to make a roux. Cook several minutes, stirring constantly. Gradually blend in the hot broth and bring to a boil. Add the broccoli, carrot, celery, onion, garlic, thyme, salt, and pepper. Cover and simmer 8 minutes or until the vegetables are tender.

Blend together the cream and egg in a separate bowl. Gradually blend several tablespoons of the soup into the mixture. Return this to the pot and cook until thickened. Blend in the cheese, stirring until melted, and serve immediately.

SERVES 6 TO 8.

POTATO, LEEK, AND FONTINA CHEESE SOUP

This is a gourmet soup—rich, creamy, and fancy.

4 medium-sized leeks

2 small onions

2 cloves garlic

2 teaspoons unsalted butter

1 teaspoon olive oil

4 large russet potatoes, peeled

3 cups chicken stock

2 cups heavy cream

1 pound grated Fontina cheese

Salt and white pepper to taste

Chopped fresh chives

Wash the leeks thoroughly and cut the white part only into ¼-inch slices. Cut the onions and garlic into ¼-inch slices. In a Dutch oven over medium-high heat, melt the butter with the oil. Add the leeks, onion, and garlic and cook 5 minutes.

Cut the potatoes into ¼-inch slices, add to the leek mixture, and cook 5 minutes. Add the stock, bring to a boil, reduce the heat, and simmer for 20 minutes. Stir in the heavy cream and simmer 10 minutes longer.

Remove from the heat and add the cheese, stirring until melted. Cool slightly and puree in a blender until smooth. Season with salt and pepper, ladle into bowls, and garnish with chopped chives.

SERVES 6.

Mountain View Inn
WAITSFIELD, VERMONT

WINTER DAY VEGETABLE SOUP

An unusual and elegant soup. The cumin and sweet potatoes add a special touch.

1 cup chopped onion

¼ cup butter or margarine

3 medium-sized sweet potatoes, peeled and chopped

3 medium-sized zucchini, chopped

1 bunch broccoli, chopped

2 medium-sized potatoes, peeled and chopped

2 stalks celery, chopped

2 quarts chicken broth

1 to 2 teaspoons ground cumin

1 teaspoon salt

1 teaspoon pepper

2 cups milk or evaporated milk

In a large soup pot, sauté the onion in the butter or margarine until transparent. Add the sweet potato, zucchini, broccoli, potato, and celery and sauté for 5 minutes. Stir in the broth and simmer 15 minutes, or until the vegetables are tender. Add the cumin, salt, pepper, and milk or evaporated milk and heat through.

SERVES 10 TO 12.

Alehouse Crab, Cheddar, and Cauliflower Soup

"We developed this recipe to showcase the ales we brew ourselves here at the inn. We serve this hearty soup with plenty of crusty French bread."

2 tablespoons plus 1 cup unsalted butter, divided

½ cup chopped carrot

½ cup chopped celery

1 cup chopped onion

1 cup ale (hearty New England microbrew or imported ale)

2 quarts chicken stock

1 small head cauliflower, chopped

24 ounces crabmeat (fresh, frozen, or canned—each has a different taste)

1 pound grated sharp cheddar cheese

1 cup all-purpose flour

1 cup heavy cream

Salt and pepper to taste

Melt 2 tablespoons of the butter in a large saucepan. Add the carrot, celery, and onion and simmer on medium heat until very soft. Add the ale, stock, and cauliflower and simmer for 30 minutes more.

Remove from the heat and cool. Puree in a blender in batches, pour back into the saucepan, and reheat. Over low heat, add the crabmeat and cheese, stirring constantly.

Make a roux by melting the remaining 1 cup butter in a saucepan. Add the flour and cook, stirring constantly, over medium heat for 5 minutes. Add the roux to the soup and mix well. Stir in the cream, add salt and pepper, and heat until piping hot but do not boil.

Serves 10 to 12.

RED CLAM SOUP

"This freezes nicely without the pasta. Serve it with red wine and garlic bread or a dry white wine."

2 tablespoons olive oil or butter

2 to 3 cloves garlic, minced

1½ to 2 cups chopped onion

2 medium-sized green bell peppers, chopped

2 large cans (28 ounces each) Italian plum tomatoes, chopped

1 cup tomato sauce

Freshly ground pepper

1 bay leaf

1 teaspoon dried oregano

1 teaspoon dried thyme

1 tablespoon dried basil

2 cups water

1 cup canned clam juice

1 cup dry white wine

½ cup dry sherry

2 cups fresh clams, shucked, with 2 cups juice from clams (two 10-ounce cans baby clams with juice can be substituted)

Small seashell pasta, cooked

In a large stockpot, heat the oil or butter and sauté the garlic, onion, and bell pepper until softened. Add the tomato, tomato sauce, pepper, bay leaf, oregano, thyme, basil, water, and clam juice. Simmer 2 hours.

Add the wine, sherry, and clams and cook 10 minutes longer. Stir in the pasta, heat through, and serve.

VARIATION: For a special meal, add shrimp or other seafood. A few open clams in their shells make a pretty presentation.

SERVES 12.

POTATO, LEEK, AND BACON CHOWDER

This soup can be left peasant style (chunky, not pureed) or half can be pureed and the other half left chunky. The cream is optional, so you can reduce the fat content, if desired.

4 slices bacon, diced

2 leeks, cleaned and thinly sliced

2 medium-sized Idaho potatoes, peeled and cut into 1-inch cubes

5 cups chicken stock

½ to 1 cup light or heavy cream (optional)

Salt and pepper to taste

Fresh chives or scallions for garnish

Sauté the bacon in a large soup pot until golden. Add the leeks and continue to cook 2 to 3 minutes. Add the potato and stock and bring to a boil. Reduce the heat and simmer 20 minutes or until the potato is tender.

Skim the soup, cool slightly, and puree in a blender in batches until smooth. Add the cream, if desired, and season with salt and pepper.

Pour into bowls and garnish each with chives or scallions. Serve with a crusty bread and salad.

SERVES 6.

Highland Lodge

SOLE AND POTATO CHOWDER

"When sole fillets are a good buy, we combine them with our locally grown potatoes and sweet cream to make this robust soup."

1 large yellow onion, diced

2 tablespoons unsalted butter

2 tablespoons all-purpose flour

3 medium-sized red potatoes, peeled, sliced, and kept in water

3½ cups water

12 ounces fresh sole fillets, cut into 1-inch squares

1 cup heavy cream or half-and-half

Sea salt and freshly ground pepper to taste

1 tablespoon finely chopped fresh parsley

In a large saucepan, sauté the onion in butter over medium heat until translucent. Sprinkle in flour, stirring constantly.

Drain the potato slices and arrange atop the onion. Add enough water to bring the level 1 inch above the potatoes. Bring to a slow boil over low heat and cook uncovered until the potatoes are just barely tender, about 12 minutes.

Arrange the sole over the potatoes and poach covered over low heat until cooked, about 5 minutes.

Add the cream or half-and-half and heat through. Season with salt and pepper and sprinkle each serving with the parsley.

SERVES 4 TO 6.

SEAFOOD ASPARAGUS CHOWDER

This is a pretty yet pricey chowder, so it's best saved for special occasions.

2 pounds fresh asparagus

1 medium-sized onion

1 bunch celery

½ pound bacon, chopped

1 stick butter

1 cup all-purpose flour

2 quarts boiling chicken stock

8 medium-sized red potatoes, diced and steamed

1 small can (8 ounces) baby corn

5 ounces fresh swordfish, cooked

5 ounces fresh scallops, cooked

5 ounces fresh salmon, cooked

6 ounces fresh lobster meat, cooked

½ cup light cream

Salt and pepper to taste

Cut off the asparagus stems, saving the tips. Run the stems through a grinder or food processor. Grind the onion and celery and add them to the stems.

Fry the bacon in a large skillet until the fat is rendered. Remove the bacon but leave the fat in the skillet. Add the butter and melt over low heat, stirring constantly. Stir in the ground asparagus, celery, and onion and sauté for 10 minutes, stirring occasionally. Add the flour and blend well. This should have the consistency of a paste. Cook at low heat for 20 minutes. Add the stock and stir constantly until thickened. Let simmer for 10 minutes.

Steam the asparagus tips until just tender and add to the soup along with the potato, corn, and seafood. Stir in the cream, season with salt and pepper, and heat thoroughly but do not boil.

SERVES 10 TO 12.

Bee and Thistle Inn
OLD LYME, CONNECTICUT

BEE AND THISTLE INN CLAM CHOWDER

"This is not a wimpy chowder. For those who wish to thin it a bit, add additional clam broth."

½ medium-sized red bell pepper, diced

½ medium-sized green bell pepper, diced

1 medium-sized onion, diced

2 stalks celery, diced

½ teaspoon black pepper

1½ teaspoons dried basil

1½ teaspoons dried oregano

½ teaspoon chopped garlic

½ teaspoon dried thyme

1 stick butter

¾ cup all-purpose flour

23 ounces clam broth

5 small red potatoes, partially cooked and diced

1 pound chopped fresh clams

Salt and pepper to taste

Sauté the red and green bell pepper, onion, celery, black pepper, basil, oregano, garlic, and thyme in the butter until the onion is transparent. Add the flour and cook over low heat for 5 minutes, stirring constantly. Add the broth, a little at a time, stirring well after each addition. Add the potato, clams, and salt and pepper and simmer 20 minutes, stirring frequently.

SERVES 8 TO 10.

CORNER HOUSE INN LOBSTER AND MUSHROOM BISQUE

Excellent taste, texture, and appearance and easy to prepare, although it does require a lot of dicing. Accompany the soup with homemade bread or rolls and a fresh green salad.

¼ medium-sized green bell pepper

½ pound Spanish onions

8 ounces sliced fresh domestic mushrooms

3 ounces (¾ stick) butter or margarine

½ cup all-purpose flour

1 quart warm milk or half-and-half

1 teaspoon salt

⅛ teaspoon white pepper

½ teaspoon paprika

¼ cup chopped fresh parsley

A dash of hot pepper sauce or cayenne pepper

½ cup dry sherry

½ pound fresh lobster meat, cooked

Chopped fresh parsley or a sprinkling of paprika for garnish

Dice the green pepper and onions and sauté with the mushrooms in the butter or margarine. Slowly add the flour, stirring constantly to form a roux. Simmer several minutes on low heat. Slowly whisk in the milk or half-and-half, stirring until the roux is smooth. Simmer, stirring occasionally, and add the salt, pepper, paprika, parsley, and hot pepper sauce or cayenne. Cook until the mixture begins to thicken, stirring occasionally to prevent sticking.

Add the sherry and lobster after the bisque has thickened fully, cook for 10 minutes more, then remove from the heat. Serve immediately, garnished with parsley or paprika.

SERVES 4 TO 6.

French Fisherman's Stew

"This recipe originated in France—a peasant dish usually served as the main meal. The portions are large and plentiful, and the flavor is robust. If you love seafood, you'll love this soup."

2 tablespoons olive oil

2 tablespoons chopped garlic

1 cup chopped fennel bulb

3 cups chopped carrot

½ cup chopped green bell pepper

2 cups chopped celery

3 cups chopped leeks

3 cups chopped broccoli

1 teaspoon dried thyme

1 teaspoon dried tarragon

1 teaspoon salt

1 teaspoon pepper

2 pinches of saffron

1 cup Marsala wine

1 gallon fish stock (see Note)

1 pound fresh cod

1 cup chopped fresh clams

1 cup fresh mussels, shucked

1 cup fresh shrimp pieces

1 cup fresh lobster knuckles

8 to 10 toasted bread rounds

1 cup Aïoli (recipe follows)

2 cups grated Gruyère cheese

In a medium-sized stockpot, heat the oil and cook the garlic until light brown. Add the fennel, carrot, bell pepper, celery, leeks, broccoli, thyme, tarragon, salt, pepper, and saffron and sauté for 3 to 5 minutes. Add the wine and sauté 1 more minute. Add the stock and bring to a boil, then reduce the heat and cook over very low heat for 30 minutes.

Add the cod, clams, mussels, shrimp, and lobster and cook over very low heat for 1 hour.

In the bottom of large soup bowls, place the toast rounds topped with Aïoli and grated cheese. Ladle in the hot soup.

Aïoli

1 cup homemade mayonnaise

1 teaspoon freshly squeezed
   lemon juice

1 tablespoon chopped garlic

A pinch of white pepper

In a small bowl, mix the mayonnaise, lemon juice, garlic, and pepper until thoroughly blended.

NOTE: Be sure to use a good, flavorful fish stock. The chef at Stonehurst Manor makes his from scratch with shrimp shells, haddock and salmon bodies, lobster bodies, and clamshells.

Serves 8 to 10.

(Ice) Bouillon Cubes

NEXT TIME you make chicken stock, take a hint from Chef Steven Mongeon of the Red Lion Inn in Stockbridge, Massachusetts. Pour the stock into ice cube trays and freeze it. After it's frozen, repackage it either individually or in small quantities in Ziploc bags so that you'll have it handy when you need extra flavor in sauces, soups, rice, etc. (And it tastes so much better than bouillon cubes.)

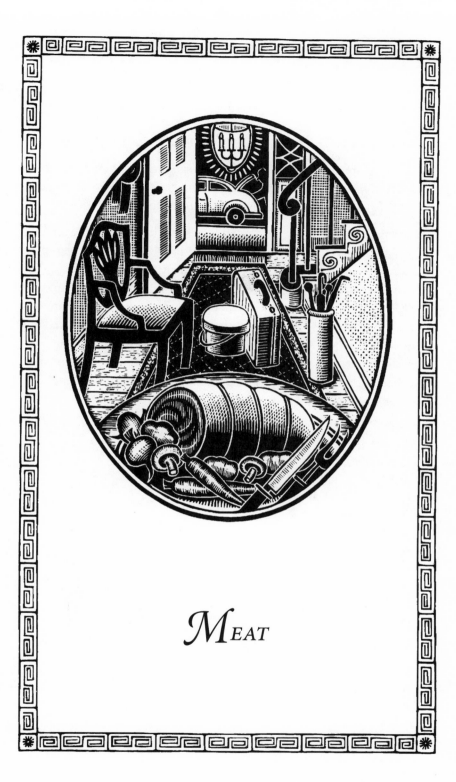

$\mathcal{M}$EAT

TENDERLOIN OF BEEF WITH MAPLE COMPOTE SAUCE

The enticing aroma of the simmering sauce will draw your guests right into the kitchen. If you prefer to cook solo, you might want to prepare the sauce the night before, since it takes a while for it to thicken.

1 small onion, chopped

2 tablespoons olive oil

1 pound whole corn kernels (if fresh not available, use frozen)

8 ounces smoked ham, diced

¼ cup chopped walnuts

2 cups chicken stock

2 cups beef stock

½ cup dry sherry

½ cup port wine

¾ cup maple syrup

2 tablespoons cornstarch dissolved in ¼ cup water

½ medium-sized red bell pepper, minced

½ cup apple cider vinegar

12 tenderloin beef steaks (3 to 4 ounces each)

Prepare the sauce by sautéing the onion in the oil until limp. Stir in the corn, ham, walnuts, chicken and beef stocks, sherry, wine, maple syrup, cornstarch mixture, bell pepper, and vinegar. Bring to a boil and simmer uncovered until reduced and thickened. Keep warm.

Grill the steaks to the desired doneness and pour about 2 ounces of the sauce over each.

SERVES 12.

First Impressions: The Centerpiece

*T*HE WAY your table looks is as important as what you're serving, and innkeepers agree that it's the details that count. A centerpiece is an easy way to add visual sparkle to the table. Freshly cut seasonal flowers, dried flowers, candles, oil lamps, and bowls of fruit in season all make fine centerpieces. But another "cool" idea is to frost fruits and flowers: Beat a couple of egg whites until stiff, dip small bunches of grapes and violets (or other edible flowers) in them, dip in sugar, put in the freezer to harden, then arrange in a bowl.

The old rule stated that centerpieces should be no higher than the diner's sight lines, and that's generally still a good idea. But rules are meant to be bent: Place tall, thin centerpieces, such as bud vases, *between* guests' sight lines so they don't have to duck around them.

BEEF TENDERLOINS WITH BOURBON

Despite the long list of ingredients, this is a quick entrée to prepare. For a fancy touch, garnish each serving with mushroom caps and parsley sprigs.

8 beef tenderloins (3 to 4 ounces each)

2 teaspoons coarsely ground pepper

2 tablespoons vegetable oil

4 green onions, chopped

¼ cup bourbon

¼ pound butter

2 tablespoons grated Parmesan cheese

2 tablespoons grated Romano cheese

1 clove garlic, minced

2 teaspoons sugar

1 teaspoon salt

¼ teaspoon dried sage

¼ teaspoon dried marjoram

¼ teaspoon dried oregano

¼ teaspoon dried thyme

¼ teaspoon paprika

A dash of ground nutmeg

Rub both sides of the tenderloins with pepper. Heat the oil in a large skillet and sauté the beef until done (5 minutes each side for medium rare), then transfer to a serving platter and keep warm.

Sauté the onion in the same skillet for 1 minute. Lower the heat and slowly add the bourbon, scraping up the brown bits in the bottom of the skillet. Stir in the butter, cheeses, garlic, sugar, salt, sage, marjoram, oregano, thyme, paprika, and nutmeg. Cook 2 minutes more.

Pour the sauce over the tenderloins and serve immediately.

SERVES 6 TO 8.

BROILED FILLET OF BEEF WITH PISTACHIOS AND PEARL ONIONS

A lavish dish that makes a lasting impression.

2 tablespoons sugar

1 tablespoon balsamic vinegar

¾ cup veal or beef stock

54 pearl onions, peeled

Salt and pepper

1 tablespoon chopped shallots

1 tablespoon butter

1 cup pinot noir

6 fillet steaks (10 ounces each)

1 cup chopped pistachios, toasted

Combine the sugar, vinegar, and ¼ cup of the veal or beef stock in a medium-sized saucepan, stirring until the sugar dissolves. Add the onions and cook slowly until the liquid is absorbed and the onions are caramelized. Season with salt and pepper and set aside to keep warm.

Sauté the shallots in the butter until soft. Add the wine and reduce until almost dry. Add the remaining stock and reduce by half.

Cook the beef until medium rare (or to your preference), coat the edges with the wine sauce, and roll in the nuts.

Place a fillet in the center of each plate and pour the sauce over it. Garnish with the caramelized pearl onions.

SERVES 6.

SALT 'N' PEPPA

YOU COULD probably count the number of dinner recipes on one hand that *don't* call for "salt and pepper to taste." Chef Steven Mongeon keeps a ready-made mixture—3 parts salt to 1 part pepper—in his kitchen at the Red Lion Inn in Stockbridge, Massachusetts. Place the blend in a clean jam or mayonnaise jar and store with your other spices.

VEAL WITH SUGAR HILL CHAMPAGNE SAUCE

"Always use fresh veal, very thinly sliced, then pound it even thinner before cooking. This is so scrumptious you'll lick your plate!"

2 pounds veal scallops, thinly sliced and pounded

¼ cup all-purpose flour

6 tablespoons butter, divided

½ pound fresh domestic mushrooms, sliced

¾ cup champagne

¼ teaspoon dried sage

¼ teaspoon dried marjoram

1½ cups heavy cream

¾ teaspoon salt

⅛ teaspoon pepper

Dust the veal with the flour. In a large skillet, sauté the veal in 4 tablespoons of the butter for 2 minutes on each side or until lightly browned. Transfer to a dish and keep warm.

Add the remaining 2 tablespoons butter to the skillet and sauté the mushrooms for 2 minutes. Using a slotted spoon, transfer the mushrooms to a dish and keep warm.

Add the champagne, sage, and marjoram to the butter in the skillet and cook until reduced by half. Add the cream and cook until reduced by one-third. Add salt and pepper and return the veal and mushrooms to the skillet only long enough to heat through. Serve immediately.

SERVES 4 TO 6.

VEAL ZURICH STYLE

"There are many variations on this classic Swiss recipe. Some call for veal cubes, which is an acceptable variation, although high-quality cutlets are most desirable."

6 veal cutlets (6 ounces each)

All-purpose flour

1 egg

1 cup milk

Fresh bread crumbs

1 tablespoon butter

1½ cups sliced fresh domestic mushrooms

1 cup brandy

1 cup sour cream

Chopped fresh parsley

Lightly pound the veal cutlets until thin. Dust the cutlets with the flour and shake to remove any excess. Combine the egg and milk. Dip each cutlet into the egg mixture and then in the bread crumbs. Lightly shake off excess crumbs and place on a clean dry plate.

In a sauté or frying pan, melt the butter over high heat until the foam that appears subsides, taking care not to burn the butter. Sauté the cutlets quickly until lightly browned on both sides. Remove from the pan and keep warm on a plate.

While the pan is still hot, add the mushrooms and sauté until soft, about 2 minutes. Remove the pan from the heat and stir in the brandy. Return the pan to the heat and allow the alcohol to evaporate. Add the sour cream, mix thoroughly, and heat to a simmer.

Pour the mixture over the cutlets, garnish with parsley, and serve.

SERVES 6.

The Churchill House Inn
BRANDON, VERMONT

CHURCHILL HOUSE'S BARBECUED BUTTERFLIED LAMB

"This is a very lean, tender, flavorful dish. Cook the meat on a very hot grill with a lid. Offer chutney and mint sauce as condiments."

2 cloves garlic

¼ cup tamari (soy sauce)

¾ cup pineapple juice

¼ cup sherry

1 tablespoon brown sugar

1 teaspoon ground ginger

1 leg of lamb, 3 to 4 pounds, butterflied (deboned) and trimmed well of all fat and gristle (this may cause the meat to come apart into sections)

Combine the garlic, tamari, pineapple juice, sherry, brown sugar, and ginger in a large shallow dish. Marinate the lamb in this mixture for up to 6 hours, turning from time to time.

Sort the meat into small, medium-sized, and large pieces, paying particular attention to thickness. Grill the large pieces for 20 minutes per side, the medium-sized for 10, and the small for 5.

Remove meat from the grill and place on a warmed platter. Slice thinly on the diagonal and serve.

SERVES 8.

GRISWOLD INN GRILLED LAMB STEAK WITH MINT AU JUS

This needs to marinate, so some advance planning is required. The actual cooking, however, couldn't be quicker or easier.

8 center-cut leg-of-lamb steaks (12 ounces each), cut from whole legs of lamb

2 cups olive or vegetable oil

5 scallions, chopped (including green part)

1 tablespoon minced garlic

1 tablespoon chopped fresh parsley

1 teaspoon pepper

Mint au Jus (recipe follows)

Place the steaks in a large shallow baking dish or large plastic storage bag. Combine the oil, scallions, garlic, parsley, and pepper and pour the marinade over the lamb. Refrigerate for 8 hours or overnight, turning the steaks occasionally to evenly coat them.

When ready to cook, remove the steaks from the marinade and either grill or broil them for 3 to 5 minutes on each side. Serve with Mint au Jus.

MINT AU JUS

3 tablespoons mint jelly

3 ounces red wine

1 tablespoon crushed garlic

1 beef bouillon cube

1 cup boiling water

Combine the jelly, wine, and garlic in a saucepan and cook over medium heat until reduced by half. Dissolve the bouillon cube in the boiling water and add to the jelly mixture. Heat until reduced by half.

SERVES 8.

LAMB CURRY

This is a tasty way to use up leftover lamb. Chicken can be substituted as well.

1 small onion, sliced

2 tablespoons butter

1 medium-sized green apple,
cored, peeled, and sliced

2 tablespoons all-purpose flour

1½ teaspoons curry powder

1 cup chicken stock

1 cup heavy cream

1 pound lamb, cooked and cut
into 1-inch cubes

Sauté the onions in the butter until soft. Add the apple and sauté for 1 minute more. Stir in the flour and curry powder and blend well. Add the stock, stirring constantly, and bring to a boil. Reduce the heat and stir in the cream. Add the lamb and cook until heated through.

SERVES 4.

CLEVER MARINADE

*M*ARINADES INFUSE flavor and sometimes tenderize cuts of meat, poultry, and fish. Deedy Marble of the Governor's Inn in Ludlow, Vermont, marinates meat in Ziploc bags and squeezes out all the air. That way, the meat is covered evenly, there's no bowl to wash, and she doesn't have to run to the refrigerator every few hours to flip the meat over.

The Governor's Inn Roast Pork

"We especially like this served with The Governor's Inn Pretty Potato Prune Pudding." (See page 225.)

2 boneless pork tenderloins (1½ to 2 pounds each)

¼ cup honey

2 tablespoons Dijon-style mustard

2 tablespoons crushed peppercorns (do not substitute)

½ teaspoon dried thyme, crushed

½ teaspoon salt

Fresh thyme and spiced crab apples for garnish

Pat dry the tenderloins. Place on a wire rack in a baking pan. Combine the honey, mustard, peppercorns, thyme, and salt, blending well. Brush two-thirds of the mixture over the pork to coat. Roast in a preheated 325°F oven for 40 minutes. Brush with the remaining mixture and bake 10 minutes more, or until a meat thermometer registers 160°F.

Remove tenderloins to a serving platter and garnish with thyme and crab apples.

Serves 8.

RARELY EVER DONE

*A*T THE RABBIT HILL INN in Lower Waterford, Vermont, Chef Russell Stannard's favorite way to serve red meat is medium rare ("The way it's supposed to be"). But no matter your preference, keep in mind that all meat continues to cook once it's been removed from the oven. It's called "carry-over cooking." The temperature of a small roast (3 to 5 pounds) will increase by around 5 degrees. A prime rib will increase by 10 degrees. And a cut of meat cooked *en croûte,* that is, wrapped in pastry—beef Wellington, for instance—will increase up to 15 degrees. Therefore, depending on how large your cut of meat is you can remove it from the oven before it reaches the correct temperature (Chef Stannard offers some general temperatures below) for the degree of doneness you want.

Rare	125° to 130°F
Medium rare	140°F
Medium well	150° to 155°F
Well done	160°F

So, for example, a prime rib that you'd like medium rare can be taken out of the oven when the internal temperature is around 130°F, because it will continue to cook to the required 140°F.

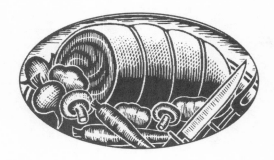

MARINATED ROAST LOIN OF PORK

"Our staff members pray there will be plenty left after dinner, for this is so good. Ghandi's Rice [see page 224] makes a fine accompaniment."

1 boneless, rolled center-cut pork roast (5 pounds)

1½ cups dry red wine

⅔ cup firmly packed brown sugar

½ cup rice wine vinegar

½ cup ketchup

½ cup water

¼ cup vegetable oil

3 tablespoons tamari (soy sauce)

4 cloves garlic, minced

2 teaspoons curry powder

1 teaspoon ground ginger

½ teaspoon freshly ground pepper

4 teaspoons cornstarch

Place the meat in a large shallow dish or Ziploc bag. Combine the wine, sugar, vinegar, ketchup, water, oil, tamari, garlic, curry powder, ginger, and pepper and pour over the meat. Cover the dish or seal the bag and set it in a shallow dish. Marinate overnight in the refrigerator, turning occasionally.

Drain the meat, reserving 2½ cups of the marinade for the gravy and using the remainder to baste the roast.

Pat the meat dry and place on a wire rack in a shallow roasting pan. Roast in a preheated 325°F oven for 2½ hours or until a meat thermometer reads 170°F. Baste the roast frequently with the marinade during the last 15 minutes of cooking.

Blend the cornstarch into the reserved 2½ cups marinade and cook, stirring constantly, until thickened and bubbly.

Remove any string from the roast, cut the meat into thin slices, and serve with the gravy.

SERVES 8 TO 10.

MEME'S PORK PIE

"Two things were always certain in my family: Christmas would come each year, and there would be pork pie to eat after midnight Mass on Christmas Eve. Lots of French families have this pie on New Year's, too!

"I learned how to make the basic pie from my mother, who learned how to make it from her mother, and so on and so on. I make it for my children and guests who are with us at the inn during the holiday season."

CRUST

2¼ cups all-purpose flour

1½ sticks cold butter, cut up

4 tablespoons cold shortening

4 tablespoons ice water

FILLING

2½ to 3 pounds lean ground pork

1 cup dry mashed potato

A dash of ground cinnamon

¾ to 1 teaspoon ground cloves (be cautious as too much ruins the pie)

Salt to taste

1 egg white beaten with a drop or two of water

To make the crust, blend the flour, butter, and shortening until the mixture resembles cornmeal. Add the water and toss until the dough forms a ball. Add a little more water, if needed. Dust the ball with flour, wrap in waxed paper, and chill for 1 hour or longer.

To make the filling, cook the meat slowly in a large skillet over low heat until done. Do not brown, just cook through (you may want to add a little water to make sure it doesn't brown). Drain off all the water and fat. Mix in the potato, cinnamon, cloves, and salt.

Divide the dough in half, roll out both halves, and place one in the bottom of a 9-inch pie plate. Add the filling, cover with the top crust, brush the egg wash over the crust, and sprinkle lightly with salt.

Bake in the bottom half of a preheated 375°F oven until the crust is golden brown. Serve hot.

NOTE: This pie can be made ahead and reheated. It freezes well, too.

SERVES 8 TO 10.

First Impressions: Food Presentation

*W*E SAVOR food with our eyes before we taste it with our mouth. New England innkeepers keep that maxim in mind as they create their culinary works of art. Here are some of the rules they follow:

* *Keep it simple.* This is the cardinal rule of food presentation; there's no need to spend hours molding chopped liver into a bust of your guest of honor. Aim, instead, for simple elegance.

* *Garnishes should be edible.* Paper booties on a rack of lamb and toothpicks with plastic strands may seem clever, but they add nothing to the flavor of the meal. Flowers are beautiful, but use only edible varieties. Natural garnishes, such as herbs, fruits, and vegetables, add color, and they taste good, too.

* *Don't overload the plates.* Remember, less is more. An overloaded plate looks unappetizing.

* *Leave a clean rim on the plate.* Visualize the food you're serving as a photograph or painting and imagine the plate as the frame. A clean rim leads your eye to the food at the center.

* *Balance.* Distribute the food evenly on the plate so it does not appear lopsided.

* *Strive for a variety of colors and shapes.* Add color with garnishes or vary the colors of the foods themselves. Keep shape in mind, too. If you serve a round vegetable (peas or brussels sprouts, for instance) serve another of a different shape.

* *Use your imagination.* One chef likes to serve a plate of spaghetti with a sprig of dill sticking out of the top like a tree. Another serves jam and jellies in a cucumber that's been cut in half lengthwise and hollowed out. A third wraps scallion leaves around filled crepes and ties a bow.

Maple Mustard Baked Rabbit

"We serve locally raised rabbit at the lodge often. It is low in fat and can be adapted to most chicken recipes. One of our most popular menus includes this recipe."

2 farm-raised rabbits (3 pounds each), cut up

⅔ cup butter or margarine, melted

⅔ cup maple syrup

4 tablespoons whole grain mustard

½ teaspoon salt

2 teaspoons freshly ground pepper

2 teaspoons curry powder

Rinse the rabbit pieces in cold water, pat dry with paper towel, and place in a shallow roasting pan. Mix the butter or margarine, maple syrup, mustard, salt, pepper, and curry powder in a small bowl and pour over the meat.

Bake in a preheated 350°F oven for 1 to 1¼ hours, turning and basting occasionally until browned. Serve with baked or mashed potatoes and coleslaw.

Serves 6.

LEG OF VENISON WITH CAPE COD CRANBERRY GLACÉ

The pronounced flavor of venison is balanced beautifully by the tartness of cranberries.

1¾ pounds venison leg, boneless and trimmed of all fat

All-purpose flour

¼ cup olive oil

1 package (4 ounces) dried shiitake mushrooms

½ cup red wine

¾ cup cranberry juice cocktail

1 beef bouillon cube

4 tablespoons fresh cranberries

Slice the venison into 2- to 3-ounce pieces. Gently pound the meat to flatten it, then dredge with flour. Shake off excess and set aside.

Heat the oil in a large skillet over medium-high heat. Add the venison and cook for 3 to 4 minutes. Turn the meat, add the mushrooms, and cook for another 2 to 3 minutes. Pour in the wine and bring to a boil. Add the cranberry juice and bouillon and bring to a boil. Reduce the heat and simmer 2 to 3 minutes. Add the cranberries and simmer another 2 to 3 minutes or until the sauce is reduced to a thin glaze.

To serve, place the venison on warm plates and pour the sauce over the meat, dividing the mushrooms and cranberries evenly for each serving.

SERVES 4.

POULTRY

BLACKBERRY CHICKEN

"Both blackberries and red raspberries are very abundant in our area. Bushes line East Lake Road and Red Bridge Road by Lake Rescue and our backyard. I freeze the berries whole to use year-round. You can easily substitute raspberries for the blackberries called for in this recipe."

4 boneless, skinless chicken breast halves (6 ounces each)

2 tablespoons butter

¼ cup chopped onion

3 tablespoons raspberry jelly

½ cup blackberries, fresh or frozen

3 tablespoons apple cider vinegar

¼ cup heavy cream

Rinse the chicken breasts and pat dry with paper towel. Melt the butter in a large skillet and sauté the breasts for about 10 minutes over medium heat. Add the onion and cook until the chicken is done, about 5 to 10 minutes more. Remove the chicken and keep warm. Add the jelly, blackberries, and vinegar to the skillet, scraping the bottom while stirring. Boil about 1 minute to slightly reduce the liquid. Add the cream and heat. Pour the sauce over the chicken and serve.

SERVES 4.

CHICKEN DIABLE

Although the inn serves this for breakfast, it is a honey of a dish for dinner, too.

4 boneless, skinless chicken breast halves (6 ounces each)

4 tablespoons butter or margarine

½ cup honey

¼ cup Dijon-style mustard

1 teaspoon salt

1 tablespoon curry powder (or to taste)

Rinse the chicken breasts and pat dry. Melt the butter or margarine in a large shallow baking pan and stir in the honey, mustard, salt, and curry powder. Roll each chicken breast in the mixture and arrange in a pan in a single layer.

Bake in a preheated 350°F oven for 15 to 20 minutes or until golden.

SERVES 4.

COOKS' Q & A

Why do some recipes tell you to let meat rest after it's been removed from the oven?

CHEF ROGER KEROACK of the Griswold Inn in Essex, Connecticut, explains it this way: When meat cooks, the muscle tissue contracts. If you cut meat or poultry when it's hot, the juices get squeezed out and the meat becomes dry. When the meat rests, however, the muscles relax enough so that the juices stay in. Chef Roger recommends allowing roasts and poultry to rest for between 15 and 45 minutes, depending upon the size of the cut of meat.

CHICKEN WITH STILTON CHEESE SAUCE

Blue cheese fanatics will love this dish.

4 boneless, skinless chicken breast halves (6 ounces each)

All-purpose flour

¼ cup olive oil

½ cup white wine

½ pint heavy cream

6 ounces crumbled Stilton or blue cheese

Salt and pepper to taste

Rinse the chicken breasts, pat dry, and pound to flatten. Dredge with the flour, shake off any excess, and set aside.

Heat the oil in a large skillet over medium-high heat, add the chicken, and sauté for 3 to 4 minutes. Turn the chicken over and cook another 3 to 4 minutes or until done. Remove from the skillet and keep warm.

Add the wine to the skillet and bring to a boil. Stir in the cream and return to a boil. Reduce the heat to medium and simmer 3 to 4 minutes or until the sauce begins to thicken. Add the cheese, salt, and pepper and stir gently until the cheese melts.

Place the chicken on warm plates, pour the sauce over it, and serve.

SERVES 4.

DEEP FREEZE

*L*IKE MOST OF US, Carol Copeland of The Maine Stay in Kennebunkport, Maine, purchases food in large quantities when it's practical to save money. But she freezes food—soups, stews, meat, and poultry—in small amounts, sometimes in single servings. Small portions defrost more quickly than larger ones and, best of all, she's able to defrost only what she knows she will use.

MAPLE CHICKEN

A great dish for entertaining. The maple syrup–sweetened sauce is spiked with Dijon-style mustard and smoothed with heavy cream.

6 boneless, skinless chicken breast halves (6 ounces each)

All-purpose flour

1 tablespoon butter, melted

2½ cups heavy cream

¼ cup maple syrup

1 tablespoon Dijon-style mustard

Salt and pepper to taste

6 slices bacon, cooked and crumbled

2 teaspoons chopped fresh parsley

Rinse the chicken breasts, pat dry, and lightly pound to flatten them to a uniform thickness (make sure the breasts are free of any cartilage). Dredge each with flour and shake to remove any excess.

In a large skillet, melt the butter over high heat until the foam that is produced subsides. Do not burn the butter. Sauté the breasts in the hot butter and cook thoroughly, turning frequently to avoid burning. Remove to plates and keep warm.

Reduce heat under the skillet and add the cream, syrup, mustard, salt, and pepper. Simmer until reduced by half, stirring constantly.

Pour equal amounts of the sauce over each breast, garnish with the bacon and parsley, and serve.

SERVES 6.

Camden Harbour Inn

CURRIED CHICKEN AND MAINE CRABMEAT

A different and delectable main dish that will be in demand year-round.

4 boneless, skinless chicken breast halves (6 ounces each)

Salt and pepper to taste

2 teaspoons mild curry powder, divided

¼ cup all-purpose flour

2 ounces clarified butter or peanut oil

2 ounces fresh Maine crabmeat

2 ounces shredded mild cheddar cheese

¼ cup dry sherry

¾ cup heavy cream

Rinse the chicken breasts and pat dry. Cover with a piece of plastic wrap and pound into thin cutlets with a tenderizing hammer. Cut each cutlet into two medallions. Season with salt, pepper, and 1 teaspoon curry powder. Dip the medallions in the flour to cover completely.

Place a 10-inch skillet over high heat for about 30 seconds. Add the butter or oil and slide the medallions into the hot butter. Sauté both sides until cooked through.

Remove the medallions from the skillet and place in a broiler pan. (Reserve the juices in skillet.) Overlap the medallions and top with the crabmeat and cheddar cheese. Preheat the broiler for melting the cheese and heating the crabmeat.

Place the skillet over medium-high heat, add the sherry, and allow to bubble for a few seconds. Add the cream and when it begins to boil you might need to lower the heat so the cream does not boil over. Season the sauce with the remaining 1 teaspoon curry powder. When the bubbles of the sauce become large and shiny, the sauce is almost complete. (If the sauce overcooks, it will "break," or curdle. Sometimes adding a tablespoon of cream will bring it back together again.)

Reheat the chicken under the broiler. Coat a dinner plate with the sauce and place the finished medallions in the center.

SERVES 4.

CHICKEN EGREMONT

"The most popular entrée served at the inn, this is our own concoction."

8 small boneless, skinless chicken breast halves (4 ounces each)

½ stick butter or margarine

1 package (10 ounces) frozen spinach or 1 bag (10 ounces) fresh, cooked and well drained

4 ounces Alouette, Boursin, Rondele, or any herbed cream cheese, divided into eight portions

½ cup all-purpose flour

½ teaspoon salt

⅛ teaspoon ground nutmeg

2 eggs, beaten

1 stack Ritz crackers, crushed

Rinse the chicken breasts and pat dry.

Melt the butter or margarine in an ovenproof baking dish that is large enough to hold the chicken without pieces touching. Lay out four pieces, cover each with one-fourth of the spinach, top with one portion cheese, then lay the four remaining pieces on top to make a sandwich and press down.

Mix together the flour, salt, and nutmeg. Dip each "sandwich" in the flour mixture, then in the eggs, and then in the cracker crumbs.

Place in the prepared baking dish and bake in a preheated 500°F oven for 12 to 15 minutes or until lightly browned and completely cooked. Place on a serving plate and top each breast with a portion of the remaining cheese.

SERVES 4.

Fowl Play

WHEN IT COMES to buying chicken, parts is *not* parts. Different birds are bred to have different qualities. Generally speaking, though, the younger the bird, the more tender and flavorful the meat.

- *Broilers and fryers* are generally the same bird. They weigh around 2½ to 3 pounds and the average age is six weeks.

- *Roasters* are bred to produce a lot of white meat and so have larger breasts. At 6 to 7 pounds, they are double the size of broilers. The age of a roaster is eight to nine weeks.

- *Capons* are male birds that have been castrated and specially fattened up. Capon meat is tender and flavorful and more expensive than that of other birds. The bird can be of various ages but weighs in at about 5 to 8 pounds.

- *Hen, fowl, or stewing chickens* are older birds, more than ten months. They weigh from 4 to 6 pounds and are good for making stocks and stews.

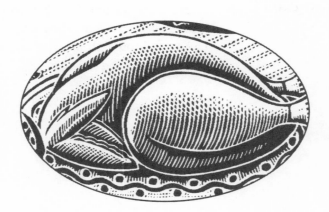

CHICKEN PUGLIA

"This creation was inspired by a trip to Puglia, a beautiful region in southern Italy where Frank's ancestors came from [Frank is one of the innkeepers and the chef's husband]. The chicken breast, stuffed with prosciutto and Fontina cheese and topped with a creamy pesto sauce, is truly wonderful."

4 boneless, skinless chicken breast halves (6 ounces each)

2 slices prosciutto ham

4 slices Fontina cheese

Salt and pepper

½ cup all-purpose flour

2 to 3 tablespoons olive oil

2 shallots or ½ medium-sized red onion, minced

2 tablespoons dry vermouth

1 tablespoon brandy

1 cup chicken stock

½ cup heavy cream

2 tablespoons pesto (store-bought or homemade; see Note)

Tomato slices and fresh basil leaves for garnish

Rinse the chicken breasts, pat dry, then carefully cut a pocket in each one. Cut the prosciutto in half and place 1 slice meat and 1 slice cheese in each pocket. Using a toothpick, pin the opening closed. Lightly sprinkle each breast with salt and pepper and dredge with flour, shaking off any excess.

Heat the oil in a large skillet and quickly brown the breasts over high heat, turning once. This is to seal the opening shut and the juices in; the chicken will finish cooking later. Remove the chicken and keep warm.

In the same skillet, sauté the shallots or red onion for 10 minutes or until soft (adding a bit of the stock, if needed). Whisk in the vermouth, brandy, and stock and reduce by half. Whisk in the cream and reduce again. Quickly whisk in the pesto, return the chicken to the skillet, cover, and simmer gently for 5 minutes on each side.

Remove the toothpicks, top each breast with some of the sauce, and garnish with 2 tomato slices and a basil leaf. Serve at once. *Viva Italia!*

NOTE: To make your own pesto, puree in a food processor or blender 2 cups chopped fresh basil, 3 cloves chopped garlic, 1 cup walnut pieces, 1 cup extra-virgin olive oil, 1 cup grated Parmesan cheese, and salt and pepper to taste.
SERVES 4.

Sugar Hill Inn

FRANCONIA, NEW HAMPSHIRE

Elegant Stuffed Chicken Breasts

Tasty and tender, these are great for a special luncheon.

5 tablespoons butter

10 ounces chopped spinach, fresh or frozen

8 ounces bread crumbs

1 egg, beaten

1 cup shredded Swiss cheese

½ teaspoon pepper

½ teaspoon salt

4 boneless chicken breast halves, skin on (6 to 8 ounces each)

2 tablespoons honey

Melt the butter in a medium-sized saucepan over medium heat. Add the spinach and cook until tender, about 2 to 3 minutes, stirring frequently. Remove from the heat and add the bread crumbs. Stir in the egg, cheese, pepper, and salt and let cool.

Rinse the chicken and pat dry. Carefully loosen the skin on each breast by pushing your fingers between the skin and the meat to form a pocket. Spoon some of the stuffing into each pocket.

Place the chicken in a 13- by 9-inch pan, brush on the honey, and bake in a preheated 350°F oven for 30 to 35 minutes or until the skin is golden brown.

NOTE: Brushing honey over the breasts right before baking not only contributes a subtle sweetness but also turns the skin a beautiful golden brown. To make the application easier, warm the honey slightly before using.

Serves 4.

Chicken Riddle

*H*ow is it that a dish as basic as chicken can be so tricky to roast? It's because white meat, which has little fat, cooks more quickly than dark meat, which is relatively fatty. When you cook them together, it's easy to end up with a dry breast but moist dark meat.

The most obvious way to cope with the problem is to cook chicken pieces separately, but to an internal temperature of 180°F. (Some cooks feel that if 180°F is done, then 190°F must be *really* done. But all they end up with is really dry meat.)

Chef Stuart London of the Old Lyme Inn in Old Lyme, Connecticut, spreads a little butter underneath the breast skin to trap moisture; he also recommends basting the breast meat regularly as it cooks. Chef Stuart sometimes even roasts larger birds upside down so that as the bird cooks the juices are pulled down into the breast.

Red Clover Inn at Woodward Farm

MENDON, VERMONT

STUFFED CHICKEN BREASTS À LA RED CLOVER INN

Instead of a bread-based stuffing, these are filled with a divine mixture of goat cheese, bacon, rosemary, and pignoli nuts.

4 small whole boneless, skinless chicken breasts (8 ounces each)

4 ounces chevre (goat cheese)

3 slices bacon, cooked and finely chopped

2 fresh sprigs of rosemary, finely chopped

¼ cup chopped pignoli nuts or almonds

Salt (optional)

Pepper to taste

1 teaspoon olive oil

Rinse the chicken breasts and pat dry. Position each breast so that it is laying flat, with what would have been the skin side down. Using a small knife, score the thicker part of the meat on each side of the breast.

Combine the cheese, bacon, rosemary, nuts, salt (if desired), and pepper. Divide the mixture evenly among the breasts, placing it on one half (or side) of the breast and pressing it firmly onto the breast. Fold over the other half and press firmly.

Heat the oil in a large skillet and sear the breasts until lightly browned. Place them in a large ovenproof dish and bake in a preheated 400°F oven for 9 to 10 minutes, turning once halfway through the cooking process.

SERVES 4.

VERMONT APPLE, SAUSAGE, AND CHEDDAR STUFFED CHICKEN

Although this can be enjoyed any time of the year, it is especially appealing in fall and winter, when appetites are hale and hearty.

6 small whole boneless, skinless chicken breasts (8 ounces each)

4 ounces butter

4 ounces sweet sausage (Italian or veal), removed from casing and crumbled

2 ounces diced green or red bell pepper

2 ounces diced celery

4 ounces diced Spanish onion

1 to 2 medium-sized McIntosh apples, peeled, cored, and diced

1 ounce white wine

Dried sage, tarragon, basil, and poultry seasoning to taste

3 to 4 slices white bread, cut into ½-inch cubes

3 to 4 slices whole wheat bread, cut into ½-inch cubes

3 ounces grated cheddar cheese

Melted butter

White wine

Lay each chicken breast down so that what would have been the skin side is facing up. Cover with plastic wrap and pound with a mallet to a uniform thickness. Refrigerate until ready to stuff.

Melt the butter in a large skillet and sauté the sausage, pepper, celery, onion, and apple until soft. Add the wine, sage, tarragon, basil, and poultry seasoning and cook for 5 minutes. Pour into a bowl and cool. Add the bread and cheese to the bowl and toss to combine. (If too wet, add more bread.)

Lay out the pounded breasts so that what would have been the skin side is now facing down. Place 3 to 4 ounces of the stuffing on one half (or side) of each breast and fold the other half over the stuffing. Brush with a small amount of melted butter and a splash of wine.

Bake in a preheated 350°F oven for about 20 minutes and serve.

SERVES 6.

BLUEBERRY HILL STUFFED CHICKEN WITH CHAMPAGNE SAUCE

"I have chosen to use chicken breasts for this recipe to simplify it, but if you are daring, try this with whole, deboned Rock Cornish game hens as we do at the inn. Although it is far more time-consuming, the results are well worth the effort."

2 tablespoons canola oil

8 ounces ground chicken breast

2 teaspoons cracked fennel seeds

½ teaspoon kosher salt

¾ cup minced red onion

2 cloves garlic, minced

1 stalk celery, minced

6 ounces fresh spinach or watercress (or 3 ounces each)

⅛ teaspoon crushed red pepper

¼ teaspoon pepper

2 teaspoons chopped fresh sage

2 ounces Gorgonzola cheese

6 boneless, skinless chicken breast halves (6 ounces each)

Blueberry Hill Champagne Sauce (recipe follows)

Fresh watercress for garnish

Heat 1 tablespoon of the oil in a large skillet over medium heat. Add the ground chicken and sauté along with the fennel and salt until the chicken is cooked through. Transfer to a bowl and set aside.

Return the skillet to the heat, add the remaining oil, and sauté the onion, garlic, and celery until soft. Stir in the spinach and/or watercress. Cook until about half of the liquid released from the greens has reduced. Lower the heat and add the red and black peppers. Add the chicken mixture, sage, and cheese, stirring over low heat until combined and the cheese has melted. Adjust the salt and pepper to taste and set aside to cool while you prepare the breasts.

Make sure all the fat and skin have been removed from each breast, then rinse them and pat dry. Lay the breasts one at a time on a clean work surface with what would have been the skin side up. Lay plastic wrap over the breast and pound with a mallet until about ¼ inch thick. Repeat with each breast.

When the stuffing has cooled, lay the breasts with what would have been the skin side down. Place 1 to 2 tablespoons of the stuffing in the center of each breast. Fold the edges of the chicken around the stuffing, forming a ball. Set on a greased baking sheet, seam side down. (This may be done 1 hour ahead and refrigerated.) Bake, covered with aluminum foil, in a preheated 350°F oven for 20 to 25 minutes.

Place a breast in the center of each dinner plate. Ladle a small amount of Champagne Sauce over it and garnish with fresh watercress.

BLUEBERRY HILL CHAMPAGNE SAUCE

3 cups chicken stock (preferably homemade)

1½ cups brut champagne

1¾ cups heavy cream

2 cups chopped fresh spinach or watercress, rinsed, dried, and stems removed

Salt to taste

¼ teaspoon white pepper

1 tablespoon freshly squeezed lemon juice

In a medium-sized saucepan, combine the stock and champagne. Cook on high heat until reduced to 2½ cups. Lower to medium heat and whisk in the cream. Add the spinach or watercress and reduce until the sauce coats the back of a spoon. Add salt, pepper, and lemon juice.

SERVES 6.

Tamworth Inn Champagne Chicken and Shrimp

A luscious combination of chicken and shrimp in a rich and creamy champagne sauce. Serve this over rice with a sprinkling of minced fresh parsley.

1 pound fresh large shrimp (16 to 20) or 1½ to 2 pounds small shrimp, peeled and deveined

2 green onions or ½ medium-sized yellow onion, chopped

3 tablespoons lemon juice

Salt and pepper to taste

3 tablespoons margarine

8 boneless, skinless chicken breast halves (6 ounces each)

¾ cup sliced fresh mushrooms

1 cup chicken broth

⅓ cup all-purpose flour

1½ cups half-and-half

¾ cup champagne

Combine the shrimp, onion, lemon juice, salt, and pepper and set aside.

In a large sauté pan, melt the margarine and cook the chicken until browned, about 10 minutes. Remove and keep warm.

Cook the mushrooms in the same pan for about 5 minutes. Remove with a slotted spoon and keep warm.

In the same pan, cook the shrimp until pink, about 5 minutes. Remove and set aside.

Combine the broth and flour and pour it into the sauté pan, blending thoroughly. Gradually add the half-and-half and the champagne. Cook until the mixture thickens and boils. Stir in the mushrooms, heat through, and combine with the chicken and shrimp. Serve over rice.

Serves 8.

GRENADINE CHICKEN

This dish can easily be increased or decreased—to feed a crowd or only two people. The amounts of grenadine and brandy also are variable and can be added according to personal preference.

1 cup all-purpose flour

1 teaspoon freshly ground pepper

1 teaspoon turmeric

½ teaspoon garlic salt

½ teaspoon seasoned salt

1 whole chicken (about 6 pounds), cut into serving pieces

½ cup butter

1 large onion, chopped

1 large can (6 ounces) sliced mushrooms, drained

1½ cups grenadine

1 cup brandy

Combine the flour, pepper, turmeric, garlic, and seasoned salt in a Ziploc bag. Add the chicken, seal the bag, and shake, making sure to coat each piece of chicken thoroughly.

In a large skillet, melt the butter and brown the chicken on both sides. Remove the chicken and set aside. Sauté the onion and mushrooms in the same skillet, cooking until tender.

In a deep ovenproof baking dish, place a layer of half the chicken and another layer of half the onion-mushroom mixture. Combine the grenadine and brandy and pour on half. Repeat the layers of chicken and onion-mushroom mixture and pour the remaining grenadine-brandy mixture over all.

Cover and bake for 1 to 1½ hours in a preheated 350°F oven, basting occasionally.

SERVES 4 TO 6.

Chicken and Leek Pot Pie

You'll never be tempted to buy a commercial brand chicken pot pie again after you make this one. It blends together just the right ingredients (don't omit the hot pepper sauce) in just the right amounts.

1 whole chicken (about 6 pounds)

4 quarts water

½ pound carrots, cut into 1-inch sticks

2 large leeks, rinsed, split, and chopped

2 cups chicken stock

2 tablespoons chopped fresh tarragon

½ cup white wine

2 cups light cream

Roux made of ½ cup flour mixed with 6 tablespoons butter

½ teaspoon hot pepper sauce

½ teaspoon ground dried thyme

1 teaspoon salt (less if using canned chicken stock)

½ teaspoon white pepper

1 frozen puff pastry sheet

1 egg

2 tablespoons milk

Split the chicken across the stomach cavity and break its back so that the legs are separated from the breast and wings. Bring the water to a simmer, add the leg portions of the chicken, and poach for 25 minutes. Add the breasts and continue poaching for another 25 minutes. The chicken should be just cooked. Remove from the broth and cool.

Pull the meat from the bones, cut into chunks, and set aside.

Simmer the carrots and leeks separately in the stock. Remove them with a slotted spoon and add to the chicken, along with the tarragon.

Add the wine to the stock and simmer to remove the alcohol. Add the cream and bring to a boil. Slowly add the roux, stirring constantly (check the thickening carefully, as you may not need all the roux). Add the hot pepper sauce, thyme, salt, and white pepper. Cool the sauce, check for seasoning, pour over the chicken and vegetables, and stir together. (May be prepared up to this point a day ahead of time.)

Place the mixture in a 13- by 9-inch baking dish. Cut the thawed pastry into 6 squares and place on the chicken. Mix the egg and milk together and brush over the crust. Bake in a preheated 400°F oven for about 15 minutes or until the filling is hot and the crust is puffed and golden brown.

SERVES 6.

COOKS' Q & A

What's the difference between phyllo dough and puff pastry?

CHEF FRANCIS BROOK SMITH of the Bee and Thistle Inn in Old Lyme, Connecticut, explains that they are two completely different products. Phyllo (also spelled filo) is a paper-thin pastry made from oil, flour, and water. Impossible to make at home, the thin sheets are available in the frozen section of grocery stores and are used primarily in sweet dishes such as turnovers and baklava.

Puff pastry is made up of more than a thousand layers of butter and flour. When it's baked, it "puffs." The pastry is sturdier than phyllo dough and used to make croissants as well as in main dishes such as beef Wellington.

1785 RASPBERRY DUCKLING

Absolutely fantastic! Serve this for a special occasion with wild rice and fresh vegetables. The sauce also can be used with roast chicken or turkey.

2 ducks (4½ to 5 pounds each), dressed

1 small onion, chopped

2 stalks celery, chopped

1 medium-sized carrot, chopped

1 medium-sized apple, peeled, cored, and chopped

2 medium-sized oranges, peeled, pithed, and chopped

½ cup tamari (soy sauce)

2 cloves garlic, sliced

1785 Raspberry Sauce (recipe follows)

Remove the neck, gizzards, and fat pads inside the cavity of both ducks. Cut off the excess neck skin. Place the ducks on a wire rack in a large roasting pan. Fill the cavity of each with onion, celery, carrot, apple, and orange. Pierce the skin with a sharp fork at 2-inch intervals. Coat the skin with tamari and place slices of the garlic on the breasts (1 clove per duck).

Roast in a preheated oven at 325°F for 3 to 3½ hours (the duck is done when a leg turns easily). Remove the vegetables from the cavities and allow the ducks to cool slightly.

Using a large knife, slice down through the middle of the breast to open the duck. Cut through on each side of the backbone. Take each half and with your fingers gently remove the rib cage.

Place the ducks breast side up on baking sheets and bake in a preheated 350°F oven for 10 to 15 minutes to heat thoroughly. Remove from the oven and transfer to serving plates. Pour heated 1785 Raspberry Sauce over the ducks and serve.

1785 RASPBERRY SAUCE

¼ pound butter

1 cup sugar

2 tablespoons all-purpose flour

1 cup apple cider vinegar

2 ounces Chambord (raspberry liqueur)

1½ cups frozen raspberries

Melt the butter in a medium-sized saucepan. Add the sugar and stir until well blended. Cook over low heat until the sauce starts to darken slightly, stirring frequently. When the mixture is a light brown color, add the flour and stir until well mixed. Add the vinegar and stir until the sugar dissolves. Bring to a slow boil and cook until the mixture reduces to half its original volume. The sauce will have a thick, syrupy consistency.

Remove from the heat and stir in the Chambord and raspberries.

SERVES 4.

AMERICA'S FIRST DINNER PARTY?

THERE ARE few contemporary accounts of the original harvest feast we now call Thanksgiving. In fact, only two survive and neither of those mentions anything about turkey with stuffing, candied yams, and pumpkin pie. So what did the Pilgrims feast upon during their three-day celebration with Massasoit and other Indians? Venison, fowl (the variety is not mentioned), cod, bass, and grains. It wasn't until the mid- to late nineteenth century—after President Lincoln declared Thanksgiving a public holiday in 1863—that turkey entered the picture. The now-ubiquitous pumpkin pie became a standard even later, in the early twentieth century.

Holiday Duckling

"This was the best duck I've ever had—anywhere!" reported the recipe tester. The duck is moist and tasty, the cranberries retain their consistency, and it is surprisingly easy to make, considering the spectacular results.

2 ducks (5½ pounds each)

1 medium-sized orange

Cranberry Orange Glaze (recipe follows)

Remove the giblets from the cavity of each duck, rinse each duck, and pat dry. Using a fork, poke holes through the skin. Place the ducks on a wire rack in a large roasting pan. Cut the orange in half, squeeze the juice from one half over one duckling, then place the half inside its cavity. Repeat with the other duck and orange half.

Bake in a preheated 325°F oven for approximately 3 to 3½ hours. Remove from oven and allow to cool.

Quarter the ducks and place them on aluminum foil–lined baking sheets, skin side up. Brush liberally with Cranberry Orange Glaze and bake at 425°F for 30 to 40 minutes. Serve with additional glaze.

Cranberry Orange Glaze

1 cup chicken stock

2 tablespoons coarsely grated orange rind

1 pound fresh cranberries

½ teaspoon fresh ginger

6 ounces currant jelly

¾ ounce Grand Marnier

¼ cup sugar

1 tablespoon cornstarch

¼ cup warm water

Place the stock, rind, three-fourths of the cranberries, the ginger, jelly, Grand Marnier, and sugar in a medium-sized saucepan. Bring to a boil, reduce the heat, and simmer 45 minutes.

Combine the cornstarch and water and stir into the cranberry mixture, cooking until slightly thickened. Remove from the heat, add the remaining cranberries, and proceed with the recipe.

Serves 4 to 6.

CORNISH GAME HEN WITH APPLE CRANBERRY STUFFING

You can present this stuffing in two different ways. Bake it separately from the hens, as described, and when both stuffing and hens are done either fill the hens with the baked stuffing and serve or spoon a portion of the stuffing on each dinner plate, place the hen on top of the stuffing, and serve.

STUFFING

1 cup chicken stock

1 loaf day-old white bread

¼ cup finely diced McIntosh apple

⅓ cup finely diced onion

¼ cup finely diced celery

¼ cup clarified butter

½ cup whole berry cranberry sauce

½ cup cooked ground breakfast sausage

1 tablespoon dried sage

1 tablespoon poultry seasoning

2 eggs, beaten

GAME HENS

6 Cornish game hens (10 to 16 ounces each)

½ cup honey

½ cup Marsala wine

2½ cups chicken stock

⅓ cup cornstarch

½ cup water

To make the stuffing, pour the stock over the bread and set aside to soak for several minutes. Meanwhile, sauté the apple, onion, and celery in the butter for 4 minutes over medium heat.

Break up the bread and combine it in a large bowl with the sautéed ingredients, cranberry sauce, sausage, sage, poultry seasoning, and eggs, mixing well. Bake in a greased or sprayed 8-inch square pan in a preheated 350°F oven for approximately 1 hour.

To prepare the hens, remove the giblets, rinse the hens, and pat dry. Combine the honey, wine, and stock in a saucepan and bring to a rolling boil. Dissolve the cornstarch in the water and add to the wine mixture, whisking until smooth. Return to a rolling boil and simmer for 2 minutes, then remove from the heat.

Place the hens in a large roasting pan and bake in a preheated 350°F oven for approximately 30 minutes. When the hens are slightly brown, begin to baste with the wine sauce and continue to baste and cook for another 30 minutes or until the hens are done. Serve with the stuffing, as desired. *SERVES 6.*

MARINATED TWIN QUAIL WITH WILD MUSHROOM RAGOUT

"You can use whatever mushrooms are available—including dehydrated mushrooms. To rehydrate them, follow the directions on the package. We serve this with saffron rice pilaf and a medley of seasonal vegetables."

8 quail (3½ ounces each)

1½ cups vegetable oil

2 tablespoons finely chopped shallots

1 orange slice with rind

½ cup diced tomato

Salt to taste

2 teaspoons pepper

½ cup orange juice

½ cup white wine

1 tablespoon dried rosemary

Wild Mushroom Ragout (recipe follows)

Sliced scallions for garnish

Place the quail in a large roasting pan. Mix together the oil, shallots, orange, tomato, salt, pepper, orange juice, wine, and rosemary and pour over the quail. Refrigerate for 3 to 4 hours or overnight, turning from time to time.

Remove the quail from the marinade and place on a preheated grill. Basting with the marinade and turning occasionally, cook for about 20 minutes or until all the juices are translucent and the quail are crispy and tender.

Spoon the ragout onto dinner plates, top with 2 quail each, and garnish with sliced scallions.

WILD MUSHROOM RAGOUT

1 tablespoon olive oil

½ cup chopped fresh
 chanterelle mushrooms

½ cup chopped fresh shiitake
 mushrooms

½ cup chopped fresh porcini
 mushrooms

½ cup seeded, skinned, and
 diced tomato

¼ cup sliced scallions

1 tablespoon finely chopped
 garlic

1 tablespoon finely chopped
 shallots

¼ cup white wine

¼ cup tomato juice

Salt to taste

1 teaspoon pepper

2 tablespoons butter (optional)

Heat the oil in a large pan, add all the mushrooms, and sauté lightly. Add the tomato, scallions, garlic, and shallots and continue to sauté. Deglaze the pan with the wine and tomato juice and season with salt and pepper. Reduce some of the liquid by simmering the ragout uncovered until all ingredients are tender. Stir in the butter (if desired), then set aside the ragout and keep warm until the quail are cooked.

SERVES 4.

FISH AND SHELLFISH

Griswold Inn
ESSEX, CONNECTICUT

WINTER FLOUNDER WITH TOMATO BASIL CREAM SAUCE

Professional-looking, great tasting, and simple to prepare, this dish has all the best qualities.

3 tablespoons butter or margarine, melted

3 tablespoons lemon juice

3 tablespoons white wine

6 to 8 fresh flounder or sole fillets (6 to 8 ounces each)

Pasta or rice

Tomato Basil Cream Sauce (recipe follows)

Fresh basil leaves and chopped fresh parsley for garnish

Combine the butter or margarine, lemon juice, and wine. Pour half of the mixture in a large shallow baking pan. Arrange the fish fillets in the dish, pour the remaining mixture over the fish, and bake in a preheated 325°F oven for 10 to 15 minutes or until the fish flakes easily with a fork.

Serve the fillets over your favorite pasta or rice, ladle Tomato Basil Cream Sauce over the fish, and garnish with fresh basil and chopped parsley.

TOMATO BASIL CREAM SAUCE

1 cup white wine

2 cloves garlic, minced

1 shallot, minced

1 bay leaf

½ cup chopped fresh basil or 4 teaspoons dried

1 jar (30 ounces) tomato or spaghetti sauce

½ cup heavy cream

In a large saucepan, combine the wine, garlic, shallot, bay leaf, and basil. Simmer until reduced to one-fourth its original volume, approximately 20 minutes. Add the sauce and simmer 10 minutes. Add the cream and simmer 10 minutes more. Strain the sauce into another pot and keep warm on low heat, stirring occasionally, until ready to ladle over the fillets.

SERVES 6 TO 8.

PAN-FRIED RAINBOW TROUT FILLETS WITH SWEET RED PEPPER AND SAGE SAUCE

"This sauce is good with any fish!"

4 tablespoons clarified butter or any frying oil, divided

2 tablespoons rubbed sage, divided

¼ cup dry vermouth or white wine

¼ cup chicken broth

¼ cup light cream

¼ cup diced roasted red bell pepper

Pinch of salt and pepper

½ cup all-purpose flour

1 teaspoon pepper

¼ cup crushed almonds

2 rainbow trout fillets (8 ounces each), fresh or frozen

2 teaspoons finely chopped fresh red bell pepper

To make the sauce, heat 2 tablespoons of the butter or oil in a saucepan. Add 1 tablespoon of the sage, the vermouth or wine, broth, cream, roasted bell pepper, and salt and pepper. Cook over moderate heat until thick and bubbly.

In a large shallow baking pan, mix the flour, pepper, almonds, and remaining tablespoon sage. Dredge each fillet on both sides with the flour mixture and fry in 2 tablespoons of the butter or oil, skin side down, for 2 minutes or until crispy. Turn and fry for 1 minute.

Place each fillet on a plate and pour sauce over the top. Garnish with fresh bell pepper.

SERVES 2.

Bradford Inn
BRADFORD, NEW HAMPSHIRE

SALMON IMPERIAL

An excellent dinner entrée. Garnish with fresh parsley and a lemon slice.

4 to 6 salmon steaks or fillets (8 ounces each), fresh or frozen

2 tablespoons butter, melted

2 tablespoons lemon juice

4 to 6 teaspoons anchovy paste

1 teaspoon dry mustard

1 clove garlic, crushed

½ teaspoon paprika

Place the salmon on a greased broiler pan. Combine the butter, lemon juice, anchovy paste, mustard, garlic, and paprika and brush the salmon with the mixture. Broil approximately 5 inches from the heat for 6 minutes; turn, brush again with the mixture, and broil an additional 4 to 5 minutes or until the fish flakes easily with a fork.

SERVES 4 TO 6.

HOW FRESH IS THAT FISHY IN THE WINDOW?

*T*HE GOSNOLD ARMS INN in New Harbor, Maine, is so close to the ocean that the fish practically swim right to the inn's kitchen. Lucy Martin buys all her fish right at the dock, so she's sure it's fresh. But how can you be sure the fish at your grocery store hasn't been sitting in the cooler for days? Here are Lucy's guidelines:

🐟 Most important is odor—fresh fish shouldn't have any. As Lucy puts it, "A fish shouldn't smell like a fish if it's fresh."

🐟 Next, if you're buying a whole fish make sure that the eyes are clear, not cloudy. And finally, the flesh should be firm, not mushy.

🐟 Use fresh fish as soon as possible after you buy it; keep it in the refrigerator for no more than a day or two.

🐟 To freeze fish, make sure it's wrapped tightly and be sure to use it within one month. Once fish thaws, use it immediately and—just as with most other foods—don't refreeze it.

SAUTÉED SALMON WITH RED PEPPER SAUCE

The satiny smooth sauce adds a touch of class and distinctive taste to the tender, moist fillets of salmon.

2 tablespoons olive oil

2 fresh boneless, skinless salmon fillets (8 ounces each)

All-purpose flour

Salt and pepper to taste

Red Pepper Sauce (recipe follows)

Heat the oil in a pan. Dust the salmon with flour and season with salt and pepper.

When the oil begins to smoke, put the salmon in the pan and sauté 2 to 3 minutes; turn and sauté another 2 to 3 minutes. The salmon should still be slightly pink in the center. Serve immediately with Red Pepper Sauce.

RED PEPPER SAUCE

1 tablespoon minced shallots

¼ teaspoon minced garlic

1 tablespoon olive oil

1 medium-sized red bell pepper, cored, seeded, and diced

¼ cup white wine

½ cup chicken stock

¼ cup heavy cream

Salt and pepper to taste

Sauté the shallots and garlic in the oil for 2 minutes. Add the bell pepper and sauté for 3 more minutes. Add the wine, bring to a boil, then simmer for 3 minutes. Stir in the stock and cream, bring to a boil, and reduce by half.

Cool slightly and puree the sauce in a blender or food processor, then strain through a fine-meshed sieve. Season with salt and pepper.

To serve, ladle some of the sauce on each dinner plate and place the salmon on top.

SERVES 4.

Planning a Dinner Party

*H*AVING FRIENDS and family to dinner is a wonderful way to spend an evening. Unfortunately, the cook usually spends the night in the kitchen instead of visiting with his or her guests. Innkeepers and chefs throw dinner parties every night, so who better to turn to for advice? Here are some of their best timesaving tips.

- Find out ahead of time what your guests won't eat. Plan on a "safe" entrée—one that most people will eat, such as chicken or pasta. This isn't the occasion to resurrect your tripe and okra casserole (it died for a reason). Likewise, don't try a new recipe when you're having company—too much could go wrong.

- Decide on a menu a week or so in advance. That will give you time to make changes. And plan the menu with seasonal ingredients in mind; they'll be fresh and easy to find.

- Figure out the logistics of the meal ahead of time. Make lists of ingredients you need to purchase. Consider how the food will be prepared and whether you've got the space and equipment necessary. For example, a sautéed dish works well for small numbers of people, but for larger groups you'll probably have to prepare a baked or roasted dish. Plan to prepare some dishes on the stove top and others in the oven. If you have only one oven, you won't be able to prepare three or four different baked items simultaneously.

- When it's time to start cooking, have all of the ingredients ready to go. Arrange all the spices on the counter, chop all the vegetables you need. The pros have a phrase for it: *mise en place*. And while you're cooking, clean up as you go: It saves time and keeps your work space tidy.

- Finally, taste the food as you cook. If you like it, chances are everyone else will, too (unless you *really* like that tripe and okra casserole).

FRESH SALMON IN GINGER LIME SAMBUCA SAUCE

Salmon lends itself to all manner of sauces, such as this innovative and zesty combination.

8 fresh salmon fillets (8 ounces each), cut 1 inch thick

1-inch piece fresh ginger, peeled

1 teaspoon lime zest

½ cup unsalted butter, softened

¼ teaspoon salt

4 tablespoons freshly squeezed lime juice, divided

¼ cup Sambuca (coffee liqueur)

8 lime slices for garnish

Wipe the salmon with a damp cloth and place the fillets in a single layer in a lightly greased broiler pan. In a food processor fitted with a steel blade, blend the ginger, zest, butter, salt, and 2 tablespoons of the lime juice until smooth. Set aside.

In a small saucepan, cook the remaining 2 tablespoons lime juice with the Sambuca over moderate heat for about 5 minutes. Add the ginger-butter mixture, a little at a time, and cook 5 minutes over low heat.

Brush the salmon with the sauce and broil about 4 inches from the heat for 5 minutes. Turn the fillets, brush with more sauce, and broil for another 5 minutes or until the salmon flakes easily when prodded in the thickest portion with a fork. Serve garnished with lime slices.

SERVES 8.

The 1785 Inn

SMOKED SALMON RAVIOLIS

Exotic, tasty, and quick presentation—the complexity and originality of this recipe is impressive. If you aren't experienced with making pasta, you may want to try this once before committing to it for a dinner party.

PASTA

2 cups all-purpose flour

2 eggs, beaten

2 egg yolks, beaten

MOUSSE

1 pound smoked salmon

2 eggs

1 cup chilled whipping cream

½ teaspoon coarsely ground pepper

2 tablespoons chopped fresh chives

Egg wash (1 egg beaten with 1 tablespoon water)

SAUCE

1 pound grated Gruyère cheese, divided

1 cup heavy cream, divided

To make the pasta, place the flour in a mound on a smooth work surface and make a well in the center. Pour the eggs and yolks into the well and slowly pull the flour into the eggs until it is all incorporated. Finish kneading by hand, adding more flour if needed for a smooth consistency.

Divide the pasta in half and roll out each half or feed through a pasta roller (No. 6 setting on a machine) until thin.

For the mousse, puree the smoked salmon and eggs together until smooth. Slowly add the cream, pepper, and chives.

Assemble the raviolis on a floured surface. Lay out the pasta and divide the mousse into twenty-four equal-sized portions. Place these portions 2 inches apart on one sheet of pasta. Brush the egg wash on the pasta between the mounds of mousse and cover with the other sheet of pasta. Cut the raviolis apart and refrigerate or freeze until ready to use.

Bring a large pot of lightly salted water to a boil, add the raviolis, and cook about 6 minutes. Meanwhile, add to each of eight ovenproof plates 1 ounce of the cheese and 2 tablespoons cream. Heat under the broiler until the cheese melts, add the raviolis, and sprinkle 1 ounce more Gruyère on top. Place under the broiler until the cheese browns lightly.

MAKES 24.

SALMON LASAGNA

Easy elegance, this dish uses uncooked lasagna noodles, which greatly reduces preparation time.

1 pound ricotta cheese

1½ ounces fresh basil leaves, cut chiffonade style

1 pound grated Mozzarella cheese

½ pound freshly grated Parmesan cheese

2 pints heavy cream, divided

Salt and pepper to taste

¾ pound lasagna noodles

2¼ pounds fresh salmon, cut into long, ¾-inch-wide slices (see Note)

Mix together the ricotta, basil, Mozzarella, Parmesan, 1 pint of the cream, and salt and pepper. Pour a thin layer of the remaining heavy cream in the bottom of a 13- by 9-inch pan. Place a layer of uncooked lasagna noodles over the cream, then add half the ricotta mixture and half the salmon. Repeat the layering of noodles, ricotta, and salmon, finishing with a layer of noodles. Pour the remaining cream over the top layer of noodles, covering it completely. Cover with aluminum foil and bake in a preheated 350°F oven for 50 to 60 minutes or until the noodles are soft.

NOTE: Be sure to check the fish carefully for bones.

SERVES 8 TO 10.

SHRIMP SCAMPI

A new twist to a familiar dish, this scampi includes sausage. Serve it over linguine, rice, or spinach.

1 medium-sized red bell pepper

2 stalks celery

1 medium-sized carrot

1 teaspoon olive oil

1¼ pounds fresh large shrimp

5 ounces sausage (andouille or milder)

2 teaspoons chopped garlic

1 teaspoon lemon juice

1 teaspoon white wine

3 ounces butter

Cut the bell pepper, celery, and carrot into julienne strips and set aside.

Place a skillet over high heat, add the oil, and reduce the heat to medium. Stir in the shrimp, sausage, and garlic and cook until the shrimp begin to turn color. Add the vegetables and sauté until the shrimp are firm. Stir in the lemon juice and wine and bring to a boil for just a few seconds. Remove from the heat and add the butter, stirring until creamy.

SERVES 6 TO 8.

SHRIMP ON THE HALF SHELL

This couldn't be simpler. For an attractive presentation, serve it on a platter along with a mound of fluffy rice and spears of steamed asparagus or broccoli.

12 fresh jumbo shrimp (1 pound)

3 tablespoons sesame oil

1 clove garlic, finely minced

1 teaspoon minced ginger

3 tablespoons minced scallions

2 tablespoons tamari (soy sauce)

2 tablespoons whiskey

¼ cup chicken stock

Split the shrimp in half lengthwise, shells and all. Wash out the veins but leave the shrimp in the halved shells. Heat the oil in a heavy skillet, arrange the shrimp shell side down in the skillet, and cook gently for 5 minutes. Add the garlic, ginger, scallions, tamari, whiskey, and chicken stock, cover, and simmer gently until tender, about 10 minutes. Serve in the shells.

SERVES 4.

CHEF DUFFINA'S SHRIMP ROYALE

Shrimp stuffed with crabmeat and blue cheese and topped with a creamy champagne sauce—awesome!

12 fresh large shrimp

1 cup fresh crabmeat

6 ounces blue cheese

2 teaspoons chopped garlic

Salt and pepper to taste

Norwich Inn Champagne Sauce
   (recipe follows)

Peel and devein the shrimp, leaving on the tails. Slice down the back three-fourths of the way through and set aside.

Put the crabmeat, blue cheese, and garlic in a mixer and blend well. Add salt and pepper. Stuff the shrimp with the mixture and place in a buttered casserole dish. Bake in a preheated 400°F oven for 15 minutes or until the shrimp are cooked.

Place 3 shrimp each on four dinner plates, spoon sauce over, and serve.

NORWICH INN CHAMPAGNE SAUCE

1 ounce butter

½ teaspoon chopped shallots

3 ounces champagne

1 cup heavy cream

A pinch each of salt and pepper

Melt the butter in a sauté pan, add the shallots, and cook until soft. Stir in the champagne and cook until reduced by half. Add the cream, salt, and pepper and cook until reduced by half.

SERVES 4.

SHRIMP WRAPPED IN PANCETTA WITH LENTILS

A new and unusual way to cook shrimp, this dish can be served as an entrée or a first course, depending on the size of the portions.

16 slices pancetta

16 fresh medium-sized shrimp, peeled and deveined

Salt and pepper to taste

1 tablespoon butter

1 tablespoon minced garlic

1 tablespoon minced shallots

1 cup cooked lentils

Fresh sprigs of Italian parsley for garnish

Wrap a slice of the pancetta around each of the shrimp to completely cover. Season with salt and pepper and grill on both sides until the pancetta is crisp and the shrimp are cooked.

Meanwhile, in a pan melt the butter and sauté the garlic and shallots until translucent. Add the lentils and cook until hot. Spoon in the middle of a serving platter, arrange the shrimp around the lentil mixture, and garnish with parsley.

SERVES 2 TO 4.

GRILLED BOURBON SHRIMP KEBABS

Utterly delicious! Vegetable lovers may want to increase the amount of vegetables in order to have more on each kebab.

1 clove garlic, minced

½ cup olive oil

½ cup tamari (soy sauce)

½ cup red wine vinegar

1 tablespoon tomato sauce

1 tablespoon bourbon

1 tablespoon brown sugar

2 tablespoons chopped scallion greens

Salt to taste

Freshly ground pepper to taste

24 fresh large shrimp, peeled, deveined, and cut butterfly style

6 scallions, trimmed and cut to include 3 inches of greens

1 medium-sized red bell pepper, seeded and cut into sixths

1 medium-sized zucchini, cut into sixths

6 cherry tomatoes, washed and stemmed

6 artichoke hearts (preferably unmarinated), drained and halved or left whole

Combine the garlic, oil, tamari, vinegar, tomato sauce, bourbon, brown sugar, scallions, salt, and pepper in a medium-sized bowl, mixing well. Place the shrimp and cut-up vegetables in the bottom of a large shallow dish and cover with the marinade. Cover with plastic wrap and marinate in the refrigerator at least 1 hour, stirring occasionally.

Prepare the fire and let burn until the coals are medium hot and glowing. Remove the shrimp and vegetables from the refrigerator and make up kebabs by alternating vegetables and shrimp on skewers. Grill until done, basting occasionally with marinade.

NOTE: If you use wooden skewers, soak them in water for about 10 to 15 minutes before stringing on the shrimp and vegetables. This prevents the wood from burning as you cook the kebabs.

SERVES 4 TO 6.

SHRIMP AND SCALLOPS IN BASIL, CREAM, AND CRAB SAUCE

This is a special-occasion dish, when cost and calories don't count.

1½ cups heavy cream

1 cup chicken stock or 1 tablespoon chicken base

⅓ cup Marsala wine

⅓ cup Madeira wine

2½ tablespoons finely chopped fresh basil

1 tablespoon chopped fresh parsley

A pinch of pepper

½ pound fresh crabmeat

1 tablespoon butter

2 tablespoons all-purpose flour

1 tablespoon vegetable oil

8 fresh medium-sized to large shrimp, peeled and deveined

16 fresh large sea scallops

Combine the cream, stock, wines, basil, parsley, pepper, and crabmeat in a large saucepan and simmer for 20 minutes. In a separate pan, melt the butter and stir in the flour to make a roux. Add to the cream sauce and cook until the sauce thickens slightly.

Heat the oil in a large skillet and sauté the shrimp and scallops until firm but not rubbery. Drain and add to the sauce. Pour over cooked, drained pasta and serve.

SERVES 4.

IN THE NICK OF THYME

*I*F YOU FIND yourself preparing a recipe calling for fresh herbs and all you have are dried, or vice versa, Kathy Bender of The Tamworth Inn in Tamworth, New Hampshire, offers this rule of thumb: The ratio of dried herbs to fresh is 1 to 3. So in a recipe calling for 1 teaspoon of dried basil, you would substitute 1 tablespoon of fresh.

SCALLOPS ROMA

"If you like scallops and you like sweet Italian sausage, then you are going to love this dish!"

1 pound fresh sea scallops

2 cups milk

4 links sweet Italian sausage

¼ cup diced onion

¼ cup heavy cream

¼ cup mild salsa

2 tablespoons Dijon-style mustard

¼ cup white wine

1 cup grated Fontina cheese

Place the scallops in a large colander and the colander in a mixing bowl large enough to hold it comfortably. Rinse the scallops with tepid water, turning them gently with your hands. Remove the colander and empty the water from the bowl slowly. Check the bottom of the bowl for sand and other residue. Continue this process until there is nothing left in the bowl after rinsing.

Place the colander with the scallops into the empty mixing bowl one last time and pour the milk over the scallops. Let the scallops marinate for 2 hours, refrigerated, turning occasionally. (The milk bath makes the scallops extra tender.)

Remove the casings from the sausage and pinch bite-sized pieces into a large skillet. Fry the sausage until just cooked. Add the onion and cook until the sausage is browned. Add the cream, salsa, mustard, and wine and cook, reducing the mixture until it is thick and bubbly.

Drain the scallops and toss them in the heated sauce for 1 minute. Divide the scallops and sauce evenly among four gratin dishes. Bake in a preheated 400°F oven for 30 minutes or until done to your preference.

Remove the dishes from the oven, sprinkle with cheese, and place under the broiler until the cheese bubbles.

SERVES 4.

GRILLED SCALLOPS ON WATERCRESS BLACK BEAN SALAD WITH CILANTRO CURRY DRESSING

If you can't find watercress, don't let that stop you from making this exquisite dish. Buttercrunch lettuce makes a fine substitution.

SALAD

1 pound black beans, soaked in cold water for 24 hours

2 quarts homemade chicken stock

½ cup diced red bell pepper

½ cup diced yellow bell pepper

½ cup diced red onion

3 tablespoons chopped fresh cilantro

¼ cup lime juice

⅓ cup extra-virgin olive oil

Salt and pepper

DRESSING

1 cup heavy cream

Juice of 1 medium-sized lime

2 tablespoons dried cilantro

4 drops of hot pepper sauce

½ teaspoon curry powder

Salt and pepper

2 pounds fresh large sea scallops

4 bunches fresh watercress

Lime wedges for garnish

To make the salad, drain the presoaked beans and place them in a stockpot with the chicken stock. Simmer for approximately 45 minutes or until tender but not mushy. When the beans are done, drain and let them cool. Add the peppers, onion, cilantro, lime juice, oil, salt, and pepper. Refrigerate until thoroughly chilled.

To make the dressing, whip the cream by hand or with a mixer until it starts to stiffen. Add the lime juice, cilantro, hot pepper sauce, curry powder, salt, and pepper. Set aside.

Grill the scallops to a golden brown. Remove the large stems from the watercress, wash, and then dry in a lettuce spinner.

Spoon the salad onto a large platter. Toss the watercress with some of the dressing and place in the center of the platter. Then arrange the scallops around the watercress and spoon some dressing over them. For garnish, add lime wedges.

SERVES 4 TO 6.

POACHED OYSTERS AND SEA SCALLOPS WITH GINGER AND MUSTARD SAUCE

"This imaginative, creative dish is a real winner," wrote the recipe tester. "The appearance is beautiful, the taste is superb, and the texture is perfect. I had some reservations concerning the beets, but they were the perfect garnish."

2 cups heavy cream

1 small knob celery root (celeriac), cut into julienne strips

1 leek, cut into julienne strips

18 plump fresh oysters, shucked

18 fresh sea scallops

2 tablespoons grated fresh ginger

A dash of cayenne pepper

1 tablespoon coarse mustard

2 small cooked beets, cut into julienne strips

In a small saucepan, reduce the heavy cream over medium heat to 1 cup.

Meanwhile, in another saucepan, bring 3 cups water to a boil. First blanch the knob celery root and then the leek. Transfer the vegetables to a casserole dish but reserve the cooking liquid.

In the same liquid, poach the oysters with their juices for 1 minute, then remove from the liquid. Repeat with the scallops. Place the oysters and scallops in a separate ovenproof casserole dish, partially covered.

Reduce the poaching liquid by half and strain into a clean saucepan. Strain in the cream, add the ginger and cayenne, and keep the mixture warm over low heat, whisking occasionally.

Place the two casserole dishes in a preheated 350°F oven for 5 minutes to heat. Divide the vegetables into six warmed soup plates and add the oysters and scallops to each.

Strain the liquid from the oysters and scallops into the cream mixture. Swirl the mustard into the mixture and pour the sauce into the soup plates. Sprinkle with the julienned beets.

SERVES 4 TO 6.

MAINE MUSSELS WITH LINGUINE

This is a simple pasta dish. The red tomatoes, fresh basil, and shiny mussel shells give it a festive appearance.

1 pound linguine

2 tablespoons olive oil

1 tablespoon chopped fresh basil

½ cup dry white wine

1 cup chopped tomato

¼ cup tomato juice

2 tablespoons chopped garlic

Salt and pepper to taste

4 pounds fresh Great Eastern mussels, rinsed and debearded

Grated Parmesan cheese

Cook the pasta according to package directions. Drain, return to the cooking pot, and toss with the oil and basil.

In another large pot, combine the wine, tomato, tomato juice, garlic, salt, pepper, and mussels. Cover and bring to a boil. Steam for about 5 minutes or until the mussels open.

Place the pasta in a warm serving bowl, pour the mussels over the pasta, and serve with freshly grated Parmesan cheese and garlic bread.

SERVES 6 TO 8.

PASTA PERFECT

*I*F YOU FIND yourself absentmindedly adding your expensive olive oil to the water when you're boiling pasta, stop! Chef Bill Okesson of the Boulders Inn in New Preston, Connecticut, says that there's no need to add olive oil (or any oil, for that matter) to the water: It only floats on top and then gets poured down the drain! But if you need to let the pasta sit for a while or store it, do coat it with a thin film of olive oil and place it in an airtight container or Ziploc bag. The oil keeps the pasta from sticking to itself. To reheat, submerge the pasta in boiling water for just a few seconds.

Andover Inn
ANDOVER, MASSACHUSETTS

MAINE LOBSTER SHANGHAI

Although rice noodles are more appropriate for this dish, some may prefer a familiar noodle or pasta like angel hair.

4 fresh lobsters (1 pound each)

¼ cup olive oil

1 package (4 ounces) dried
  shiitake mushrooms

¾ cup white wine

2 cloves garlic, minced

3 tablespoons tomato paste

1 pint heavy cream

6 ounces snow peas

2 ounces rice noodles, soaked to
  soften

Fresh sprigs of cilantro for
  garnish

In a large stockpot, bring 1½ to 2 gallons of water to a boil, drop in the lobsters, and cook over high heat for 8 to 10 minutes. Remove the lobsters and cool to room temperature. Remove the meat from the shells and set aside.

Heat the oil in a large skillet over medium-high heat. Add the mushrooms and cook, stirring frequently, for 1½ to 2 minutes. Add the wine and bring to a boil. Stir in the garlic, tomato paste, and cream, mixing well, and bring to a boil. Reduce the heat and simmer for 3 to 4 minutes or until the sauce starts to thicken.

Add the snow peas and lobster and simmer 2 to 3 minutes, until the meat is hot. Add the noodles, stir well to coat with sauce, and heat for 1 minute.

To serve, remove the noodles with a pasta fork or tongs and divide evenly onto warm plates. Pour the remaining sauce, lobster, and snow peas over the noodles. Garnish each serving with a large sprig of cilantro.

SERVES 4.

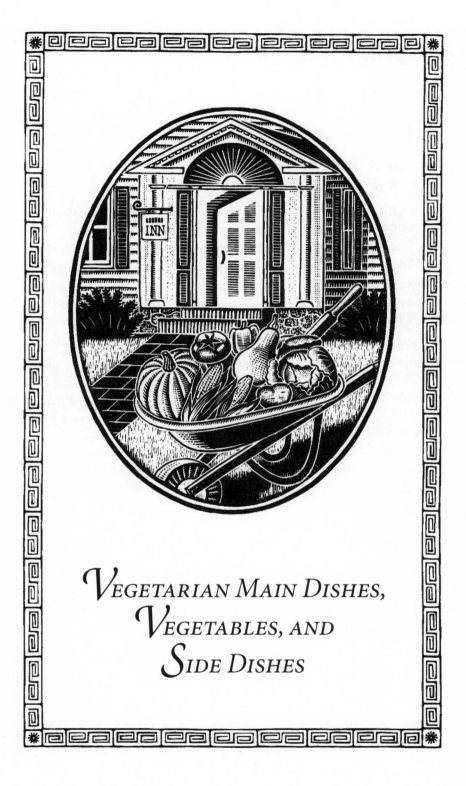

Vegetarian Main Dishes, Vegetables, and Side Dishes

Pasta Provençal

Festive and flavorful, this is great for the holidays, Super Bowl Sunday, or whenever you want something a little special and unusual.

1 pint cherry tomatoes, quartered

½ cup chopped sun-dried tomatoes

4 cloves garlic, chopped

4 scallions, minced

½ cup chopped fresh parsley

½ cup shredded fresh basil

¼ cup capers, rinsed and drained

½ cup pitted and chopped oil-cured olives

¼ cup balsamic vinegar

⅔ cup olive oil

1 pound penne or linguine

Pepper to taste

Parmesan cheese

Combine the tomatoes, garlic, scallions, parsley, basil, capers, olives, and vinegar and mix well. Slowly stir in the oil. Let the dressing stand at room temperature for 30 to 40 minutes before using it.

Cook the pasta al dente, then toss with the sauce. Serve with a sprinkle of pepper and cheese.

NOTE: This recipe can be made up to two days in advance. If you do, add a little more oil and vinegar to perk up the flavors.

Serves 6 to 8.

SUMMER VEGETABLE OMELET

This can be made throughout the year, of course, but nothing compares to the flavor of fresh-picked, homegrown vegetables.

2 tablespoons butter

1 medium-sized onion, chopped

1 medium-sized green bell pepper, chopped

1 small zucchini, thinly sliced

1 small yellow squash, thinly sliced

2 medium-sized tomatoes, peeled and cut into chunks

½ teaspoon salt

½ teaspoon pepper

½ teaspoon dried oregano

½ teaspoon dried thyme

Butter or vegetable oil

10 eggs

Melt 2 tablespoons butter in a large skillet. Sauté the onion and bell pepper until they begin to soften. Add the zucchini and yellow squash and cook until tender. Add the tomato and sauté until the juice is released. Stir in the salt, pepper, oregano, and thyme.

In an omelet pan, melt the butter or heat the oil, tilting the pan to coat the entire surface. Beat together 2 eggs at a time and pour into the pan. When the eggs are almost cooked, add a portion of the sautéed vegetables, fold the omelet in half, and cook until done.

SERVES 5.

VERMONT CHEDDAR PIE

Perfect for potluck suppers—it's substantial and eye-catching, and it travels well.

2 to 3 cups diced, parboiled potato

½ cup chopped onion, divided

1 teaspoon salt-free lemon-herb seasoning

½ teaspoon garlic powder

¾ cup chopped steamed spinach

⅓ cup crumbled feta cheese

¼ cup grated Romano or Parmesan cheese

½ cup grated cheddar cheese

2 eggs

½ cup low-fat milk

Dried parsley flakes

Paprika

Combine the potato and ¼ cup of the onion and press into the pie plate as a crust. Sprinkle with the seasoning and garlic. Carefully spread a layer of spinach in the bottom, sprinkle with crumbled feta cheese, and top with Romano or Parmesan cheese and then cheddar cheese.

Beat the eggs and milk together and pour carefully over the ingredients in the crust. With the remaining onion, make a small circle in the center of the pie. Sprinkle parsley in a larger circle around the onion, then paprika around the parsley.

Bake in a preheated 350°F oven for 1 hour.

NOTE: To keep the onion and parsley toppings from drying out, you might want to bake this covered for the first 30 to 40 minutes, then remove the cover and complete cooking.

SERVES 6.

SMOKED CHEDDAR AND ONION PIE

"This pie can be served as an appetizer or as a light main course for lunch or dinner."

4 tablespoons butter

1 medium-sized onion, sliced

1 unbaked 9-inch pie shell

3 eggs, beaten

¾ cup sour cream

2½ cups grated smoked cheddar cheese

⅛ teaspoon white or cayenne pepper

Chopped fresh parsley or chives (optional)

Melt the butter in a skillet over medium heat, add the onion and sauté slowly just until the onion starts to color. Place in the pie shell.

Mix together the eggs, sour cream, cheese, and pepper until combined. Pour over the onion in the shell.

Bake in a preheated 350°F oven for 40 minutes or until a knife inserted in the center comes out clean. Sprinkle with fresh herbs as a garnish, if desired, and serve warm with a salad.

SERVES 6 TO 8 AS A MAIN DISH.

APPLE CINNAMON QUICHE

"Yankee Magazine featured this in an April 1992 article, 'Breakfasts to Crow About.' Our guests asked for it before the write-up, but now they demand it."

1 medium-sized tart apple, peeled, cored, and grated

2 tablespoons butter

7 ounces grated aged Vermont cheddar cheese

1 unbaked 10-inch pastry shell

1 tablespoon sugar

½ teaspoon ground cinnamon

3 large eggs

1½ cups whipping cream

Sauté the apple in the butter for 5 minutes. Combine with the cheese and scatter evenly over the bottom of the pastry shell. Combine the sugar and cinnamon and sprinkle over the apple-cheese mixture.

In a medium-sized bowl, lightly whisk together the eggs and whipping cream and pour over the apple-cheese mixture. Bake in a preheated 375°F oven for 35 to 40 minutes or until set.

SERVES 6 TO 8.

SPINACH CASSEROLE

For a simple yet substantial supper, serve this with a loaf of crusty bread and green salad with a light dressing.

SPINACH LAYER

1 package (10 ounces) frozen chopped spinach, thawed and drained

2 tablespoons butter

1¼ cups ricotta cheese

½ cup grated Parmesan cheese

1 egg, beaten

1 cup pignoli nuts

¼ teaspoon ground nutmeg

TOMATO SAUCE

3 to 4 medium-sized tomatoes

3 tablespoons olive oil

1 teaspoon finely chopped garlic

¼ cup grated Parmesan cheese

BÉCHAMEL SAUCE

2 tablespoons butter

2 tablespoons all-purpose flour

1 cup milk

½ teaspoon salt

¼ teaspoon pepper

¼ cup Parmesan cheese

For the spinach layer, sauté the spinach in the butter over medium heat, stirring until all liquid evaporates. Add the cheeses, egg, nuts, and nutmeg, blending well. Spread in a buttered 2-quart casserole.

To make the tomato sauce, plunge the tomatoes briefly in boiling water, then slip off and discard the skins and seed and chop the tomato pulp.

Heat the oil over medium heat in a small pan and cook the garlic for 2 minutes. Sprinkle Parmesan cheese over the spinach layer and cover with the tomato and then the garlic.

To make the béchamel sauce, melt the butter in a saucepan, slowly stir in the flour, and cook for about 1 minute, stirring constantly. Gradually add the milk, stirring until thickened. Season with the salt and pepper. Pour over the tomato layer and sprinkle with Parmesan.

Bake in a preheated 350°F oven for 45 minutes.

SERVES 6 TO 8.

Cheese Soufflé with Red and Green Peppers

"This is a favorite dish of our guests."

4 tablespoons butter

4 slices white bread, crust removed and cut into 1-inch cubes

5 ounces grated sharp cheddar cheese

3 eggs, beaten

1½ cups milk

2 tablespoons chopped red bell pepper

2 tablespoons chopped green bell pepper

Paprika

Melt the butter in an 11- by 7-inch casserole. Evenly distribute the bread over the bottom and sprinkle the cheese over it. Mix the eggs and milk together and pour over the bread and cheese. Sprinkle the chopped bell peppers over the mixture, dust with paprika, cover, and refrigerate overnight.

Bake in a preheated 350°F oven for 1 hour.

VARIATION: Leave out the bell peppers or add 1 teaspoon crushed hot red pepper flakes, or for a pleasant, enigmatic flavor, add 4 thin slices of Genoa salami, finely chopped.

SERVES 6.

MARLBOROUGH EGG-STUFFED BAKERS

"This is easy to make. Accompany with warm corn muffins spread with green pepper jelly."

6 large baking potatoes, scrubbed

1 stick butter, melted

12 eggs, beaten

2 cups broccoli, chopped, cooked, and drained

2 tablespoons diced green onion or fresh chives

1½ cups grated Monterey Jack cheese

Bake the potatoes in a preheated 400°F oven for 45 to 60 minutes. Test with a fork for doneness (they should be cooked but firm). Cool slightly.

Cut the potatoes in half lengthwise. Run a knife around the inside edge of each potato, about ¼ inch inside the skin, to loosen the pulp. Scoop out the pulp with a spoon, leaving a shell. (Save the pulp for home fries or hash.)

Using a pastry brush, brush some of the butter on the inside and outside of the potato shells. Place the shells on a cookie sheet and return to the oven for 15 minutes to brown slightly.

Meanwhile, pour the remaining butter into a large skillet and heat until bubbly. Add the eggs and stir until firm but not dry. Turn off the heat, add the broccoli and onion or chives, and mix well.

When the potato shells have browned, remove them from the oven and fill with the egg-broccoli mixture, dividing it equally among the twelve shells. Top with the grated cheese and place under a broiler until the cheese is bubbly. Serve hot.

NOTE: Egg substitute can be used in place of whole eggs, margarine in place of butter, and low-sodium/low-fat cheese instead of regular cheese for a very heart-healthy entrée. The potatoes can be prepared a day ahead and kept covered with aluminum foil and refrigerated. They need only to be browned and stuffed before serving.

SERVES 6 TO 12.

BAKED STUFFED ACORN SQUASH

"A wonderfully tasty and nutritionally balanced dish for our vegetarian guests."

2 acorn squash

½ cup brown rice

1 teaspoon salt

1½ cups water

3 tablespoons canola oil

⅓ cup diced onion

1 clove garlic, diced or crushed

1 teaspoon curry powder

¼ cup diced red bell pepper

¼ cup diced green bell pepper

10 fresh mushrooms, chopped

½ cup extra-firm tofu, cut into ¼-inch cubes

4 tablespoons pine nuts, toasted

Salt and pepper to taste

1 tablespoon minced fresh parsley

Cut the squash in half crosswise to obtain a scalloped rim. Scoop out and discard the seeds and slice off just enough of the bottom of each so the squash will sit level. Place the squash, cut side down, in a large shallow baking dish filled halfway with water. Bake in a preheated 350°F oven for 1 hour or until soft. Turn right side up and let cool.

Meanwhile, combine the rice, salt, and water in a small pot, cover tightly, and cook for about 20 minutes. Set aside. (These first two steps can be done a day or two ahead of time.)

In a large frying pan, heat the oil and sauté the onion until translucent, about 15 minutes. Add the garlic and curry powder and sauté 1 minute longer. Add the peppers and mushrooms and sauté about 5 minutes, adding a little water if needed.

Turn the mixture into a large bowl and mix in the tofu, pine nuts, rice, salt, and pepper.

Sprinkle the acorn bowls lightly with salt and brush the rims with a bit of oil. Fill the cavities with the tofu mixture, rounding the top and keeping the rims free.

Place squash in a large roasting pan with ½ inch of water and reheat in the oven for 15 minutes. Garnish with parsley and serve.

SERVES 4.

Ahead of the Game: The Day Before

*I*F THERE'S ONE THING that every last innkeeper and chef agrees about, it's that the more you can do in advance of having guests for dinner the better. And that means more than setting the table the morning of your party. Here are some dishes that can be readied the day before a dinner.

 • *Hors d'oeuvres.* Wash and cut vegetables for crudités a day in advance. Place them on a tray, top them with wet paper towel and plastic wrap, and store in the refrigerator.

 • *Vegetables.* If you're serving sautéed vegetables with dinner, blanch them in broth or water the day before and keep in the refrigerator. Finish cooking before dinner.

 • *Pasta.* Cook pasta in boiling water as usual. Drain, then coat with a thin film of olive oil, and store in the refrigerator in a Ziploc bag or other airtight container. To reheat, immerse in boiling water for a few seconds. (This method does not work for homemade or fresh pasta.)

 • *Potatoes.* You can peel—but not slice—potatoes a day ahead. Store them in the refrigerator in a container filled with cold water. You can even bake and stuff potatoes a day ahead. To reheat, wrap in aluminum foil and bake at 120°F until just heated (if they get too hot, they'll implode).

 • *Meats.* If your main course for dinner is going to be sautéed or braised meat, you can begin cooking it the day before.

NOODLE CARROT TOSS

This moist and nourishing side dish makes a colorful accompaniment to any entrée.

1 package (12 ounces) medium-sized egg noodles

⅓ cup butter or margarine

1 to 2 teaspoons salt, divided

3 cups shredded carrots

⅓ cup finely chopped fresh parsley

2 eggs, slightly beaten

½ cup plus 2 tablespoons milk

¼ teaspoon pepper (or more to taste)

In a large pot, cook the noodles in boiling water for only 3 to 4 minutes. Drain and return to the pot. Add the butter or margarine, stirring until melted, and set aside.

In a large saucepan, stir ½ to 1 teaspoon of the salt into ½ inch of water and bring to a boil. Add the carrot and cook 1 to 2 minutes, stirring occasionally. Drain well, then add the carrot and parsley to the noodles.

In a medium-sized bowl, beat together the eggs, milk, pepper, and remaining ½ to 1 teaspoon salt. Add to the noodles and blend well.

Pour mixture into a well-greased casserole, cover, and bake in a preheated 375°F oven for 25 to 30 minutes, stirring occasionally.

NOTE: This recipe can be doubled or tripled to feed a large gathering.

SERVES 6.

CHEDDAR CHEESE AND GRITS SOUFFLÉ

Not really a soufflé in the true sense of the word, but delicious nevertheless.

1 cup grits, regular or instant

¼ teaspoon Worcestershire sauce

1 tablespoon butter

A dash of dry mustard

Salt and pepper to taste

2 cups grated sharp cheddar cheese

2 eggs, well beaten

Cook the grits according to package directions, but add the Worcestershire, butter, mustard, salt, and pepper to the water. Remove from the heat and stir in the cheese. Let cool slightly. When the cheese has melted, stir the eggs into the grits.

Pour into a greased 1½-quart baking dish and bake in a preheated 350°F oven for 1 hour.

SERVES 6.

LEMON GARLIC ASPARAGUS

Quick and easy, this is a tasty way to spruce up asparagus. Garlic fanciers will love it!

4 tablespoons unsalted butter

2 teaspoons minced garlic

Juice of 1 medium-sized lemon

16 to 20 asparagus spears, cooked and chilled

1 hard-boiled egg, chopped

1 teaspoon chopped fresh tarragon

Salt and pepper to taste

Melt the butter in a small saucepan, then remove from the heat. Stir in the garlic and lemon juice. Pour over the asparagus, sprinkle with the egg, tarragon, salt, and pepper, and serve.

SERVES 4.

MEL'S ASPARAGUS CORDON BLEU

Served drizzled with hollandaise sauce, this also makes a great breakfast topped with a dropped egg.

4 slices boiled ham

4 slices Swiss cheese

16 fresh asparagus spears

1 cup fine bread crumbs

1 tablespoon dried parsley

⅛ teaspoon pepper

½ cup all-purpose flour

1 egg, beaten

¼ cup butter, melted

Top each ham slice with a slice of cheese, then 4 asparagus spears. Roll the ham and cheese around the asparagus and trim the ends of the asparagus to fit (see Note).

Combine the bread crumbs with the parsley and pepper. Dredge each roll with flour, dip in egg, then dip in bread crumbs. Sauté in the butter over medium heat for 4 minutes on each side or until golden brown. Serve at once.

NOTE: Depending on the size of the asparagus and the texture you desire, you may want to blanch the spears briefly before wrapping them in the ham and cheese. This will also enhance the green color.

SERVES 4.

SUN-DRIED TOMATO TIP

MARNIE DUFF of the 1811 House in Manchester Village, Vermont, never buys jars of sun-dried tomatoes: "You're paying for oil and a jar." Instead, she purchases the dried tomatoes and soaks them herself.

BROILED TOMATOES

Simply delicious! These take little time to prepare and even less to cook—but do keep an eye on them so the tops don't burn.

3 medium-sized tomatoes, sliced ¼ inch thick (discard stems)

½ cup bread crumbs

½ cup grated Parmesan cheese

2 tablespoons chopped fresh chives

¼ cup chopped fresh parsley

3 tablespoons butter, melted

Place the tomato slices in an ovenproof dish. In a small bowl, combine the bread crumbs, cheese, chives, and parsley. Stir in the butter, mixing until thoroughly blended. Spread the mixture over the tomatoes and place under a preheated broiler until the tops are browned.

SERVES 6.

Trail's End, A Country Inn

WILMINGTON, VERMONT

OVEN-FRIED POTATOES

"These potatoes are similar to western fries. The kitchen smells so good while they're baking!"

4 medium-sized baking potatoes

¼ cup vegetable oil

1 tablespoon grated Parmesan cheese

¼ teaspoon garlic powder

¼ teaspoon paprika

¼ teaspoon pepper

¼ teaspoon salt

Cut the potatoes into wedges, leaving the skins on. Place in a single layer in a 13- by 9-inch pan. In a small bowl, combine the oil, cheese, garlic, paprika, pepper, and salt. Brush over the potato wedges.

Bake in a preheated 375°F oven for 45 minutes, basting occasionally.

SERVES 4.

Griswold Inn

ESSEX, CONNECTICUT

GRISWOLD INN GRILLED VEGETABLES

Serve these to the people you know who say they hate vegetables, and watch them ask for second helpings.

2 medium-sized zucchini

2 medium-sized yellow summer squash

2 tablespoons olive or salad oil

2 tablespoons chopped fresh basil

1 tablespoon crushed garlic

Salt and pepper to taste

Wash and dry the zucchini and summer squash. Trim the ends and slice lengthwise into thirds. Beat together the oil, basil, and garlic and brush on both sides of the vegetables.

Cook on a hot grill for 3 minutes, turn, and grill another 3 minutes. Sprinkle with salt and pepper, cut diagonally, and serve immediately.

SERVES 4.

Cooks' Pantry: Oil

$\mathcal{N}$OT ALL cooking oils are created equal. Some should not be heated, others are suitable for frying but aren't good choices for salads. Most oils keep for about a year if they're kept in a cool, dark place. The exception is almond oil, which requires refrigeration.

* *Almond oil.* The imported variety has a light, toasted almond flavor and is wonderful in salads and other cold dishes. It should not be heated. Stored in the refrigerator, almond oil will keep for about a year.

* *Avocado oil.* This versatile oil has a mild flavor that makes it appropriate for frying, in salad dressings, and in baked products.

* *Corn oil.* With a high smoke point, this is a dependable choice for frying. While high in polyunsaturated fats, it's bland and therefore not very popular for salad dressings. Stored in the refrigerator, corn oil will keep for about a year.

* *Olive oil.* This fragrant, fruity oil is terrific for sautéing, in salad dressings, or just drizzled on bread or vegetables. It also is high in polyunsaturated fats, making it a heart-healthy choice, too. Don't waste extra-virgin olive oil on sautéing; choose a lower grade instead.

* *Peanut oil.* Often used in Chinese cooking, it's good for sautéing, frying, and in salads.

* *Safflower oil.* This virtually flavorless oil has a high smoke point, making it well suited for deep-frying. While high in polyunsaturated fats, it's too heavy for salads.

* *Sesame oil.* Also commonly used in Chinese cooking, sesame oil is best when cold. Stored in the refrigerator, it will keep for a year, and in a cool, dry place for six months. Also high in polyunsaturated fats.

* *Soybean oil.* Inexpensive and high in polyunsaturated fats, this oil adds little taste to foods, making it a good choice for frying.

ROBBIN CHURCHILL BEANS

"Wonderful for any picnic, pig roast, or informal party."

3 medium-sized apples, cored, chopped, but not peeled

1½ cups chopped onion

2½ medium-sized green bell peppers, chopped

¼ cup bacon drippings

5 cans (16 ounces each) dark red kidney beans, drained

2½ cups firmly packed brown sugar

3½ tablespoons curry powder

Parmesan cheese

Sauté the apple, onion, and bell pepper in the bacon drippings until they begin to soften. In a large casserole, combine the beans, brown sugar, and curry powder with the sautéed ingredients, stirring to blend. Sprinkle the top with the cheese.

Bake uncovered in a preheated 350°F oven for about 30 minutes.

NOTE: This recipe freezes well and can be made in even larger quantities.

SERVES 12 TO 14.

TARRAGON RICE PILAF

"This dish is filled with delightful surprises to tickle the palate."

½ cup brown basmati rice

½ cup wild rice

3 cups chicken stock

½ cup long-grain white rice

1 scallion, finely chopped

1 clove garlic, minced

¼ cup red wine vinegar

2 tablespoons fruit juice (any variety)

1 tablespoon salad oil

1 teaspoon tamari (soy sauce)

¼ cup chopped walnuts

⅓ cup red seedless grapes, quartered

1 tablespoon chopped fresh tarragon or 1 teaspoon dried

1 tablespoon chopped fresh parsley or 1 teaspoon dried

1 tablespoon chopped fresh chives or 1 teaspoon dried

Place the basmati and wild rices in a heavy 2-quart saucepan. Add the stock and bring to a boil. Cover and simmer on very low heat for 30 minutes. Add the long-grain rice and stir lightly with a fork to mix. Cover again and continue to simmer 25 minutes or until the liquid is absorbed. Remove from the heat and let stand covered.

Place the scallions and garlic in a jar with a tight lid. Add the vinegar, fruit juice, oil, and tamari and shake well.

Toast the walnuts in a preheated 350°F oven for 5 to 10 minutes. Transfer to a large bowl and toss with the grapes, tarragon, parsley, and chives. (If dried herbs are used, add them to the dressing in the jar and shake well.)

Add the rice to the nut mixture, using a fork to mix, and pour the dressing over all, fluffing with a fork.

SERVES 6.

The Austin Hill Inn

WEST DOVER, VERMONT

GHANDI'S RICE

"For some reason, my kids started calling me Ghandi, and because I have made this versatile and well-received rice dish so many times they named it Ghandi's Rice."

2 tablespoons butter
3 cloves garlic, minced
1 cup long-grain white rice
2 cups warm chicken broth
Freshly ground pepper

Melt the butter in a large saucepan and sauté the garlic until softened. Add the rice and stir to coat with the butter. Add the chicken broth and pepper and bring to a boil. Reduce the heat, cover, and simmer for 20 minutes.

VARIATION: Add pine nuts, slivered almonds, sautéed mushrooms, bits of blanched carrot or broccoli, or chopped fresh parsley.

SERVES 4.

Trail's End, A Country Inn

WILMINGTON, VERMONT

PINEAPPLE PUDDING

"This is a perfect side dish for ham, but it could also be used as a dessert."

½ cup milk
3 eggs, beaten
6 slices white bread, cut into
  ¾-inch cubes
½ cup sugar
1 large can (20 ounces) crushed
  pineapple, drained
¼ cup butter, melted
Ground cinnamon

Mix together the milk, eggs, bread, sugar, pineapple, and butter. Pour into a greased baking dish, sprinkle with cinnamon, and bake in a preheated 350°F oven for 40 to 45 minutes.

SERVES 4.

THE GOVERNOR'S INN
PRETTY POTATO PRUNE PUDDING

"While experimenting in our kitchen with mashed potatoes, we developed this lovely dish. (It works only with fresh potatoes, not instant.) We bake it in a charlotte or soufflé mold, unmold it onto a platter, and garnish around the base with fresh parsley and a few yellow daylilies. This is especially good with roast pork."

2 cups mashed white potato

2 eggs plus 2 egg yolks, divided

⅓ cup fine cornmeal (see Note)

½ cup unsalted butter, melted

Salt and freshly ground white pepper to taste

2 cups mashed sweet potato

15 dried, pitted prunes (fresh and soft)

½ cup whole berry cranberry sauce (optional)

In a large bowl, combine the white potato, 1 egg, 1 egg yolk, half the cornmeal, half the butter, and salt and pepper. In a separate bowl, repeat the procedure with the sweet potato. Set aside both bowls.

Prepare the prunes by snipping them into quarters. Spread the white potato mixture in the bottom of a generously buttered mold. Arrange the prunes over the top, add the cranberry sauce (if desired), and cover with the sweet potato mixture.

Cover the top of the pudding with a piece of buttered waxed paper and place in a large roasting pan.

Place the mold in a preheated 325°F oven and pour enough hot water into the pan to come halfway up the sides of the mold. Bake for 1½ to 2 hours or until a knife inserted in the center comes out clean and is hot to the touch. Unmold the pudding onto a platter, slice or scoop the pudding, and serve.

NOTE: To achieve *fine* cornmeal, pour the cornmeal into a food processor with the motor running, using a steel blade. Grind until it is of a fine consistency.

SERVES 6 TO 8.

DESSERTS

Grunberg Haus Bed and Breakfast

MAPLE-BAKED APPLES

Baked apples are an appealing dessert any time but especially after a rich and heavy meal. Often topped with whipped cream or ice cream, these use French vanilla yogurt instead, which complements the sweet yet slightly tart flavor of McIntosh apples and doesn't leave you with that too-full feeling. These are fantastic for breakfast, too.

4 medium-sized McIntosh apples

1 cup raisins

½ teaspoon caraway seeds, divided

4 teaspoons chopped walnuts, divided

4 tablespoons maple syrup, divided

4 tablespoons French vanilla yogurt, divided

Core the apples, remove and discard the peel from the top one-third, and place the apples in individual ovenproof baking cups. Fill each apple two-thirds full with raisins, then top with ⅛ teaspoon caraway seeds, 1 teaspoon walnuts, and 1 tablespoon maple syrup.

Bake in a preheated 350°F oven for 1 hour. Top each with 1 tablespoon yogurt and serve.

SERVES 4.

MAPLE-BAKED PEARS IN A JIFF

"Bartlett, Comice, or any type of pear that is ripe and in season will work well. We serve these topped with a splash of heavy cream and garnish each with a pansy."

4 tablespoons butter

2 tablespoons granulated sugar

4 medium-sized pears

2 tablespoons maple syrup

2 tablespoons brown sugar

A dash of allspice

Rub the butter in the bottom of a medium-sized clear glass or ceramic baking dish, leaving the extra butter in the dish, then dust with the granulated sugar. Peel the pears and trim a sliver off the bottom of each so they sit up straight. Drizzle the tops of the pears with the maple syrup, sprinkle with brown sugar, then dust with allspice.

Bake in a preheated 325°F oven for 15 minutes (the juice from the pears mixes with the butter and sugars to create a caramel coating). Place each pear in a small dessert bowl, spoon juices from the baking dish over each, and serve.

SERVES 4.

 *The Blue Hill Inn*

BLUE HILL, MAINE

FRESH FRUIT WITH ORANGE ZABAGLIONE

This is so simple yet so elegant. Use only the freshest fruits that are ripe yet not bruised or blemished.

1 medium-sized orange, seeded and sliced

Sugar

Assorted fresh fruits, sliced

4 egg yolks

½ cup sugar

¼ cup Grand Marnier

Fresh sprigs of mint for garnish

Run one of the orange slices around the rims of 4 chilled wine glasses, then dip the rims in sugar. Fill with the fresh fruit.

Beat the yolks with the sugar until pale and creamy. Place over a double boiler, continue beating, and slowly add the Grand Marnier. Cook until thick.

Spoon over the fruit and garnish each with an orange slice and a sprig of mint.

SERVES 4.

 *Eggemoggin Reach Bed and Breakfast*

BROOKSVILLE, MAINE

HARVEY'S FAVORITE FRUIT

Light and luscious, this makes a beautiful display.

Medium-sized oranges (1 per person)

Medium-sized kiwifruit (1 per person)

Pomegranate seeds from fresh pomegranates

Cointreau (orange liqueur) or kirsch (cherry liqueur)

Peel the oranges and cut into ¼-inch slices. Peel and slice the kiwis crosswise. Arrange the oranges and kiwis in a circular pattern on individual dessert plates. Pile the pomegranate seeds in the center, drizzle with Cointreau or kirsch, and serve immediately.

SERVINGS BASED ON AMOUNT OF FRUIT USED.

COUPE ELIZABETH

You'll never want plain vanilla ice cream again once you've tasted it with this deep burgundy sweet-tart sauce. Even those who demand chocolate sauce on their ice cream will find this irresistible.

1 can (16 ounces) Bing cherries

½ cup Cherry Herring (cherry liqueur)

1 tablespoon cornstarch

1½ quarts vanilla ice cream

Whipped cream

Ground cinnamon

Drain the cherries, reserving 1 cup of the juice. In a small bowl, combine the cherries and Cherry Herring and let stand for about 1 hour.

In a large saucepan, dissolve the cornstarch in ½ cup of the reserved cherry juice. Add the remaining ½ cup juice and bring to a boil, stirring constantly. Reduce the heat and simmer, stirring frequently, until thickened and translucent, about 5 minutes. Remove from the heat and let cool. Then add the cherries and Cherry Herring to the thickened juice, mixing well.

Scoop ice cream into bowls, pour the cherry sauce over it, top with a ruffle of whipped cream (using a pastry bag with a No. 6 decorating tip), and sprinkle lightly with cinnamon. Serve at once.

SERVES 6.

VANILLA ICE CREAM WITH HOT STRAWBERRY AMARETTO SAUCE

"If you have the freezer space, spoon the ice cream into individual champagne glasses and freeze until serving."

1 stick butter

¾ cup firmly packed brown sugar

¼ teaspoon ground cinnamon

¼ cup lemon juice

2 tablespoons orange juice

1 package (10 ounces) frozen whole strawberries

½ cup amaretto (almond liqueur)

Vanilla ice cream

Melt the butter in a large skillet. Stir in the brown sugar and cook slowly until it dissolves. Add the cinnamon, lemon juice, and orange juice and simmer for 1 minute. Add the frozen strawberries and stir gently over medium heat until they soften and separate.

Remove the skillet from the heat and stir the amaretto into the sauce. Scoop the ice cream into six bowls and spoon on some of the sauce. Serve immediately.

VARIATION: Other fruits can be substituted for the strawberries. Try making it with four ripe bananas.

SERVES 6.

FOLIAGE CHAMOMILE SORBET

Distinctive yet not at all difficult, this smooth sorbet is a real winner. See if your guests can figure out the various ingredients.

¾ cup sugar

4 cups freshly steeped chamomile tea

1 to 2 tablespoons Grand Marnier

2 whole cloves

1 medium-sized to large bay leaf

½ cinnamon stick

Zest and juice of 1 medium-sized lemon

Zest of 1 medium-sized orange

Fresh sprigs of mint for garnish (optional)

Stir the sugar into the hot tea and stir to dissolve. Combine with the Grand Marnier, cloves, bay leaf, cinnamon, lemon zest and juice, and orange zest and let steep for 1 hour.

Strain into a 13- by 9-inch pan and freeze for 4 hours, breaking the crystals that form on the sides every 30 minutes.

Thirty minutes before serving, transfer to a food processor or blender and process until smooth. Refreeze. When ready to serve, scoop into wine goblets and garnish each serving with a sprig of mint, if desired.

SERVES 6.

Captain Dibbell House

CLINTON, CONNECTICUT

AWARD-WINNING APPLE PIE

This pie was judged to be the best in New England in Yankee Magazine's *Great New England Inns Apple Pie Contest in 1991.*

CRUST

2 cups all-purpose flour

1 teaspoon salt

⅔ cup cold shortening

2 tablespoons cold butter

4 tablespoons cold water

FILLING

½ to ⅔ cup firmly packed light brown sugar

1 to 1½ tablespoons cornstarch

¾ teaspoon ground cinnamon

1 teaspoon apple pie spice

7 cups peeled, cored, and sliced apples (see Note)

1½ tablespoons butter, cut into small pieces

Milk

Sugar

For the crust, mix the flour and salt together in a large bowl. Combine the shortening and butter and work half of it into the flour and salt until it resembles cornmeal. Work the remaining half into the dough until it is pea-sized. Sprinkle with the water and blend in lightly until the dough cleans the sides of the bowl. Handle as little as possible.

Divide the dough in half. Using a lightly floured pastry cloth and roller stocking, roll the dough from the center out in one direction at a time until it is about 2 inches larger than the pie plate. Fold it in half, lay it in the pie plate, then unfold.

For the filling, mix the brown sugar, cornstarch, cinnamon, and spice together. Stir gently into the apples. Spread the mixture over the bottom crust and dot with butter.

Roll out the remaining dough to 1 inch larger than the pie plate. Place it on top of the apples, press it down gently around the apples, and seal the edge with a fork. Prick the upper crust, brush with milk, and sprinkle with sugar. Place strips of aluminum foil around the edge to prevent excessive browning.

Bake in a preheated 450°F oven for 10 minutes. Reduce the heat to 350°F and bake for 35 to 45 minutes or until golden brown and juice starts to bubble through slits. Remove the foil for the last 15 minutes.

NOTE: Pick an apple that is slightly tart and firm. Good choices include Red Romes, Ida Reds, and Macouns. The amount of sugar, cornstarch, and spice depends on the tartness of the apple. You are striving for a slightly tart, not too sweet taste.

SERVES 6 TO 8.

COOKS' Q & A

What are the differences between butter, vegetable shortening, and lard in pie crust?

EVERY COOK has his or her pet method for making pie crust. Some insist on butter, some won't use anything but shortening, and some still rely on good old-fashioned lard. Mark Hodesh of the Castine Inn in Castine, Maine, offers some guidelines. Lard makes a very flaky pie crust, but the lard sold at the grocery store is likely to be of a lower quality than what works best (and it's not exactly a health food). Butter is delicious and makes a flaky crust, but it's difficult to work with because it melts easily. Vegetable shortening is easiest to work with and tastes better if you add a little butter.

NORWICH INN APPLE CRANBERRY CRUMB PIE

This recipe tied for first place for Vermont in Yankee Magazine's *Great New England Inns Apple Pie Contest in 1991. A high pie, it carries a generous amount of crumb topping.*

CRUST

1½ cups all-purpose flour

½ cup cold butter

3 tablespoons granulated sugar

1 egg, beaten

1 tablespoon vanilla extract

1 tablespoon cold water

FILLING

6 to 8 medium-sized Granny Smith apples, peeled, cored, and thinly sliced

⅔ cup firmly packed brown sugar

Zest and juice of 1 medium-sized lemon

1 tablespoon ground cinnamon

1 teaspoon ground nutmeg

¼ cup all-purpose flour

4 tablespoons butter, melted

1 cup fresh cranberries

TOPPING

¾ cup butter

⅔ cup firmly packed brown sugar

1½ cups all-purpose flour

1½ teaspoons ground cinnamon

½ teaspoon ground nutmeg

To make the crust, mix the flour with the butter until crumbly. Add the granulated sugar, egg, vanilla, and water, mixing until the dough forms a ball. Chill in the refrigerator for at least 1 hour. Roll out a single crust that overlaps a 10-inch pie plate by about 1 inch.

To make the filling, lightly toss the apples, brown sugar, lemon zest and juice, cinnamon, nutmeg, flour, butter, and cranberries in a mixing bowl until the apples and cranberries are thoroughly coated. Pour the filling into the pie crust, mounding it high.

To make the topping, mix the butter, brown sugar, flour, cinnamon, and nutmeg together until crumbly. Distribute over the top of the pie.

Bake in a preheated 400°F oven for 45 to 60 minutes or until the topping is golden brown.

SERVES 8.

Tamworth Inn Sour Cream Apple Pie

"This pie is a variation of the traditional apple pie and should be served warm."

FILLING

2 eggs

½ cup granulated sugar

1 cup sour cream or plain yogurt (see Note)

1½ tablespoons all-purpose flour (if using yogurt, increase to 2 tablespoons)

½ teaspoon vanilla extract

¼ teaspoon salt

4 medium-sized to large tart apples, peeled, cored, and thinly sliced

1 unbaked 9-inch pie shell

TOPPING

6 tablespoons brown sugar

½ cup all-purpose flour

3 tablespoons butter or margarine, softened

To make the filling, beat the eggs in a medium-sized bowl. Add the granulated sugar, sour cream or yogurt, flour, vanilla, and salt, mixing well. Add the apples and toss until the slices are thoroughly coated with the mixture. Turn into the pie shell and bake in a preheated 400°F oven for 30 minutes.

Meanwhile, make the topping by combining the brown sugar, flour, and butter or margarine, mixing until crumbly. After the pie has baked 30 minutes, remove it from the oven, lower the temperature to 350°F, sprinkle the topping evenly over the top, and return to the oven for 15 minutes.

NOTE: Substituting plain yogurt for sour cream does not affect the richness of this dessert. Vanilla yogurt can also be used.

SERVES 6 TO 8.

AUGUSTUS SNOW HOUSE SOUR CREAM APPLE PIE

A fine pie to make for a holiday dinner, church supper, or bake sale. Rich and filling, it should be served in small slices.

CRUST

2½ cups all-purpose flour

5 tablespoons sugar

½ teaspoon salt

¾ teaspoon ground cinnamon

6 tablespoons butter

6 tablespoons shortening

4 to 6 tablespoons apple cider, apple juice, or water

FILLING

5 to 6 medium-sized tart apples, peeled, cored, and sliced

⅓ cup sugar

¼ teaspoon salt

1 cup raisins

1 egg, well beaten

1 teaspoon vanilla extract

⅔ cup sour cream

TOPPING

3 tablespoons brown sugar

3 teaspoons ground cinnamon

3 tablespoons granulated sugar

1 cup chopped walnuts

½ cup all-purpose flour

1 cup oatmeal

1 stick butter

To make the crust, combine the flour, sugar, salt, and cinnamon in a large bowl. Add the butter and shortening and cut in until crumbly. Gradually stir in the cider, juice, or water until the dough forms a ball. Roll out onto a lightly floured surface to fit a 10-inch springform pan.

To make the filling, toss the apples, sugar, salt, and raisins together in a large bowl. In a small bowl, combine the egg, vanilla, and sour cream, blending well. Pour over the apples and stir until thoroughly coated. Pour into the crust.

To make the topping, combine the brown sugar, cinnamon, granulated sugar, walnuts, flour, and oatmeal. Add the butter and cut into the mixture until crumbly. Spread over the filling.

Bake in a preheated 400°F oven for about 1 hour.

NOTE: To keep the topping from over-browning, you may need to cover it with aluminum foil for the last 15 minutes or so of baking.

SERVES 12 TO 14.

BLUEBERRY SUPREME

"A group that has been to the inn at least ten times always requests this dessert. Serve it with whipped cream or French vanilla yogurt."

CRUST

1⅓ cups graham cracker crumbs

¼ cup sugar

⅓ cup butter or margarine, melted

FILLING

2 eggs, beaten

⅓ cup sugar

1 package (8 ounces) cream cheese, softened

TOPPING

2 cups fresh blueberries, divided

½ cup sugar

2 tablespoons cornstarch

¾ cup water

¼ teaspoon orange extract

To make the crust, mix the crumbs, sugar, and butter or margarine together until thoroughly combined. Pat into an 11- by 7-inch Pyrex dish.

For the filling, combine the eggs, sugar, and cream cheese in a food processor or with an electric mixer. Pour over the crust and bake in a preheated 350°F oven for 20 minutes. Cool.

Meanwhile, prepare the topping by combining 1 cup of the blueberries, the sugar, cornstarch, water, and orange extract in a saucepan. Cook over medium heat until clear and thick, stirring frequently.

After the pie has cooled completely, cover it with the remaining 1 cup of blueberries. Pour the blueberry mixture over the berries and chill.

SERVES 8.

Lincoln House Country Inn

DENNYSVILLE, MAINE

CRANBERRY ORANGE PECAN PIE

"Serve this warm or cooled with a dollop of whipped cream or ice cream. The pie freezes very nicely."

1 cup sugar

1½ tablespoons all-purpose flour

¼ cup butter, softened

1 teaspoon grated orange rind

½ teaspoon ground nutmeg

2 eggs

¾ cup light corn syrup

¼ teaspoon salt

1 teaspoon vanilla extract

1 cup chopped pecans or walnuts

1 cup cranberries, fresh or frozen

1 unbaked 9-inch pie shell

Whipped cream (try a drop of Grand Marnier instead of vanilla) or ice cream

Cream together the sugar, flour, butter, orange rind, and nutmeg. Add the eggs, corn syrup, salt, and vanilla and beat until well blended. Stir in the pecans or walnuts and cranberries. Pour into the pie shell.

Bake in a preheated 350°F oven for 60 to 70 minutes or until a knife inserted halfway between the center and the edge comes out clean.

SERVES 8.

FITZWILLIAM INN NUTTY PIE

Vanilla ice cream and Fitzwilliam Inn Caramel Sauce are just the right additions to this sweet delight. The sauce recipe makes a large amount, but you'll be happy to have extra on hand.

1 tablespoon sliced almonds

3 eggs

1 cup sugar

1 teaspoon baking powder

¼ teaspoon salt

1 teaspoon vanilla extract

1 cup graham cracker crumbs

1 cup chopped walnuts

Vanilla ice cream

Fitzwilliam Inn Caramel Sauce
(recipe follows)

Sprinkle the almonds on the bottom of a greased or sprayed 9-inch pie plate. Beat the eggs, then add the sugar, baking powder, salt, and vanilla, mixing until thoroughly blended. Fold in the crumbs and nuts. Pour the mixture into the pie plate.

Bake in a preheated 350°F oven for 25 to 30 minutes, being careful not to overbake. Serve topped with the ice cream and Caramel Sauce.

FITZWILLIAM INN CARAMEL SAUCE

1 cup firmly packed brown
sugar

¼ cup granulated sugar

½ cup corn syrup

1 cup evaporated milk

A few grains of salt

½ teaspoon butter

Combine the sugars, syrup, milk, and salt in a double boiler and cook until the sugars dissolve and the mixture is smooth and a bit thickened. Remove from the heat and stir in the butter.

SERVES 8 TO 10.

Stafford's in the Field
CHOCORUA, NEW HAMPSHIRE

CHOCOLATE WALNUT PIE

When you feel like splurging on calories and indulging in chocolate, this is a quick and easy solution that tastes like a special treat.

1 stick unsalted butter, softened

1 cup granulated sugar

3 large eggs, lightly beaten

¾ cup light corn syrup

1 teaspoon vanilla extract

2 squares unsweetened chocolate, melted

1 cup chopped walnuts

1 unbaked 9-inch pie shell

Beat the butter and sugar together until smooth. Add the eggs, syrup, and vanilla, beating to blend thoroughly. Stir in the chocolate, then the nuts, and pour into the pie shell.

Bake in a preheated 375°F oven for 40 to 50 minutes.

SERVES 8.

The Boulders Inn
NEW PRESTON, CONNECTICUT

BERRY CRUMBLE

An easy and excellent fruit dessert that can vary with the seasons.

½ cup all-purpose flour

½ cup sugar

½ teaspoon ground nutmeg

1 tablespoon ground cinnamon

A pinch of salt

4 tablespoons butter

4 cups mixed fresh berries (blueberries, raspberries, strawberries, etc.)

Vanilla ice cream

Stir together the flour, sugar, nutmeg, cinnamon, and salt. Cut in the butter until crumbly.

Butter a 1-quart square glass baking dish and sprinkle with sugar. Arrange the berries in the dish and cover with the crumbled mixture. Bake uncovered in a preheated 350°F oven for 25 minutes. Serve warm with ice cream.

SERVES 6 TO 8.

NINA'S BLUEBERRY TORTE

"This makes a great breakfast treat, too."

1 cup all-purpose flour

¼ teaspoon salt

1 teaspoon baking powder

½ cup butter, softened

1 cup sugar

2 eggs

2 cups or more fresh
    blueberries tossed with
    sugar

¼ wedge of lemon

Blueberry Torte Topping (recipe
    follows)

In a medium-sized bowl, mix together the flour, salt, and baking powder and set aside.

In a large bowl, cream the butter and sugar until smooth. Beat in the eggs one at a time. Add the flour mixture and stir until blended. Turn into a greased and floured 8-inch springform pan, pressing the dough over the bottom and ½ inch up the sides. Pour the blueberries over the dough and squeeze the juice from the lemon over the berries. Cover with the topping.

Bake in a preheated 350°F oven for 1 hour or until firm. Serve with ice cream.

BLUEBERRY TORTE TOPPING

1 tablespoon all-purpose flour

2 tablespoons sugar

1 teaspoon ground cinnamon

In a small bowl, mix the flour, sugar, and cinnamon until well blended.

VARIATION: One-half cup fresh raspberries can be mixed into the blueberries, or sliced Italian plums may be substituted for the berries.

SERVES 8.

APPLE PANDOWDY

When you're in the mood for apple pie but don't want to fuss with making a pretty crust, this is the dessert to turn to.

1 cup all-purpose flour

¾ cup sugar, divided

1½ teaspoons baking powder

¼ teaspoon salt

3 tablespoons margarine or shortening

⅓ cup milk

2 cups water

½ teaspoon ground cinnamon

8 medium-sized apples, peeled, cored, and sliced

Cream or half-and-half (optional)

In a large bowl, combine the flour, ¼ cup of the sugar, baking powder, and salt. Add the margarine or shortening, and with floured fingers gently crumble the ingredients until the consistency of coarse cornmeal. Add the milk and stir just until the dough clings together. Knead gently (10 to 12 strokes) on a lightly floured surface. Roll or pat the dough until it is about ½ inch thick and will fit the top of the baking dish you will be using. Cover dough with a clean towel and set aside.

In a Dutch oven, heat the water, remaining ½ cup sugar, and cinnamon over medium-high heat until the sugar dissolves. Add the apples and blanch for 4 to 5 minutes or until they are just soft enough to pierce easily with a fork.

Leave the apple mixture in the Dutch oven or transfer to a 13- by 9-inch baking dish. Place the dough on top of the apples and bake in a preheated 450°F oven for 7 minutes. With the back of a spoon, press down on the dough in several places to allow the apple syrup to spread over the top. Continue baking for about 5 more minutes, until the top is golden brown.

Spoon into serving bowls and divide any remaining syrup equally among them. Float a small amount of cream or half-and-half in the syrup, if desired.

SERVES 8.

APPLE STRUDEL

Although just about any kind of apple can be used, this is especially good with McIntosh or Granny Smith.

2 cups all-purpose flour

6 tablespoons sugar, divided

½ teaspoon salt

4 teaspoons baking powder

¼ cup plus 2 tablespoons shortening

⅔ cup milk

2½ cups peeled, cored, and chopped apple

½ teaspoon ground cinnamon

2 tablespoons butter, cut into bits

Apple Strudel Frosting (recipe follows)

Sift the flour, 2 tablespoons of the sugar, salt, and baking powder together in a large bowl. Cut in the shortening until crumbly in consistency. Add the milk and blend well. Roll the dough out to a ½-inch thickness.

In another bowl, combine the apple, remaining 4 tablespoons sugar, cinnamon, and butter. Spread over the dough, fold the sides over, and seal.

Bake in a preheated 400°F oven for 30 minutes. Remove from the oven and spread with the frosting while the strudel is still hot.

APPLE STRUDEL FROSTING

2 tablespoons hot water

1½ cups confectioners' sugar

1 teaspoon vanilla extract

Combine the water, sugar, and vanilla in a bowl, beating until smooth. If the frosting seems too thick to spread easily, thin it with a bit more water or use apple cider or apple juice for additional flavor.

SERVES 8 TO 10

Captain Ezra Nye House

SANDWICH, MASSACHUSETTS

Peach Kuchen

This tastes just fine with canned peaches, but nothing compares to fresh, ripe, juicy ones.

¼ cup flaked coconut, toasted lightly

1 cup all-purpose flour

2 tablespoons plus 2 teaspoons sugar, divided

A pinch of salt

1 stick unsalted butter

1½ cups sliced peaches

¼ teaspoon cinnamon

½ cup sour cream

½ lightly beaten egg

For the crust, combine the coconut, flour, 2 tablespoons sugar, and salt. Cut in the butter until crumbly. Lightly press into the bottom and ½ inch up the sides of an 11- by 7-inch pan. Bake in a preheated 350°F oven for 18 minutes.

Remove from oven and arrange the peach slices in two rows down the length of the crust. Combine the remaining 2 teaspoons sugar and cinnamon and sprinkle over the fruit. Blend the sour cream and egg and pour over the top. Bake another 18 minutes and serve.

SERVES 6.

TAKE IT OFF!

NEED TO PEEL peaches, nectarines, or tomatoes? Chef Frank Duffina of the Norwich Inn in Norwich, Vermont, recommends carving a small X in the skin and then dipping the fruit in boiling water for about one minute: The skins come right off!

SWEETHEART CREPES

A very rich and tasty treat ideal for Valentine's Day!

½ cup light or dark rum

½ cup brandy

1 tablespoon cornstarch mixed with 1 tablespoon water

1½ cups granulated sugar, divided

1 cup water

1 can (16 ounces) any variety sweet cherries (Bing, for example), drained and juice reserved

16 ounces ricotta cheese

1 package (8 ounces) cream cheese, softened

1 teaspoon ground cinnamon

½ cup chopped pecans

½ cup shredded, sweetened coconut

2 cups whipping cream

2 teaspoons vanilla extract

4 tablespoons confectioners' sugar

8 crepes, using any sweet dessert crepe recipe

4 teaspoons brown sugar

To make the topping, combine the rum, brandy, cornstarch-water mixture, 1 cup granulated sugar, water, and reserved cherry juice in a saucepan. Cook until the sauce thickens, 30 to 40 minutes.

Meanwhile, to make the filling combine the cheeses, cinnamon, and remaining ½ cup granulated sugar, beating until the mixture is smooth. Add the pecans and coconut and mix until just combined. Set aside.

Whip the cream until it begins to thicken. Add the vanilla and whip. Add the confectioners' sugar just before the cream is fully whipped, then refrigerate until ready to use.

To assemble, set out a crepe and spread one-eighth of the filling evenly down the middle of the crepe, then place an eighth of the cherries on top of the filling. Fold the sides of the crepe over the filling and turn right side up. Repeat. Refrigerate for at least 1 hour, layered between sheets of waxed paper and covered.

When ready to serve, place each crepe on a dessert plate, spoon on some sauce, top with a dollop of fresh whipped cream, and sprinkle with brown sugar.

Serves 8.

APPLE CREPES À LA MODE

Another treat with a split personality—terrific for dessert as well as breakfast.

2 tablespoons butter or margarine

3 cups chopped apple

⅓ cup raisins

½ cup chopped almonds

⅓ cup firmly packed brown sugar

½ teaspoon ground cinnamon

6 crepes, room temperature

Vanilla ice cream

Fresh mint leaves

In a large skillet, melt the butter or margarine and sauté the apple, raisins, and nuts for 5 minutes or until the apple is tender, stirring frequently. Stir in the brown sugar and cinnamon and sauté 2 more minutes.

Remove from the heat and spoon one-sixth of the mixture onto a crepe. Fold over the sides, tuck in the ends, and place seam side down on a plate. Work quickly so the mixture does not soak through the crepe before you turn it over. Repeat five more times and garnish with a scoop of ice cream and a mint leaf.

SERVES 6.

APPLE MERINGUE PUDDING

"The pudding will look very odd when it comes out of the oven because the meringue forms an irregular crust on the top. This unique, sweet dessert is quick and easy to prepare."

1 egg

¾ cup sugar

4 teaspoons all-purpose flour

1¼ teaspoons baking powder

⅛ teaspoon salt

1 teaspoon vanilla extract

½ cup cored, peeled, and chopped apple

½ cup chopped walnuts

Whipped cream spiked with apple brandy

Beat the egg lightly in a large bowl. Add the sugar and beat until the mixture is creamy and pale.

In a separate bowl, sift together the flour, baking powder, and salt. Blend into the sugar mixture. Stir in the vanilla, apple, and nuts. Pour into an ungreased 7-inch square baking pan.

Bake in a preheated 350°F oven for 30 minutes. To serve, spoon out the pudding into dessert dishes, allowing the meringue to intermix with the apple pudding without breaking up too much. Top with a dollop of spiked whipped cream.

SERVES 2.

STONECREST BASIC BREAD PUDDING

This old-fashioned bread pudding includes a new twist—dried cherries. Top with your favorite ice cream, frozen yogurt, or fruit sauce.

5 to 6 cups French bread cut into 1-inch cubes

⅔ cup sugar

6 eggs

3 cups milk

2 teaspoons vanilla extract

1 cup plumped dried cherries (soak in warm water 20 minutes)

Place the bread in a large bowl. In a separate bowl, gradually whisk the sugar into the eggs. Add the milk and vanilla and pour over the bread cubes. Let stand 25 to 30 minutes. Stir the cherries into the bread mixture and pour into a buttered 9- by 5-inch loaf pan.

Place in a larger pan and add enough boiling water to come halfway up the sides of the loaf pan (this is called a water bath or bain-marie). Bake in a preheated 350°F oven for 45 to 50 minutes or until a knife inserted in the center comes out clean.

Remove the pudding from the bath and let stand 15 minutes (or overnight) before unmolding. Slice and serve with a topping of your choice.

SERVES 5 TO 6.

MAPLEHEDGE BREAD PUDDING WITH STRAWBERRY SAUCE

"This recipe has received the most comments and requests. In July, in Charlestown, there is an abundance of strawberries for picking, and it's at this time that I especially like to make the bread pudding, using fresh strawberries. By using skim milk, margarine, and only two eggs for eight servings, this dish is low in fat and cholesterol."

French bread (preferably day-old), sliced ½ inch thick

½ cup currants

2 eggs, beaten

¾ cup sugar

1 quart skim milk

½ cup margarine, melted

1 tablespoon vanilla extract

1 teaspoon ground nutmeg

Strawberry Sauce (recipe follows)

Place one layer of bread in the bottom of a 9-inch square greased pan. Sprinkle with half of the currants. Place another layer of bread on top and sprinkle with the remaining currants. Mix together the eggs, sugar, milk, margarine, vanilla, and nutmeg and pour gently over the bread and currants, making sure all in the top layer is saturated. Cover and refrigerate at least 8 hours.

Bake in a preheated 350°F oven uncovered until the custard is set and the top is lightly browned, about 45 minutes. Cut into servings and top with Strawberry Sauce.

STRAWBERRY SAUCE

1 pint fresh strawberries or 1 large package (16 ounces) frozen

¼ cup orange juice

3 tablespoons lemon juice

¼ cup sugar

2 tablespoons cornstarch

Place the strawberries, orange juice, and lemon juice in a medium-sized saucepan and cook on low until the berries are softened. Puree one-third of the strawberry mixture, then return to the whole. Combine the sugar with the cornstarch and add to the strawberries. Cook, stirring constantly until slightly thickened.

SERVES 6 TO 8.

Pumpkin Custard

Light, airy, and delectable but very rich, so small portions are best.

3 eggs

1 cup mashed, cooked pumpkin

2 cups half-and-half

½ cup firmly packed brown
   sugar

⅛ teaspoon salt

⅛ teaspoon ground nutmeg

¼ teaspoon ground ginger

1 teaspoon ground cinnamon

1 teaspoon vanilla extract

Gently beat the eggs in a medium-sized bowl. Add the pumpkin and mix. Stir in the half-and-half, brown sugar, salt, nutmeg, ginger, cinnamon, and vanilla and mix thoroughly.

Pour the mixture into custard cups or small ovenproof dishes, place in a 2-inch-deep baking pan, and slowly add enough hot water to fill the baking dish halfway.

Bake in a preheated 325°F oven for 45 minutes or until a toothpick inserted near the rim of one of the cups comes out clean (the middle will firm up when the custard cools). Remove the cups and let cool on a wire rack. After the custards are cool, refrigerate or serve at room temperature.

Serves 6 to 8.

CHOCOLATE MOUSSE AND GRAND MARNIER MASCARPONE

For an extra-fancy touch, garnish each parfait with a rosette of mascarpone, fresh berries, and a mint leaf.

MOUSSE

1 pound bittersweet chocolate

6 large eggs

1 cup warm heavy cream

3 cups whipped cream

MASCARPONE

1½ pounds mascarpone

¼ cup confectioners' sugar

2 teaspoons Grand Marnier

To make the mousse, melt the chocolate in a double boiler. In a separate double boiler, whisk the eggs until creamy to make a sabayon. Add the cream to the chocolate and fold the eggs into it. Then fold the whipped cream into the chocolate mixture and chill.

To make the mascarpone, combine the mascarpone, sugar, and Grand Marnier, beating until thoroughly blended.

Layer parfait glasses with the chocolate mousse, then mascarpone, and finish with chocolate mousse.

SERVES 12.

Stafford's in the Field

CHOCORUA, NEW HAMPSHIRE

MAPLE FRANGO

Smooth, elegant, and easy.

3 large egg yolks

½ cup maple syrup (medium amber grade is suggested for flavor)

2 cups heavy cream, whipped stiff

In a large bowl, beat the yolks until light colored and thick. In a small saucepan, bring the maple syrup to a boil, but watch carefully as it will quickly bubble over once it boils. Slowly pour the hot syrup into the yolks, beating constantly. When all is well mixed, let cool. Fold in the whipped cream and freeze 3 to 4 hours before serving.

SERVES 6.

The Forest—A Country Inn

INTERVALE, NEW HAMPSHIRE

THE FOREST'S APPLE CAKE

This is a great multi-occasion cake that can be whipped together at the last minute. It's attractive, moist, and yummy.

1¾ cups sugar

1 cup vegetable oil

3 eggs

2 cups all-purpose flour

1 teaspoon ground cinnamon

1 teaspoon baking soda

1 teaspoon salt

5 medium-sized McIntosh apples, peeled, cored, and cut up

In a large bowl, cream together the sugar and oil. Add the eggs one at a time, beating well after each addition. Combine the flour, cinnamon, baking soda, and salt and add to the sugar-egg mixture. Stir in the apple. Pour into an ungreased 13- by 9-inch pan.

Bake in a preheated 350°F oven for about 1 hour.

SERVES 14 TO 16.

CRAB APPLE INN APPLE CAKE

Top this with ice cream or whipped cream for a terrific dessert; for breakfast or brunch, use French vanilla yogurt.

1 stick butter or margarine, melted and cooled

1½ cups sugar, divided

2 large eggs

1 cup all-purpose flour

1 teaspoon baking powder

1 teaspoon vanilla extract

1½ teaspoons ground cinnamon

4 to 5 medium-sized tart apples (Cortland or Granny Smith), peeled, cored, and thinly sliced

Combine the butter or margarine, 1 cup of the sugar, and the eggs in a mixing bowl and beat thoroughly. Add the flour, baking powder, and vanilla and beat until well blended. Spread the mixture evenly in a greased 8-inch square baking dish.

For the topping, combine the remaining ½ cup sugar and the cinnamon in a bowl. Add the apples and stir to coat thoroughly. Arrange the apples on top of the batter in overlapping rows, pressing them lightly into the batter.

Bake in a preheated 350°F oven for 1 hour or until golden brown and a toothpick inserted in the center comes out clean. Cut into squares and serve hot.

SERVES 6 TO 8.

GRAM'S APPLESAUCE CAKE

"An attractive presentation is to thinly slice the chilled applesauce cake (using a sharp knife), spread with apple butter, and make little sandwiches. Arrange on a doily-lined serving plate and garnish with yellow pansies and fresh green mint."

2 cups sifted all-purpose flour

1 teaspoon baking soda

1 teaspoon ground cinnamon

½ teaspoon ground cloves

½ teaspoon ground nutmeg

¼ teaspoon salt

½ cup unsalted butter, softened

1 cup firmly packed brown sugar

1 cup unsweetened applesauce, warmed

1 cup raisins

½ cup chopped nuts

Apple Butter (recipe follows)

Sift together the flour, baking soda, cinnamon, cloves, nutmeg, and salt and set aside. Cream the butter until soft and fluffy and add the brown sugar gradually, beating until the mixture is light. Alternately add the dry ingredients and the warm applesauce, blending well after each addition. Mix in the raisins and nuts. Pour into three small greased loaf pans (6 by 3½ inches).

Bake in a preheated 350°F oven for 45 to 50 minutes or until done. Cool in the pans for 15 minutes. Remove, wrap, and chill before slicing. Serve with Apple Butter.

APPLE BUTTER

2 cups unsweetened applesauce

½ cup sugar

1 teaspoon ground cinnamon

¼ teaspoon ground allspice

A pinch of ground ginger

A pinch of ground cloves

Combine the applesauce, sugar, cinnamon, allspice, ginger, and cloves in a medium-sized saucepan. Bring to a boil and simmer for 1 hour, stirring occasionally. Cool and spread on slices of the cake.

MAKES 3 SMALL LOAVES.

APRICOT CHEESE FRUITCAKE

This is a dense, moist cake that makes a fine alternative to traditional fruit-cake. Other kinds of dried fruit can be used as well, with excellent results.

2 cups water
½ cup chopped dried apricots
½ cup golden raisins
2 cups sugar, divided
1 package (8 ounces) cream cheese, softened
1 cup butter, softened
1½ teaspoons vanilla extract
4 eggs
2 cups all-purpose flour
1½ teaspoons baking powder
½ cup chopped pecans

In a medium-sized saucepan, combine the water, apricots, raisins, and ¼ cup of the sugar. Bring to a boil, reduce the heat, and simmer 15 to 20 minutes. Drain well and set aside.

In a mixing bowl, beat 1½ cups of the sugar, the cheese, butter, and vanilla until creamed. Add the eggs, one at a time, beating well after each addition. Sift the flour, baking powder, and remaining ¼ cup sugar and add gradually to the creamed mixture. Gently fold in the apricot mixture. Turn into a greased and floured Bundt pan or 9-inch angel food cake pan.

Bake in a preheated 325°F oven for 65 to 70 minutes. Cool completely on a wire rack. Wrap in aluminum foil and store overnight before serving or freezing.

SERVES 12 TO 15.

STAFFORD'S BLUEBERRY BUCKLE

For those who have childhood memories of picking blueberries, the taste of this cake will transport you immediately to those carefree days of summer.

2 cups all-purpose flour

4 teaspoons baking powder

½ teaspoon salt

½ stick butter, softened

¾ cup sugar

1 large egg

½ cup milk

1 cup fresh blueberries

Blueberry Buckle Topping
(recipe follows)

Sift the flour, baking powder, and salt together. In a separate bowl, cream the butter and sugar, then beat in the egg. Add the milk and dry ingredients alternately to the creamed mixture, finishing with the milk. Fold in the blueberries and spread into a greased 9-inch square baking pan. Sprinkle the topping over the batter.

Bake in a preheated 350°F oven for about 30 minutes or until done.

BLUEBERRY BUCKLE TOPPING

½ cup sugar

½ teaspoon ground cinnamon

½ stick butter

Using a pastry knife or food processor, combine the sugar, cinnamon, and butter until the consistency of cornmeal.

SERVES 16.

CRANBERRY MELT-IN-YOUR-MOUTH CAKE

A buttery shortbread cake with a base of tart cranberries and crunchy nuts.

2 cups fresh cranberries, rinsed, picked over, and patted dry

1½ cups sugar, divided

½ cup chopped nuts

2 eggs

1 stick margarine, melted and cooled

½ stick butter, melted and cooled

1 cup all-purpose flour

Mix the berries, ½ cup sugar, and nuts and pour into a greased 10-inch pie plate.

Beat together the eggs and remaining 1 cup sugar. Add the margarine and butter and the flour, stirring to blend well. Pour the batter over the cranberry mixture.

Bake in a preheated 325°F oven for 50 to 60 minutes. Serve plain or with vanilla ice cream.

SERVES 8.

Rowell's Inn
SIMONSVILLE, VERMONT

Rowell's Inn Old Vermont Cocoa Cake

Impressive and special, this is a celebration cake. The layers are thin and fragile, so be careful when removing them from the pans.

½ cup unsweetened cocoa powder

½ cup boiling water

¼ cup butter, softened

¼ cup shortening

2 cups sugar

⅛ teaspoon salt

1 teaspoon vanilla extract

2 eggs

1½ teaspoons baking soda

1 cup buttermilk

1¾ cups all-purpose flour

2 tablespoons sour cream

1 tablespoon maple syrup

⅓ cup chopped walnuts

Cocoa Maple Frosting (recipe follows)

Combine the cocoa and water and set aside.

Cream the butter, shortening, sugar, salt, and vanilla until fluffy. Add the eggs one at a time, beating well after each addition. Stir the baking soda into the buttermilk and add alternately with the flour to the creamed mixture.

Measure 1⅔ cups batter into a small bowl and stir in the sour cream, maple syrup, and nuts. Pour into two greased, waxed paper–lined 9-inch cake pans. Blend the cocoa-water mixture with the remaining batter and pour into a third prepared cake pan.

Bake in a preheated 350°F oven for 25 to 30 minutes. Cool 5 minutes before removing from the pans.

Spread Cocoa Maple Frosting between the layers, on the sides, and over the top of the cake.

Cocoa Maple Frosting

½ cup butter

½ cup unsweetened cocoa powder

2 tablespoons corn syrup

1 teaspoon maple syrup

3 cups confectioners' sugar

6 tablespoons milk

Combine the butter, cocoa, and syrups. Add the sugar alternately with the milk. Beat until smooth.

Serves 12.

Cake Walk

ONE NIGHT a few years ago, Diana Smith of The Marlborough in Woods Hole, Massachusetts, had a 5-pound chocolate cake disappear from her refrigerator. It wasn't until the next morning that the mystery was solved when three guests, all sporting chocolate hangovers, confessed to the crime. It's safe to say that Diana knows a thing or two about cake baking. Here are some of her pointers:

* Make sure that all of the ingredients called for in the recipe are at room temperature before you mix them. That goes for butter, eggs, and milk, none of which will spoil in the short time that they're warm.

* Don't use dry measuring cups for liquids or vice versa. Although the volume is the same, you can't get a level dry measure from a liquid cup.

* If your recipe calls for "4 cups sifted flour," sift the flour before you measure it and don't tap the cup on the counter to pack the flour. It defeats the purpose of sifting in the first place.

* Follow the recipe to the letter and don't substitute ingredients. For example, it's not a good idea to substitute margarine for butter because the liquid content in the two products are not comparable.

* Place the rack in the center of the oven so that the heat can flow evenly around the cake.

* If the temperature in the oven is too cool, the cake will turn out mushy; too hot and the cake will have a hump in the middle. Why guess? Invest in a good oven thermometer.

* Loud noises and jumping children will *not* cause a cake to fall (when Diana was a child, her mother would insist that she whisper if there was a cake in the oven); drastic changes in the oven temperature will. Resist the urge to open the oven door every five minutes to check on your cake.

DIANA'S FAVORITE CHOCOLATE CAKE

"I once made this for guests who came to the inn for the World Famous Falmouth Road Race. I told everyone when they checked in that they could help themselves to cake. I wasn't too surprised to discover the next morning that the whole cake had disappeared. What was surprising is that four women had stayed up visiting and talking the entire night and had eaten all the cake by themselves! Needless to say, they had a very light breakfast!"

1 cup sifted unsweetened cocoa powder

2 cups boiling water

3 cups sifted all-purpose flour

2 teaspoons baking soda

½ teaspoon baking powder

¾ teaspoon salt

1 cup butter, softened

2½ cups sugar

4 eggs

1½ teaspoons vanilla extract

Chocolate Butter Cream Filling (recipe follows)

Whipped Cream Frosting (recipe follows)

Combine the cocoa and water until thoroughly blended and set aside to cool.

Sift together the flour, baking soda, baking powder, and salt. In a separate bowl, cream the butter, sugar, eggs, and vanilla, beating for 5 minutes. Add the flour mixture alternately with the cocoa liquid to the creamed mixture, stirring to blend, but do not overmix. Pour into three greased and floured 9-inch cake pans.

Bake in a preheated 350°F oven for 30 minutes or until a knife inserted in the center comes out clean. Remove from the pans to cool on wire racks.

Use all the filling between the layers and frost the top and sides of the cake with all the frosting. Chill for 24 hours.

CHOCOLATE BUTTER CREAM FILLING

1 cup butter, softened

½ cup sifted unsweetened cocoa powder

¾ cup sifted confectioners' sugar

2 eggs

Cream together the butter and cocoa until smooth. Add the sugar and eggs and beat until fluffy.

WHIPPED CREAM FROSTING

2 cups heavy cream

¾ cup sifted confectioners' sugar

1 teaspoon vanilla extract

Whip the cream until stiff. Beat in the sugar and vanilla until thoroughly blended.

SERVES 18 TO 20.

BITTERSWEET CHOCOLATE PISTACHIO CAKE

"We have received many requests for this cake at the lodge. It is suitable for special occasions—like a chocoholic's birthday!"

12 ounces bittersweet chocolate, chopped

1¾ cups unsalted butter, cut up

9 eggs, separated

1 cup plus 2 tablespoons granulated sugar, divided

⅔ cup firmly packed brown sugar

4½ tablespoons ground, toasted pistachios

⅔ cup cake flour

¾ teaspoon cream of tartar

Pistachio Cake Icing (recipe follows)

Melt the bittersweet chocolate and the butter together in a double boiler over simmering water or in a microwave oven. Set aside but keep warm.

In a large bowl, using a blender with a whisk attachment and set on high speed, beat together the egg yolks, 1 cup of the granulated sugar, and the brown sugar until the mixture forms a slowly dissolving ribbon. Gently fold in the pistachios and flour, then the chocolate mixture. Keep warm.

In another bowl, again using the blender and whisk attachment set on high speed, beat the egg whites and tartar until foamy. Add the remaining 2 tablespoons sugar gradually and continue beating until round peaks are formed. Fold the egg whites into the chocolate batter quickly without deflating the whites. There should be no trace of whites left in the batter. Pour the batter into a 10-inch springform pan that has been buttered, lined with waxed paper, buttered again, and dusted with flour.

Bake in a preheated 375°F oven on the middle rack for 50 to 60 minutes or until the middle of the cake is almost firm (the center should be slightly runny). Set the cake on a wire rack and let cool completely.

Release the sides of the springform pan and unmold onto a cake plate. Pour the icing over the cooled cake, smoothing over the top and sides, and let it harden slightly before serving.

Pistachio Cake Icing

12 ounces semisweet chocolate, cut up

½ cup unsalted butter, cut up

¼ cup water

Melt the chocolate, butter, and water together in a double boiler over simmering water or in a microwave oven, stirring until combined and glossy.

SERVES 12 TO 14.

Cooks' Pantry: Cooking with Chocolate

*D*ESSERT WOULDN'T BE dessert at the Old Lyme Inn in Old Lyme, Connecticut, without some chocolaty treat on the menu. Chef Stuart London offers these pointers for cooking with every dessert lover's favorite.

⬧ Store chocolate covered in a cool, dry place; it should keep for several months. Don't refrigerate and never freeze it. If the chocolate develops white streaks—called a "bloom"—the quality has not been affected and it's okay to use.

⬧ Chocolate and water don't mix: Be careful not to allow any water to drip into melted chocolate because it will cause the chocolate to stiffen and be unusable.

⬧ To keep melted chocolate warm, place the bowl on a heating pad turned on low. (Be sure to read the directions on your heating pad beforehand.)

⬧ Milk chocolate, which is *very* good for eating, is usually not good for cooking. Don't substitute it for unsweetened, bittersweet, or semisweet chocolate.

The 1785 Inn

CHOCOLATE STRAWBERRY SHORTCAKE

For a change of pace, try this updated version of an all-time favorite.

SHORTCAKES

2 cups all-purpose flour

2 teaspoons baking powder

4 tablespoons unsweetened cocoa powder

⅓ cup sugar

½ teaspoon baking soda

½ teaspoon salt

5 tablespoons cold unsalted butter, cut into five portions

4 ounces chocolate chips

¾ cup milk

SAUCE

4 quarts fresh strawberries, hulled and sliced, divided

2 cups sugar

½ cup orange juice

TOPPING

2 cups heavy cream

½ cup confectioners' sugar

2 teaspoons vanilla extract

Fresh mint leaves for garnish

For the shortcakes, combine the flour, baking powder, cocoa, sugar, baking soda, and salt in a food processor. Add the butter and chocolate chips and process until crumbly. Begin processing again and add the milk, blending until the mixture is crumbly but will hold together when pinched together with your fingers. Turn the dough out onto a floured surface, shape into a ball, and flatten into a 1-inch thick circle. Using a 2-inch round cutter, make twelve shortcakes. Place on a cookie sheet lined with parchment paper. Bake in a preheated 450°F oven for 13 minutes. When slightly cooled, remove the short-cakes to a plate and cover with plastic wrap to keep moist.

For the sauce, puree 2 quarts of the strawberries in a food processor. Pour the puree into a large bowl and stir in the sugar and orange juice, then add the remaining 2 quarts berries.

For the topping, whip the cream in a bowl. When the mixture begins to thicken, beat in the sugar and vanilla.

To assemble the shortcakes, spoon a tablespoon of the sauce in the bottom of a serving dish, place the bottom half of a shortcake on the sauce, 2 tablespoons sauce on the shortcake, and 1 tablespoon whipped cream on the sauce. Add the top half of the shortcake, 2 tablespoons sauce, and 1 tablespoon whipped cream. Garnish with mint leaves.   *SERVES 12.*

UPSIDE-DOWN PEAR SKILLET CAKE

Serve this warm with vanilla ice cream, whipped cream, or pear brandy.

1 cup firmly packed brown
    sugar

6 tablespoons unsalted butter
    (¾ stick cut into four pieces)

1⅓ cups all-purpose flour

1⅓ cups sugar

2 teaspoons ground cinnamon

1¼ teaspoons baking soda

½ teaspoon salt

2 large eggs

½ cup vegetable oil

2 small pears, unpeeled, cored,
    and coarsely grated

4 medium-sized pears, peeled,
    cored, and each cut into 6
    wedges

Position the rack in the center of the oven and set the temperature to 350°F.

Sprinkle the brown sugar evenly over the bottom of a large skillet with 2½-inch-high sides. Place the butter pieces in the skillet and put in the oven until the butter melts, about 5 minutes, then remove.

Mix the flour, sugar, cinnamon, baking soda, and salt in a medium-sized bowl. Beat in the eggs and oil. Mix in the grated pear.

Whisk the butter and brown sugar in the skillet until the sugar dissolves. Arrange the pear wedges closely together in the skillet in a flower pattern. Place any remaining wedges in the center. Pour the batter over the pears, spreading it evenly.

Bake in the oven for about 1 hour or until springy to the touch. Let cool for 20 minutes. To remove the cake, flip the skillet onto a plate.

SERVES 12.

Stonecrest Farm Bed and Breakfast

WILDER, VERMONT

LEMON RICOTTA CHEESECAKE

The gingersnap crust gives this cake a unique flavor. For a stunning presentation, garnish with a berry puree and sprigs of fresh mint.

CRUST

½ cup slivered almonds

20 to 25 gingersnap cookies

¼ cup sugar

4 tablespoons unsalted butter, melted

FILLING

4 eggs

⅔ cup sugar

½ cup light cream

¼ cup all-purpose flour

2 pounds ricotta cheese

¼ cup lemon juice

2 teaspoons lemon zest

In the bowl of a food processor fitted with a metal blade, chop the almonds until coarse. Add the gingersnaps and process to a fine meal. Add the sugar and butter and pulse until well blended. Press the crust over the bottom and partially up the sides of a 9- or 10-inch springform pan.

Whisk together the eggs and sugar. Add the cream and flour and mix well. Stir in the ricotta, lemon juice, and zest and blend thoroughly. Pour the filling into the prepared crust.

Bake in the lower third of a preheated 350°F oven for 1 hour. Cool the cake thoroughly and refrigerate until ready to serve.

SERVES 10.

BAILEYS IRISH CREAM CHEESECAKE

This light and lively cheesecake needs no crust. It's basic and versatile; therefore, the liqueur you use can be varied.

3 pounds cream cheese

5 large eggs

2 cups sugar

1 cup Baileys Irish Cream

6 tablespoons all-purpose flour

Cut the cheese into small pieces and blend on low speed in a mixer using a whisk attachment. Add the eggs one at a time, beating until the mixture is smooth. Alternate adding the sugar and Baileys gradually. Mix thoroughly for about 10 minutes. Gradually add the flour until thoroughly blended. Place the mixture in a greased 12-inch springform pan.

Bake in a preheated 350°F oven for 1 hour or until the top is slightly browned. Let cool about 30 minutes in the pan before removing.

SERVES 12.

Austin Hill Cheesecake

"Over the years, every time we enjoyed cheesecake at a friend's home or dining in a restaurant I would ask for the recipe. Then I'd experiment with different ones, adding and deleting ingredients. Cheesecake was one dessert that had to be just perfect. Well, from all the wonderful comments, this one is it—creamy, light, not too sweet, and it just melts in your mouth."

2 pounds cream cheese, softened

½ cup heavy cream

4 eggs

1¾ cups sugar

1 teaspoon vanilla extract

1 tablespoon freshly squeezed lemon juice

Put the cheese, cream, eggs, sugar, vanilla, and lemon juice in a food processor fitted with a metal blade and mix for about 10 seconds. Pour the mixture into a buttered 10-inch springform pan and shake to get the bubbles out. Place the springform pan in larger pan and fill the larger one with boiling water until the water reaches halfway up the sides of the springform pan.

Bake in a preheated 300°F oven for 2 hours. Let stand 1 hour in the oven after the heat is turned off. Remove from the oven and let stand 2 hours more on a trivet. Then refrigerate until ready to serve.

VARIATION: Serve this cheesecake plain or painted with a mixture of apricot preserves that have been cooked down with a few drops of water. Top with kiwi slices and strawberries or with pureed raspberries and kiwis.

Serves 12 to 16.

TRISH'S CHEESECAKE

"The ultimate in cheesecake—rich and creamy. A sliver will do you!"

CRUST

2 cups graham cracker crumbs

½ cup sugar

½ stick butter, softened

FILLING

1 pound cottage cheese

1 pound cream cheese

1½ cups sugar

4 eggs

3 tablespoons cornstarch

3 tablespoons all-purpose flour

5 teaspoons lemon juice

1 tablespoon vanilla extract

½ stick unsalted butter, melted and cooled

2 cups sour cream

Mix the crumbs, sugar, and butter together and press three-fourths of the mixture into the bottom and up the sides of a sprayed or generously buttered 9-inch springform pan. Reserve the remaining crumbs to sprinkle on top of the cheesecake.

In a food processor, puree the cottage cheese until smooth. Add the cream cheese and blend thoroughly. Mix in the sugar and pour into a large bowl.

In another bowl, beat the eggs until lemon yellow and add them to the cheese mixture. Stir in the cornstarch, flour, lemon juice, and vanilla and combine well. Add the butter and beat in the sour cream until smooth. Pour into the prepared pan.

Bake on the middle rack of a preheated 325°F oven for 1 hour. Turn the heat off and leave the cake in the oven with the door closed for 1 hour. Then sprinkle with the remaining crumbs and chill overnight before serving.

SERVES 16 TO 20.

PEANUT BUTTER TORTE WITH CHOCOLATE SAUCE

Big kids as well as little ones will love this dessert. It's intensely rich, however, so cut the portions small.

1 cup graham cracker crumbs

1¼ cups sugar, divided

⅓ cup butter, melted

2 cups creamy peanut butter (see Note)

1 cup sugar

2 cups whipped cream

8 ounces semisweet chocolate chips

¼ cup coffee

Combine the crumbs, ¼ cup of the sugar, and butter and press into the bottom of a 9- to 10-inch springform pan.

Using a mixer or food processor, blend the peanut butter and remaining 1 cup sugar until creamy. Fold the whipped cream into the peanut butter mixture and spoon into the prepared pan. Refrigerate at least 4 hours.

When ready to serve, combine the chocolate and coffee and melt in a microwave for about 1 minute on high. Serve the torte with the sauce spooned over the slices.

NOTE: Crunchy peanut butter can be substituted for creamy.

SERVES 12 TO 16.

COLOSSAL COOKIES

"These cookies are made without any flour! Guests rave about them and always request the recipe."

½ cup butter, softened

1½ cups granulated sugar

1½ cups firmly packed brown sugar

4 eggs

1 teaspoon vanilla extract

2 cups peanut butter

6 cups rolled oats

2½ teaspoons baking soda

1 cup chocolate chips

1 cup raisins

Cream together the butter and sugars. Add the eggs one at a time, beating well after each addition. Mix in the vanilla, peanut butter, oats, baking soda, chocolate chips, and raisins, blending well.

Drop rounded spoonfuls on greased cookie sheets and bake in a preheated 350°F oven for 10 to 12 minutes or until light brown. Let cool and serve.

MAKES 6 TO 8 DOZEN.

The Hancock Inn

HANCOCK, NEW HAMPSHIRE

SCOTCH SHORTBREAD

"We serve this every afternoon at teatime to our guests."

½ pound butter, softened

½ cup sugar

2 cups all-purpose flour

Combine the butter, sugar, and flour and work together with your hands until thoroughly blended, but do not overwork. Pat into a 13- by 9-inch baking pan and prick the surface all over with a fork.

Bake in a preheated 325°F oven for 40 to 45 minutes or until lightly browned. When cooled, cut into small squares. *MAKES 2 DOZEN.*

FELICIA'S PUMPKIN COOKIES

Soft cookies with rounded tops, chockful of raisins and nuts. Pack these in school lunches, take them on a picnic, share them with a friend who's feeling blue.

2 cups butter, softened

2 cups sugar

2 eggs

2 cups mashed, cooked
   pumpkin

2 teaspoons vanilla extract

5 cups all-purpose flour

2 teaspoons baking powder

1 teaspoon baking soda

4 teaspoons ground cinnamon

2 teaspoons ground cloves

2 teaspoons ground nutmeg

1 teaspoon salt

2 cups raisins

2 cups chopped walnuts

Cream together the butter and sugar until smooth. Beat in the eggs one at a time. Add the pumpkin and vanilla, blending well.

In a separate bowl, combine the flour, baking powder, baking soda, cinnamon, cloves, nutmeg, and salt. Add to the creamed mixture, stirring well. Mix in the raisins and nuts.

Drop rounded spoonfuls on greased cookie sheets and bake in a preheated 375°F oven for 10 to 15 minutes.

MAKES 3 TO 4 DOZEN.

BISCOTTI

"These cookies range from very crisp to very hard. The amount of shortening in the recipe is the determining factor. You can omit the butter and the cookies will be slightly harder, but eaten very easily if dipped in liquid, which is traditional. We have been serving biscotti for years. We offer them at tea or as an unusual dessert to be dipped in coffee or port wine."

3¾ cups all-purpose flour

2½ cups sugar

1 teaspoon baking powder

A pinch of salt

4 eggs, divided

2 egg yolks

1 teaspoon vanilla extract

4 tablespoons unsalted butter, softened

1⅓ cups roughly chopped toasted almonds, with skins or without

Mix together the flour, sugar, baking powder, and salt. In a separate bowl, beat 3 of the eggs plus the egg yolks until frothy, then add the vanilla. Mix the dry ingredients and butter into the eggs, beating well.

Turn the mixture onto a floured surface and knead in the almonds, adding more flour as needed. Shape and roll the dough into two logs about 12 by 3 inches by 1 inch high. Place on a greased and floured cookie sheet. Whip the remaining egg and brush over the top surface of the dough.

Bake in a preheated 350°F oven for about 35 minutes. Remove from the cookie sheet and let cool until easily handled, then slice the logs on the diagonal into ¾-inch-thick slices. Place the slices back on the same cookie sheet and bake an additional 15 minutes or until lightly browned. Let cool completely and store in an airtight container.

MAKES 2 TO 2½ DOZEN.

CENTER HARBOR FIREHOUSE BROWNIES

"These were named Firehouse Brownies because I served fourteen pans of them as the dessert at our annual Center Harbor Fire Department Spaghetti Supper. My neighbor was then the fire chief of Center Harbor, and he helped me out on Christmas Eve when the pipes froze at my bed and breakfast inn. I had a full house, and it was my first Christmas in New Hampshire on my own. He spent hours in my 1772 basement crawl space, armed with a hair dryer, thawing the frozen pipes; the temperature was 10 degrees below zero! The following summer, at the time of the annual event, I felt I owed him one!"

4 squares (4 ounces) unsweetened chocolate

2 sticks butter or margarine

4 eggs

2 cups sugar

1 cup all-purpose flour

½ teaspoon salt

1 cup chopped pecans or walnuts

1 teaspoon vanilla extract

Brownies Frosting (recipe follows)

Brownies Icing (recipe follows)

Melt the chocolate and butter or margarine together and set aside.

In a large bowl, beat the eggs, then add the sugar and beat thoroughly. Combine the flour, salt, nuts, and vanilla. Stir in the chocolate mixture and then the egg-sugar mixture, blending well. Pour into a buttered 13- by 9-inch pan.

Bake in a preheated 325°F oven for 35 minutes. When cooled, spread with the frosting. With a wire whisk or fork, drizzle the icing over the frosting in quick circles or up and down and across.

BROWNIES FROSTING

2 tablespoons butter or margarine, softened

1¼ cups sifted confectioners' sugar

3 tablespoons light cream

Beat the butter or margarine until light. Add the sugar and beat thoroughly. Mix in the cream, stirring until smooth. It will not look like much, but it will be enough.

BROWNIES ICING

2 squares (2 ounces) semisweet
   chocolate

1 tablespoon butter or
   margarine

Melt the chocolate and butter or margarine together in a small pan.

NOTE: These brownies freeze very well.

MAKES 2 DOZEN.

Grafton Inn
FALMOUTH HEIGHTS, MASSACHUSETTS

GINGER COOKIES

"My mother, Edythe DeVere, passed this recipe down to me. It was one of her favorites."

¾ cup butter, softened

1 cup sugar

1 egg, beaten

¼ cup molasses

½ teaspoon ground cinnamon

1 teaspoon ground ginger

1 teaspoon salt

2 cups sifted all-purpose flour

¾ teaspoon baking soda

Sugar

Cream the butter and sugar until smooth. Add the egg and molasses and blend well. Sift together the cinnamon, ginger, salt, flour, and baking soda. Combine with the creamed mixture, stirring well.

Roll the dough into balls the size of a marble, dip in sugar, and place on greased cookie sheets. Bake in a preheated 325°F oven for about 10 minutes.

MAKES 5 DOZEN.

NANIAMO BARS

"Our guests consider these to be the perfect complement to afternoon tea or as a dessert with evening coffee."

BASE

½ cup butter, softened

¼ cup sugar

5 tablespoons unsweetened
    cocoa powder

1 teaspoon vanilla extract

1 egg, beaten

2 cups crushed graham
    crackers (about 28 squares)

¾ cup coconut

¾ cup nuts (your preference)

ICING

¼ cup butter, softened

3 tablespoons milk

2 cups confectioners' sugar

TOPPING

4 squares (4 ounces) bittersweet
    chocolate

1 tablespoon butter

To make the base, combine the butter, sugar, cocoa, vanilla, and egg in a double boiler. Stir until melted and smooth. Remove from the heat and add the graham cracker crumbs, coconut, and nuts. Pour into a 9-inch square pan.

For the icing, blend the butter, milk, and sugar until smooth. Pour on top of the graham cracker mixture.

For the topping, melt the chocolate and butter in a double boiler. Drizzle on top of the icing.

Refrigerate until ready to serve, then cut into bars.

MAKES ABOUT 30.

PECAN DIAMONDS

Fancy treats for the holidays. Serve them with praline ice cream.

SHORTBREAD

1 cup unsalted butter, softened

¾ cup sugar

½ cup shortening

3 eggs

1 teaspoon vanilla extract

1¼ cups plus 1 tablespoon cake flour

½ cup plus 3 tablespoons all-purpose flour

1 teaspoon salt

2 teaspoons baking powder

TOPPING

1 pound unsalted butter

1 pound light brown sugar

½ cup granulated sugar

¾ pound honey

½ cup heavy cream

1½ pounds pecans

To make the shortbread, cream together the butter, sugar, and shortening in a large bowl. Add the eggs one at a time, beating well after each addition. Stir in the vanilla.

In a separate bowl, combine the flours, salt, and baking powder. Add to the creamed mixture a little at a time while beating, but do not overbeat. Spread the dough in a greased 13- by 9-inch deep-dish pan. Bake in a preheated 400°F oven for 20 minutes.

For the topping, mix the butter, sugars, honey, and cream in a large pot. Bring to a simmer and cook for 4 minutes, stirring frequently. Add the nuts. Pour immediately over the cooked shortbread.

Bake at 400°F for 5 minutes. Cool, then refrigerate for 4 hours to set. Cut into diamond-shaped servings and reheat in a 400°F oven for 5 minutes before serving.

MAKES 2 DOZEN.

CATHEDRAL HOUSE LEMON SQUARES

A delicate, creamy lemon topping over a shortbread crust.

½ cup butter or margarine, softened

1 cup plus 2 tablespoons all-purpose flour, divided

¼ cup confectioners' sugar

1 cup granulated sugar

2 eggs, beaten

2 tablespoons lemon juice

½ teaspoon baking powder

Confectioners' sugar

Combine the butter, 1 cup of the flour, and ¼ cup confectioners' sugar, beating well. Pat into a 13- by 9-inch glass pan and bake in a preheated 350°F oven for 15 minutes. (If you prefer a thicker crust, bake in a 9-inch square pan.)

Meanwhile, mix together the granulated sugar, eggs, lemon juice, remaining 2 tablespoons flour, and baking powder. Pour over the crust and bake for 25 minutes more. Sprinkle with confectioners' sugar when cool. SERVES 6 TO 8.

BOOKS FOR (REALLY OLD) COOKS

ONE OF THE WORLD's earliest books of cooking instruction was a hefty twelfth-century tome titled *Bokes of Kervyne*, which instructed knights in the manly art of carving meats. Six centuries later, in 1796, America's first book of cookery, written by a woman named Amelia Simmons, was published. The title—which only barely can be recited in one breath—was *American Cookery or the art of Dressing Viands, Fish, Poultry & Vegetables and the best Modes of Making Pastes, Puffs, Pies, Tarts, Puddings, Custards & Preserves and All Kinds of Cakes from the Imperial Plumb to Plain Cake adapted to This Country & All grades of Life.* Viands, incidentally, is another word for meat.

BEAVER POND FARM INN DATE SWIRLS

"There won't be many—if any—of these left over."

1½ cups all-purpose flour

2 sticks unsalted butter, cut into small pieces

½ cup sour cream

1 box chopped dates (Dromedary is good)

½ cup water

Put the flour and butter in the bowl of a food processor and pulse until barely mixed. Add the sour cream and pulse until the mixture almost holds together. Turn the mixture out onto a floured surface and knead 8 to 10 turns. Wrap in plastic wrap and chill at least 30 minutes.

In the meantime, combine the dates and water in a saucepan. Boil until the water has almost evaporated. Set aside to cool thoroughly.

Divide the chilled dough in half. Roll each half into an 18- by 6-inch rectangle. Divide the date mixture between the two rectangles and spread evenly over the surface. Roll up the dough starting on the long side. Cut each roll into ½- to ¾-inch slices (there should be fourteen to sixteen slices per roll).

Place on greased baking sheets and bake in a preheated 375°F oven for 15 to 20 minutes or until barely golden. Remove from the oven and place on a wire rack to cool.

MAKES 28 TO 32.

CHOCOLATE PÂTÉ

A luscious and expensive treat for special occasions, this has a fudgelike texture and heavenly taste.

¾ pound butter, softened

2 cups unsweetened cocoa powder

¾ pound semisweet chocolate

1⅓ cups sugar

½ cup water

2 eggs

4 egg yolks

2 ounces Grand Marnier

1 cup pistachios

½ pound white chocolate, cut into ¼-inch chunks

½ pound milk chocolate, cut into ¼-inch chunks

In a large bowl, beat together the butter and cocoa until smooth. Melt the semisweet chocolate in a double boiler.

Bring the sugar and water to a boil in a large saucepan and add to the butter-cocoa mixture. Add the melted chocolate and mix well.

Beat the eggs and egg yolks together in another bowl. Stir a small amount of the butter-chocolate mixture into the beaten eggs, then return all to the mixture. Add the Grand Marnier, nuts, white chocolate, and milk chocolate.

Line a greased 9- by 5-inch loaf pan with parchment paper. Pour in the mixture and freeze. Slice and serve.

SERVES 12 TO 14.

CHOCOLATE PÂTÉ WITH FRESH RASPBERRY SAUCE

For such an elegant-looking dessert, this is quite simple to do. The pâté is smooth—almost like a chocolate mousse—and the sauce adds the crowning glory.

2 cups heavy cream, divided

3 egg yolks, slightly beaten

2 packages (8 ounces each) semisweet chocolate

½ cup light corn syrup

⅓ cup butter or margarine

¼ cup confectioners' sugar

1 teaspoon vanilla extract

Fresh Raspberry Sauce (recipe follows)

Whipped cream and fresh raspberries for garnish (optional)

Mix ½ cup of the cream with the yolks and set aside.

In a large saucepan, stir the chocolate, syrup, and butter or margarine over medium heat until just melted, stirring constantly to prevent scorching or burning. Add the egg-cream mixture and cook 3 minutes, stirring constantly. Cool to room temperature.

Beat the remaining 1½ cups cream, sugar, and vanilla into soft peaks. Fold into the chocolate until just mixed (do not beat). Pour into a 9- by 5-inch loaf pan lined with plastic wrap. Refrigerate overnight or chill in the freezer for 3 hours.

Turn the pâté out onto a cutting board and slice into 12 equal portions. Serve with Fresh Raspberry Sauce, garnished with whipped cream and fresh berries, if desired.

FRESH RASPBERRY SAUCE

1½ cups fresh raspberries

¼ cup superfine sugar

1 tablespoon lemon juice

1 tablespoon Chambord (raspberry liqueur)

Puree the raspberries in a blender or food processor. Stir in the sugar, then add the lemon juice and liqueur. Strain the puree through a fine-meshed sieve to remove the seeds. Cover and chill until serving.

SERVES 12.

DIRECTORY OF
NEW ENGLAND INNS

(The numbers in parentheses after the inns' names refer to the pages on which their recipes may be found.)

CONNECTICUT

Bee and Thistle Inn (136, 193, 279, 282)
100 Lyme Street
Old Lyme, CT 06371
(203) 434-1667

The Boulders Inn (88, 96, 197, 242, 267)
Route 45, East Shore Road
New Preston, CT 06777
(203) 868-0541

Captain Dibbell House (29, 234–35)
21 Commerce Street
Clinton, CT 06413
(860) 669-1646

The Croft Bed and Breakfast (74)
7 Penny Corner Road
Portland, CT 06480
(860) 342-1856

1895 House Bed and Breakfast (132)
97 Girard Avenue
Hartford, CT 06105
(860) 232-0014

Elms Inn (231)
500 Main Street
Ridgefield, CT 06877
(203) 438-2541

Greenwoods Gate Bed and Breakfast Inn (14)
105 Greenwoods Road East, P.O. Box 491
Norfolk, CT 06058
(203) 542-5439

Griswold Inn (87, 135, 149, 186, 194, 217, 220, 252)
36 Main Street
Essex, CT 06426
(860) 767-1776

The Homestead Inn (94, 95)
420 Field Point Road
Greenwich, CT 06830
(203) 869-7500

The Inn at Ridgefield (202)
20 West Lane
Ridgefield, CT 06877
(203) 438-8282

Old Lyme Inn (68, 74, 77, 217, 274)
85 Lyme Street, P.O. Box 787
Old Lyme, CT 06371
(203) 434-2600

Red Brook Inn (27)
2750 Gold Star Highway, P.O. Box 237
Mystic, CT 06372
(203) 572-0349

Stonehenge (145, 253)
Stonehenge Road, Route 7
Ridgefield, CT 06877
(203) 438-6511

Thurber House (55)
78 Liberty Way
Putnam, CT 06260
(860) 928-6776

Tolland Inn (70)
63 Tolland Green, P.O. Box 717
Tolland, CT 06084
(860) 872-0800

MAINE

Asticou Inn (181)
P.O. Box 406
Northeast Harbor, ME 04662
(207) 276-3344

Blue Hill Inn (230)
Union Street, Route 177
Blue Hill, ME 04614
(207) 374-2844

Camden Harbour Inn (164)
83 Bayview Street
Camden, ME 04843
(207) 236-4200

Castine Inn (69, 176–77)
Main Street
Castine, ME 04421
(207) 326-4365

Craignair Inn (15, 203)
533 Clark Island Road
Clark Island, ME 04859
(207) 594-7644

Dockside Guest Quarters (119)
Harris Island, P.O. Box 205
York, ME 03909
(207) 363-2868

Edgewater Farm Bed and Breakfast (62)
HC 32, Box 464
Sebasco Estates, ME 04565
(207) 389-1322

Eggemoggin Reach Bed and Breakfast
    (31, 38, 222, 230)
R.R. 1, Box 33A
Brooksville, ME 04617
(207) 359-5073

Gosnold Arms (150)
North Side Road
New Harbor, ME 04554
(207) 677-3727

Graycote Inn (19, 24, 35)
40 Holland Avenue
Bar Harbor, ME 04609
(207) 288-3044

High Meadows Bed & Breakfast (80)
Route 101
Eliot, ME 03903
(207) 439-0590

Lincoln House Country Inn (105, 240)
R.R. 1, Box 136A
Dennysville, ME 04628
(207) 726-3953

The Maine Stay (66, 72)
34 Maine Street, P.O. Box 500A-YB
Kennebunkport, ME 04046
(207) 967-2117

Pilgrim's Inn (92, 129)
Deer Isle, ME 04627
(207) 348-6615

Spruce Point Inn (121)
Box 237
Boothbay Harbor, ME 04538
(207) 633-4152

Tide Watch Inn (218)
Waldoboro, ME 04572
(207) 832-4987

MASSACHUSETTS

Academy Place Bed and Breakfast (54)
8 Academy Place, P.O. Box 1407
Orleans, MA 02653
(508) 255-3181

Addison Choate Inn (5)
49 Broadway
Rockport, MA 01966
(508) 546-7543

Anderson-Wheeler Homestead (211)
154 Fitchburg Turnpike (Route 117)
Concord, MA 01742
(508) 369-3756

Andover Inn (157, 162, 204)
Chapel Avenue
Andover, MA 01810
(508) 475-5903

Augustus Snow House (238)
528 Main Street
Harwichport, MA 02646
(508) 430-0528

Captain Ezra Nye House (53, 210, 212,
    246)
152 Main Street
Sandwich, MA 02563
(800) 388-2278

Cumworth Farm Bed and Breakfast
    (259)
472 West Cummington Road
Cummington, MA 01026
(413) 634-5529

Cyrus Kent House Inn (278)
63 Cross Street
Chatham, MA 02633
(508) 945-9104

Egremont Inn (165)
Old Sheffield Road
South Egremont, MA 02158
(413) 528-2111

Grafton Inn (277)
261 Grand Avenue South
Falmouth, MA 02540
(508) 540-8688

The Inn on Sea Street (28)
Hyannis, MA 02647
(508) 775-8030

Inn on the Sound (18)
313 Grand Avenue
Falmouth, MA 02540
(508) 457-9666

Jenkins Inn (13)
7 West Street
Barre, MA 01005
(508) 355-6444

Liberty Hill Inn on Cape Cod (245)
77 Main Street, Route 6A
Yarmouth Port, MA 02675
(800) 821-3977

The Marlborough Bed and Breakfast Inn
    (4, 21, 83, 104, 111, 154, 213, 262–63)
320 Woods Hole Road
Woods Hole, MA 02543
(508) 548-6218

Nauset House Inn (63, 243)
143 Beach Road, P.O. Box 774
East Orleans, MA 02643
(508) 255-2195

On Cranberry Pond Bed and Breakfast
    (26)
43 Fuller Street
Middleboro, MA 02346
(508) 946-0768

The Periwinkle Guest House (65)
11 India Street, P.O. Box 4
Nantucket, MA 02554
(508) 228-9267

Red Lion Inn (117)
Main Street
Stockbridge, MA 01262
(413) 298-5545

River Bend Farm (30, 57)
643 Simonds Road, Route 7 North
Williamstown, MA 01267
(413) 458-3121

Sterling Inn (147, 163)
Route 12, P.O. Box 609
Sterling, MA 01564
(508) 422-6592

The Victorian Inn (6)
South Water Street
Edgartown, MA 02539
(508) 627-4784

Weathervane Inn (127, 271)
Route 23, P.O. Box 388
South Egremont, MA 01258
(413) 528-9580

The Whalewalk Inn (248)
220 Bridge Road
Eastham, MA 02642
(508) 255-0617

NEW HAMPSHIRE

Bernerhof Inn (106)
Route 302, P.O. Box 240
Glen, NH 03838
(603) 383-4414

Birchwood Inn (50, 101)
Route 45
Temple, NH 03084
(603) 878-3285

Bradford Inn (188, 195)
Main Street, P.O. Box 458
Bradford, NH 03221
(603) 938-5309

Cathedral House Bed and Breakfast (280)
63 Cathedral Entrance
Rindge, NH 03461
(603) 899-6790

Corner House Inn (137)
Main Street, P.O. Box 204
Center Sandwich, NH 03227
(603) 284-6219

Crab Apple Inn (255)
P.O. Box 188
Plymouth, NH 03264
(603) 536-4476

Ferry Point House Bed and Breakfast (3)
100 Lower Bay Road
Sanbornton, NH 03269
(603) 524-0087

Fitzwilliam Inn (241)
On the Common
R.R. 1, Box 27
Fitzwilliam, NH 03447
(603) 585-9000

The Forest—A Country Inn (49, 254)
P.O. Box 37
Intervale, NH 03845
(603) 356-9772

The Hancock Inn (126, 273)
Main Street
Hancock, NH 03449
(603) 525-3318

Jefferson Inn (46, 47)
Route 2, RFD 1, Box 68A
Jefferson, NH 03583
(603) 586-7998

Maplehedge Bed and Breakfast (251)
Main Street, Route 12
P.O. Box 638
Charlestown, NH 03603
(603) 826-5237

Meeting House Inn (99, 114, 187, 200, 247)
35 Flanders Road
Henniker, NH 03242
(603) 428-3228

1785 Inn (178, 179, 192, 266)
Route 16, P.O. Box 1785
North Conway, NH 03860
(603) 356-9025

Snowvillage Inn (115, 122, 167, 214)
Stuart Road, P.O. Box 68
Snowville, NH 03849
(603) 447-2818

Staffords-in-the-Field (242, 254, 258, 275)
P.O. Box 270
Chocorua, NH 03817
(603) 323-7766

Stillmeadow Bed and Breakfast at Hampstead (20)
545 Main Street, P.O. Box 565
Hampstead, NH 03841
(603) 329-8381

Stonehurst Manor (138, 139)
P.O. Box 1937
North Conway, NH 03860
(800) 525-9100

Sugar Hill Inn (43, 52, 100, 120, 124, 146, 168)
Route 117
Franconia, NH 03580
(603) 823-5621

The Tamworth Inn (25, 98, 110, 174, 237)
Main Street, P.O. Box 189
Tamworth, NH 03886
(800) 642-7352

The Tuc' Me Inn Bed and Breakfast (59)
118 North Main Street, P.O. Box 657
Wolfeboro, NH 03894
(603) 569-5702

The Village House (40, 64)
Route 16A, P.O. Box 359
Jackson, NH 03846
(603) 383-6666

Watch Hill Bed and Breakfast (32, 34, 82, 276–77)
Old Meredith Road, P.O. Box 1605
Center Harbor, NH 03226
(603) 253-4334

RHODE ISLAND

Admiral Benbow Inn (61)
93 Pelham Street
Newport, RI 02840
(401) 846-4256

Admiral Farragut Inn (16, 17)
31 Clarke Street
Newport, RI 02840
(401) 846-4256

Admiral Fitzroy Inn (283)
398 Thames Street
Newport, RI 02840
(401) 846-4256

Francis Malbone House Inn (273)
392 Thames Street
Newport, RI 02840
(401) 846-0392

Melville House (42, 67)
39 Clarke Street
Newport, RI 02840
(401) 847-0640

The Richards Bed and Breakfast (7, 36, 60, 219)
144 Gibson Avenue
Narragansett, RI 02882
(401) 789-7746

Stella Maris Inn (51)
91 Washington Street
Newport, RI 02840
(401) 849-2862

VERMONT

Austin Hill Inn (86, 113, 128, 153, 224, 270)
Route 100, P.O. Box 859
West Dover, VT 05356
(802) 464-5281

Autumn Crest Inn (89, 182, 183)
Clark Road
R.R. 1, Box 1540
Williamstown, VT 05679
(802) 433-6627

Beaver Pond Farm Inn (71, 281)
Gold Golf Road, R.D. Box 306
Warren, VT 05674
(802) 583-2861

Betsy's Bed and Breakfast (2, 44–45, 244)
74 East State Street
Montpelier, VT 05602
(802) 229-0466

Birch Hill Inn (239)
West Road, P.O. Box 346
Manchester, VT 05254
(802) 362-2761

Black Lantern Inn (232)
Montgomery Village, VT 05470
(802) 326-4507

Blueberry Hill Inn (172, 173, 191, 198)
Goshen, VT 05733
(802) 247-6735

Brass Lantern Inn (123)
717 Maple Street
Stowe, VT 05672
(802) 253-2229

The Churchill House Inn (12, 125, 148, 223, 249)
R.R. 3, Box 3265
Brandon, VT 05733
(802) 247-3300

Combes Family Inn (80, 108, 112, 160)
953 East Lake Road
Ludlow, VT 05149
(800) 822-8799

Edson Hill Manor (201)
1500 Edson Hill Road
Stowe, VT 05672
(802) 253-7371

1811 House (161)
Manchester, VT 05254
(802) 362-1811

Golden Maple Inn (23)
Wolcott Village, VT 05680
(802) 888-6614

Governor's Inn (75, 84, 142, 151, 225, 256)
86 Main Street
Ludlow, VT 05149
(802) 228-8830

Grunberg Haus Bed and Breakfast (33, 208, 228)
Route 100 South, R.R. 2 Box 1595
Waterbury, VT 05676
(800) 800-7760

Hartness House Inn (81, 106)
30 Orchard Street
Springfield, VT 05156
(802) 885-2115

Highland Lodge (134, 156, 209, 264, 265)
R.R. 1, Box 1290
Greensboro, VT 05841
(802) 533-2647

Historic Brookside Farms Country Inn (175)
Route 22A
Orwell, VT 05760
(802) 948-2727

Inn at Manchester (39, 48, 116, 207, 257)
Route 7A, P.O. Box 41
Manchester, VT 05254
(800) 273-1793

The Inn at the Round Barn Farm (9, 229)
East Warren Road
Waitsfield, VT 05673
(802) 496-2276

Mad River Inn (78)
P.O. Box 75
Waitsfield, VT 05673
(802) 496-7900

Manchester Highlands Inn (8, 58)
Highland Avenue, P.O. Box 1754
Manchester, VT 05255
(802) 362-4565

Mountain Top Inn (90, 171)
Mountain Top Road, P.O. Box 407
Chittenden, VT 05737
(802) 483-2311

Mountain View Inn (130)
RFD Box 69
Waitsfield, VT 05673
(802) 496-2426

The Norwich Inn (91, 131, 180, 196, 236)
Main Street, P.O. Box 908
Norwich, VT 05055
(802) 649-1143

Rabbit Hill Inn (10, 189)
P.O. Box 55
Lower Waterford, VT 05848
(802) 748-5168

Red Clover Inn at Woodward Farm (107, 170, 233)
Woodward Road
R.R. 2, Box 7450
Mendon, VT 05701
(802) 775-2290

Rowell's Inn (260)
R.R. 1, Box 267D
Chester, VT 05143
(802) 875-3658

Silas Griffith Inn (11)
South Main Street
R.R. 1, Box 66F
Danby, VT 05739
(802) 293-5567

Silver Maple Lodge (37)
R.R. 1, Box 8
Fairlee, VT 05045
(802) 333-4326

Stonecrest Farm Bed and Breakfast (76, 79, 103, 133, 206, 250, 268)
119 Christian Street
Wilder, VT 05088
(800) 730-2425

Trail's End, A Country Inn (144, 216, 219, 224)
Smith Road
Wilmington, VT 05363
(802) 464-2727

Tulip Tree Inn (272)
Chittenden Dam Road
Chittenden, VT 05737
(800) 707-0017

The White House of Wilmington (199, 269)
Route 9, P.O. Box 757
Wilmington, VT 05363
(802) 464-2135

INDEX

HOWE LIBRARY
13 E. SOUTH ST.
HANOVER, N.H. 03755